STUDIES IN BAPTIST HISTO
VOLUME

Offering Christ to the World

Andrew Fuller (1754-1815) and the Revival of Eighteenth-Century Particular Baptist Life

To Peter and Sue,

With thanks and
prayer

Peter Morden

Andrew Fuller (1754-1815)
He was the very picture of a blacksmith William Wilberforce

A full listing of all titles in this series
appears at the close of this book

STUDIES IN BAPTIST HISTORY AND THOUGHT
VOLUME 8

Offering Christ to the World

**Andrew Fuller (1754-1815) and the Revival of
Eighteenth-Century Particular Baptist Life**

Peter J. Morden

Foreword by Ian M. Randall

PATERNOSTER PRESS

First published 2003 by Paternoster Press

Paternoster Press is an imprint of Authentic Media
P.O. Box 300, Carlisle, Cumbria, CA3 0QS, U.K.
and P.O. Box 1047, Waynesboro, GA 30830–2047, U.S.A

09 08 07 06 05 04 03   7 6 5 4 3 2 1

British Library Cataloguing in Publication Data
A catalogue record for this book is available from the British Library

ISBN 1-84227-141-5

Typeset by Peter Morden
Printed and bound in Great Britain
for Paternoster Press
by Nottingham Alpha Graphics

Series Preface

Baptists form one of the largest Christian communities in the world, and while they hold the historic faith in common with other mainstream Christian traditions, they nevertheless have important insights which they can offer to the worldwide church. Studies in Baptist History and Thought will be one means towards this end. It is an international series of academic studies which includes original monographs, revised dissertations, collections of essays and conference papers, and aims to cover any aspect of Baptist history and thought. While not all the authors are themselves Baptists, they nevertheless share an interest in relating Baptist history and thought to the other branches of the Christian church and to the wider life of the world.

The series includes studies in various aspects of Baptist history from the seventeenth century down to the present day, including biographical works, and Baptist thought is understood as covering the subject-matter of theology (including interdisciplinary studies embracing biblical studies, philosophy, sociology, practical theology, liturgy and women's studies). The diverse streams of Baptist life throughout the world are all within the scope of these volumes.

The series editors and consultants believe that the academic disciplines of history and theology are of vital importance to the spiritual vitality of the churches of the Baptist faith and order. The series sets out to discuss, examine and explore the many dimensions of their tradition and so to contribute to their on-going intellectual vigour.

A brief word of explanation is due for the series identifier on the front cover. The fountains, taken from heraldry, represent the Baptist distinctive of believer's baptism and, at the same time, the source of the water of life. There are three of them because they symbolize the Trinitarian basis of Baptist life and faith. Those who are redeemed by the Lamb, the book of Revelation reminds us, will be led to 'fountains of living waters' (Rev. 7.17).

Studies in Baptist History and Thought

Series Editors

Anthony R. Cross	Centre for Baptist History and Heritage, Regent's Park College, Oxford, England
Curtis W. Freeman	Duke University, North Carolina, USA
Stephen R. Holmes	King's College, London, England
Elizabeth Newman	Baptist Theological Seminary at Richmond, Virginia, USA
Philip E. Thompson	North American Baptist Seminary, Sioux Falls, South Dakota, USA

Series Consultants

David Bebbington	University of Stirling, Stirling, Scotland
Paul S. Fiddes	Regent's Park College, Oxford, England
Stanley J. Grenz	Carey Theological College, Vancouver, British Columbia, Canada
Stanley E. Porter	McMaster Divinity College, Hamilton, Ontario, Canada

For Anne, Rachel and Joseph,
and in memory of our baby son, Andrew

Contents

Chapter 4
The Disputes with Abraham Booth   77

Chapter 5
Fuller's Pastoral Ministry   103

Chapter 6
Fuller and the Baptist Missionary Society   128

Foreword

Andrew Fuller was the leading eighteenth-century Baptist exponent of evangelical Calvinism. He was also someone who put his beliefs into practice in a remarkably active life as a pastor and as the Secretary of the Baptist Missionary Society (BMS). The growth of Particular Baptist life in the nineteenth century owes an enormous amount to Andrew Fuller. Despite his influence and significance, however, Fuller has not been the subject of a critical scholarly biography. Peter Morden's study of Fuller, therefore, is of considerable importance.

This book does much more than tell the story of Fuller's life. It places him in his theological and ecclesiological context and shows the way in which his own thinking developed, from his early roots in High Calvinism. It is especially welcome to have such a detailed examination of Fuller's seminal work, *The Gospel Worth of All Acceptation.* Fresh and stimulating insights into the shaping of Fuller's theology are offered.

Fuller was drawn into disputes with a number of contemporaries. Some of these seem now to be rather obscure, but the way in which they are treated here is most helpful for an understanding of the crucial changes that were taking place within Baptist and wider evangelical life in the eighteenth century. The way in which Fuller responded to the Arminian stream within the evangelical revival is illuminating.

Although there is an appropriate theological focus in Peter Morden's examination of Andrew Fuller, Fuller's commitment to pastoral ministry and his unstinting efforts for the BMS are also thoroughly analysed. In addition, there is a fascinating treatment of Fuller's spirituality, an area of enquiry that is receiving increasing attention in church history. Fuller as a person, not simply as a thinker and doer, emerges clearly. Nor is this simply an account of Fuller's greatness; perceptive critical evaluation is a feature of this book.

Peter Morden has made extensive use of primary sources and has also interacted fully and confidently with those who have written about Fuller and his period. Historical work on evangelicalism has been re-orientated by David Bebbington's book, *Evangelicalism in Modern Britain;* Peter Morden has shown that Fuller fits the framework outlined by David Bebbington and that he was someone who was not only deeply affected by evangelicalism but was a creative force within the movement.

I am delighted to be able to commend this careful, readable and relevant book. I hope that it will be widely read and also that it will stimulate others to work on important figures in the Baptist story who merit scholarly study.

Ian M. Randall
Lecturer in Church History and Spirituality
Spurgeon's College, London

Preface and Acknowledgements

Working to complete this study on Andrew Fuller, which is a thoroughly revised, updated and expanded version of my MPhil thesis, has been an immensely enjoyable and challenging experience for me. I am deeply indebted to the supervisor of my thesis, Rev Dr Ian Randall, for his encouragement to pursue my initial ideas on Fuller, his penetrating comments on my work and his friendship. No one is better qualified to write the Foreword to this book, as Ian has read through almost all the material at least twice! I am also indebted to Dr Michael Haykin, firstly for the stimulus of his historical writings on eighteenth-century Particular Baptist life, and latterly for his encouragement to me personally, including his invitation for me to contribute to the work he is editing on Fuller's Apologetics, soon to be published in the Paternoster *Studies in Baptist History and Thought* series. Rev Dr Anthony Cross has been an enthusiastic and extremely supportive editor of this book. These three scholars have all taken time out of their busy schedules to give me every help and assistance, and I am very grateful.

A number of others have read through and commented on my material at different stages, or have given help and advice on specific topics. In particular I want to thank Rev Dr Stephen Holmes, Rev Darren Hirst, Rev Dr Roger Hayden and Rev Dr Derek Murray. Rev Dr Frank Rinaldi and Rev Dr Peter Naylor have kindly allowed me to read relevant sections of their forthcoming works, also to be published in the *SBHT* series. John Barclay has been more than a proof reader – as well as working meticulously through the text (for some chapters twice), he has also offered considerable insights in the area of eighteenth-century Scottish Baptist life. Jeremy Mudditt at Paternoster Press has been very supportive and encouraging at all times. Whilst acknowledging my debt to all of these individuals, I remain entirely responsible for the opinions expressed within this work, as well as any errors that remain.

I am glad to acknowledge the help I have received from the staff at various libraries and institutions. These include the Evangelical Library and Dr Williams' Library in London, where I have been given every assistance. Susan Mills has been extremely helpful whenever I have visited the Angus Library, Regent's Park College, Oxford, as has Shirley Shine at Bristol Baptist College. Philip Saunders of the Cambridge County Records Office and John Pemble of Fuller Baptist Church, Kettering have helped me track down relevant material on Fuller. I particularly want to thank Judy Powles, librarian at Spurgeon's College in London, who obtained a number of different theses from other parts of the country for me, and helped in many other ways too. Thank you.

The thesis on which this work is based was completed with the help of generous financial assistance from the Particular Baptist Fund which I am happy to acknowledge here. Instituted in 1717 for, amongst other things, 'the relief of poor ministers', this is the same fund that helped to supplement Andrew Fuller's stipend at his first pastorate at Soham, Cambridgeshire. I also want to thank the two churches it has been my privilege to serve as a pastor during the time I have been studying and writing. Victoria Baptist Church, Eastbourne, generously allowed me several periods of study leave in order to finished the bulk of my original work. Latterly Shirley Baptist Church, Solihull, agreed to grant me a three month sabbatical in order to complete this book. This is a church which Fuller's friend Samuel Pearce was instrumental in planting in 1797, and so in a real sense a fruit of the Revival which is dealt with by this study. My thanks are due to more people at these two churches than I can possibly list here, but I do want to especially acknowledge the help and support given me by Rev John Murray, the late Val Tattersall, Terry Green, my current ministerial colleague Rev Kevin White (who was converted through the work of Fuller Baptist Church in Kettering) and Carole Green.

Finally I want to thank my wife Anne, to whom I owe more than I could possibly say, and my two children, Rachel and Joseph. They have patiently endured the times when I have had to shut myself away to write, as well as the times when I have been away from home. This book is dedicated to them, as well as being in memory of our baby son, Andrew.

Peter J. Morden
Shirley, Solihull
April 2003

Chronology of Fuller's Life

6 February 1754
Fuller born at Wicken, Cambridgeshire, son of Robert and Philippa Fuller

1761
Family moved to Soham

November 1769
Fuller's conversion experience

April 1770
Baptized and joined Particular Baptist church at Soham, pastored by John Eve

May 1775
Ordained pastor of the Soham church by Robert Hall Sr

1776
Married Sarah Gardiner of Burwell, Cambridgeshire

October 1783
Inducted pastor of the Particular Baptist church at Kettering (the 'Little Meeting'), by Robert Hall Sr; John Ryland Jr preached

1784
Northamptonshire Association 'Call to Prayer' issued

1785
The Gospel Worthy of All Acceptation published

1787
A Defence of a Treatise Entitled, The Gospel of Christ Worthy of All Acceptation: Containing a Reply to Mr Button's Remarks, and the Observations of Philanthropos published

April 1791
Fuller preaches the sermon later published as *The Pernicious Consequences of Delay in Religious Concerns*, at Clipstone

August 1792
Fuller's first wife, Sarah, dies

October 1792
Baptist Missionary Society formed at Kettering. Fuller appointed secretary

January 1793
Fuller suffers slight stroke and temporary facial paralysis

December 1794
Fuller married Ann Coles of Ampthill, Bedfordshire

1799
First of five visits to Scotland on behalf of BMS

1800
The Gospel its Own Witness published

1804
Visit to Ireland on behalf of BMS

1812
Visit to South Wales on behalf of BMS

8 May 1815
Fuller dies at Kettering

Abbreviations

BQ   *Baptist Quarterly*

DEB   D.M. Lewis (ed.), *Dictionary of Evangelical Biography 1730-1860* (2 vols; Oxford: Blackwell, 1995)

DNB   L. Stephens and S. Lee (eds), *Dictionary of National Biography, from the Earliest Times to 1900* (21 vols; Oxford: Oxford University Press, 1921-22)

HEB   J. Ivimey, *History of the English Baptists* (4 vols; London: Isaac, Taylor, Hinton, 1830)

JTS   *Journal of Theological Studies*

Introduction

Soon after the formation of the Baptist Missionary Society (BMS) in 1792, Andrew Fuller (1745-1815) was in London in his capacity as the society's secretary, trying to solicit much needed funding for the new venture. One of those he approached was a 'Rev Mr Cecil, a celebrated clergyman of the Church of England'.[1] Cecil not only refused to give a donation, but also spoke 'in slighting terms' of the Particular Baptist denomination to which Fuller belonged. Cecil was prepared, however, to make an exception of the author of the theological treatise *The Gospel Worthy of All Acceptation*. This he described, without knowing that he was speaking to its author, as 'one of the most masterly productions I know'. When Fuller replied that this was in fact his own work, Cecil 'rose from his chair, expressed the most eager apologies and earnestly pressed a subscription'. But Fuller had been stung and initially refused to accept it. In concluding his account of this incident, Fuller's son and biographer, Andrew Gunton Fuller (1799-1884), recorded that 'it was not without considerable persuasion that the perhaps too sensitive collector could be induced to receive the money'.

As this incident suggests, Andrew Fuller was one of the foremost English Baptist ministers of his day. He was probably best known by his contemporaries, and certainly by later generations, for the reasons given above: he was the author of the hugely influential *The Gospel Worthy of All Acceptation* and the secretary of the BMS from its inception to his death. But in fact Fuller published on a wide range of theological and apologetic subjects, as well as spending the whole of his ministry as a local church pastor. He was a hugely influential figure in Particular Baptist life, at a time when the denomination was undergoing what Michael Haykin has termed a 'profound revitalization'.[2] Fuller lacks a

---

1   See A.G. Fuller, *Men Worth Remembering: Andrew Fuller* (London: Hodder and Stoughton, 1882), pp. 112, for this and subsequent quotations in this paragraph. The clergyman Fuller met was almost certainly Richard Cecil, a contemporary and biographer of John Newton and one of the founder members of the Evangelical Anglican Eclectic Society. The meeting was not dated by Gunton Fuller, upon whom this account rests, but it must have been in 1792 or early in 1793. For Cecil see J.H. Pratt (ed.), *The Thought of The Evangelical Leaders: Notes of the Discussions of The Eclectic Society London during the years 1798-1814* (Edinburgh: Banner of Truth, 1978 [1856]), pp. 1-2, 178-79, 424-25. Unlike his friend Newton, Cecil appears to have had a generally negative attitude towards Dissenters in general and Baptists in particular.

2   M.A.G. Haykin, 'A Habitation of God, through the Spirit: John Sutcliff (1752-

modern critical biographer, and, as Roger Hayden comments, 'it is a tragedy that no serious biography of him has been written since 1863'.[3] By any standards Fuller was a significant figure, one whose life and work have continuing relevance today. This study seeks to survey in detail the central aspects of his life and thought, drawing the contours of his ministry on the map of eighteenth- and nineteenth- century Evangelical and Particular Baptist life.

A Note on Sources

There is a rich vein of primary material waiting to be mined by the student of Fuller. Of first importance are the early 'tombstone' biographies of him, by John Ryland Jr (1753-1825) and John Webster Morris (1763-1836), both originally published in 1816.[4] Ryland was Fuller's 'official' biographer and worked with access to all his subject's private papers. Consequently he is the most important source of primary data from Fuller's diaries and letters. Morris had been a notable figure amongst the Northamptonshire Particular Baptists as pastor of the church at Clipstone. After moving to Dunstable in 1803 he became bankrupt (in 1808), due to the failure of his printing business, and had to leave the pastorate, consequently becoming estranged from Fuller, due to his lack of repentance.[5] He still wrote a generally appreciative account of his subject, but was more prepared to be critical of Fuller than Ryland. Some of his comments are, in my view, extremely perceptive. Ryland and Morris are supplemented by a later biography by one of Fuller's sons from his second marriage, Andrew Gunton Fuller,

---

1814) and the Revitalization of the Calvinistic Baptists in the Late-Eighteenth Century', *BQ* 34.7 (July, 1992), p. 306. Fuller was also a highly respected figure in the wider Evangelical world, as the incident with Cecil illustrates and this study will show.

3   R. Hayden, 'The Life and Influence of Andrew Fuller', in R.L. Greenall (ed.), *The Kettering Connection: Northamptonshire Baptists and Overseas Mission* (Leicester: Department of Adult Education, University of Leicester, 1993), p. 12.

4   Although I have worked in the main from the substantially revised and expanded second editions which came out in 1818 and 1826 respectively.

5   *DEB*, II, p. 794. Writing to the BMS missionary W.R. Ward, Fuller spoke of Morris's 'pride and extravagance' and 'shocking failure'. Fuller's comments indicate that Morris was acting 'dishonourably to his creditors', but there is also mention of other unspecified 'moral lapses'. See Fuller to W.R. Ward, 16 July 1809; 15 June 1810, bound volume of Fuller letters to Carey, Marshman, Ward etc., 1795-1815 (3/170), Angus Library, Oxford. See also M.A.G. Haykin, *One Heart and Soul: John Sutcliff of Olney, his Friends and his Times* (Durham: Evangelical Press, 1994), pp. 279-86.

published in 1882.[6] Gunton Fuller's aim was to complement the more major works with a personal, family oriented sketch of his father. It contains a significant amount of material (for example the anecdote of Andrew Fuller's meeting with Cecil), that is not in Ryland or Morris. A small biography by T.E. Fuller,[7] a grandson of his subject, adds little to these three. The 1845 American edition of Fuller's Collected Works has recently been reprinted, and this contains almost all of Fuller's theological and apologetic writings, together with many sermons and other miscellaneous pieces, as well as another, shorter, 'Memoir' by Gunton Fuller.[8] There is much additional material held in libraries and archives, particularly the Angus Library, Regent's Park College, Oxford, and the Bristol Baptist College Library. Pride of place probably goes to the collection of Fuller's letters transcribed by Ernest Payne.[9] Together, these and the other primary sources listed in the bibliography provide ample material for a study of the different aspects of Fuller's wide-ranging ministerial career.

There is also a wealth of relevant primary and secondary material available on eighteenth-century Evangelicalism, and a growing literature relating directly to English Particular Baptist life.[10] I have sought to interact with the most significant books and articles, reassessing the key aspects of Fuller's life and work in the light of recent research. The secondary material relating directly to Fuller has been limited and decidedly uneven in quality,[11] although important work has been done,

---

6   A.G. Fuller, *Men Worth Remembering*. For Gunton Fuller see, *DEB*, I, p. 415.

7   T.E. Fuller, *A Memoir of the Life and Writings of Andrew Fuller* (The Bunyan Library, 11; London: J. Heaton & Son, 1863).

8   A. Fuller, *The Complete Works of the Rev Andrew Fuller, With a Memoir of his Life by the Rev Andrew Gunton Fuller* (A.G. Fuller ed; rev. ed. J. Belcher; 3 vols; Harrisonburg, Virginia: Sprinkle Publications, 3rd edn, 1988 [1845]).

9   Fuller Letters, Angus Library, Oxford (4/5/1 & 4/5/2). Payne collected material from over 550 letters in the course of his work. Some, but by no means all, of these transcribed letters appear in the biographies already cited.

10   For some of the most important literature on eighteenth-century Evangelicalism up to his time see the select biography in G.M. Ditchfield, *The Evangelical Revival* (Introductions to History; London: UCL Press, 1998), pp. 121-30; for examples of work on eighteenth-century Particular Baptist life see many of the entries in M.A.G. Haykin (ed.), *The British Particular Baptists, 1638-1910* (2 vols; Springfield, Missouri: Particular Baptist Press, 1998-2000).

11   For example, A.H. Kirkby, 'The Theology of Andrew Fuller in its Relation to Calvinism' (PhD thesis, Edinburgh University, 1956), which is highly speculative in its views of the origins of Fuller's change of thought. Cf. A.H. Kirkby, 'Andrew Fuller, Evangelical Calvinist', *BQ* 15.5 (January, 1954), pp. 195-202.

especially recently.[12] Nevertheless, even now, the best extended treatment of Fuller's theology is probably still that contained in a series of articles for the *Baptist Quarterly* by E.F. Clipsham. But these appeared in 1963, before the recent resurgence of scholarly interest in Evangelicalism and Particular Baptist life.[13] If anything the coverage of Fuller's pastoral ministry has been even thinner.[14] Fuller's thought and life are both long overdue a detailed treatment.

The Content of this Study

This study attempts this detailed analysis of Fuller's wide ranging career, showing how he came to be shaped – in theology, pastoral practice, spirituality and work as a missionary statesman – by forces associated with the Evangelical Revival. Because of Fuller's importance for the wider story of the transformation of English Particular Baptist life, a study of this kind throws considerable light on the changes taking place in the churches. It clearly shows that it was Evangelical forces that were at work in the denomination during this period of life and growth. The writings of the American theologian and philosopher Jonathan Edwards (1703-58) were particularly important in shaping Fuller and his ministerial colleagues. But Fuller's own contribution to this story of revival[15] and renewal was also a considerable one.

The seven main chapters which form the core of the book are arranged thematically rather than chronologically. Following an opening chapter which seeks to place Fuller in his ecclesiastical context, there are three chapters which concentrate on Fuller's *thought*, specifically his

---

12   For an excellent recent addition to the literature on Fuller see M.A.G. Haykin (ed.), *Armies of the Lamb: The Spirituality of Andrew Fuller* (Classics of Reformed Spirituality, 3; Dundas, Ontario: Joshua Press, 2001).

13   E.F. Clipsham, 'Andrew Fuller and Fullerism: A Study in Evangelical Calvinism', BQ 20.1-4 (1963); '1. The Development of a Doctrine', pp. 99-114; '2. Fuller and John Calvin', pp. 147-54; '3. The Gospel Worthy of All Acceptation', pp. 215-25; '4. Fuller as a Theologian', pp. 269-76.

14   Although see D.L. Young, 'The Place of Andrew Fuller in the Developing Modern Missions Movement' (DPhil thesis, Southwestern Baptist Theological Seminary, 1981). Young's work contains much useful material, but in my judgement is flawed in a number of important respects. His thesis has never been published. I am indebted to Michael Haykin for obtaining a copy of this thesis for me.

15   In this study I have used the word Revival in upper case to denote the Evangelical Revival, and occasionally used the word in lower case as a synonym for 'revitalization'. As I am arguing that the revitalization of Particular Baptist life was part and parcel of the Evangelical Revival, the two uses actually blur into one.

theology of salvation. Chapter two analyzes the origins of the work on which his reputation as a theologian largely rested – *The Gospel Worthy of All Acceptation*, which was originally published in 1785. Fuller rejected the theology known as 'High Calvinism'[16] in favour of an Evangelical Calvinism which would come to characterize every area of his life and thought. Chapters three and four examine how his theology of salvation developed after 1785, focusing especially on the period up to and including1806, after which his most important theological writing had been completed. During this time, Fuller significantly modified his thought as he increasingly came into contact with progressive American thinking and responded to criticism from a variety of quarters. Fuller emerged from this process with a vibrant Evangelical theology. He also earned a reputation as the Particular Baptists premier theologian, and saw the Edwardsean Evangelical Calvinism which came to bear the name 'Fullerism' all but capture the denomination, although his triumph was never quite complete.

The next three chapters focus on Fuller's *life*, surveying both his ministry as a local church pastor (chapter five), his involvement in the genesis and subsequent history of the BMS (chapter six) and his devotional life (chapter seven). This second section of the study reveals that as his theological understanding shifted there were parallel developments in his ministry. What I am concerned to show is how Fuller, both in thought and life, moved from his inherited High Calvinism to an Evangelicalism that was in marked contrast to his earlier position. The order of the chapters springs from my own conviction that, although the precise relationship between Fuller's life and thought was sometimes complex, the changes in Fuller's ministry cannot be understood without an awareness of his developing theology. Indeed, the theological renewal he underwent was the motor for the corresponding renewal that took place in his pastoral practice.

As noted earlier, this study seeks to locate Fuller's place in the wider story of the revitalization of Particular Baptist life. Fuller was involved in most of the developments that Baptist historians have traditionally focused on as they have sought to describe the transformation of Calvinistic Baptist churches which took place in the last quarter of the eighteenth century. Through his life and thought Fuller was both instrumental in and illustrative of the change in outlook and theology that swept over the denomination. This study will show that the revitalization of Particular Baptist life was both fed by the Evangelical Revival and was itself part of the wider Evangelical Revival. Fuller himself was stimulated by Evangelicalism and in turn he stimulated others.

---

16   The nature of High Calvinism is discussed in chapter one.

Finally, a note on where I stand personally might be in order. It will probably become clear quite quickly that I am sympathetic to Fuller and many of his emphases. Moreover, I write as one whose primary calling is to pastoral ministry, and who has come to believe there is much in the story of Fuller and the Revival of eighteenth-century Particular Baptist life to challenge the churches of today, particularly those of the Baptist faith and order. I have been encouraged by comments such as the following by Professor Owen Chadwick, that 'a historian frigid towards his theme can hardly ever write good history',[17] but I have tried to be careful. Hagiography is an obvious pitfall, but my aim has been to write a work of analysis rather than apology or advocacy, and I have endeavored throughout to write 'good history'. In particular I would strenuously deny that I have in any sense distorted the account for the purpose of edification.[18] Where there are insights which I believe could greatly contribute to the spiritual vitality of the churches today, I have almost always refrained from pointing them out, leaving the reader to draw his or her own conclusions. My fundamental aim has always been to contribute to an understanding of Fuller and of the churches in which he worked. Nevertheless, I would not be honest if I did not say that this book is offered with the hope (and indeed the prayer), that as Fuller's story is retold, some might find resources for their own ministries today and be challenged afresh to 'offer Christ to the world'.

---

17   O. Chadwick, *The Spirit of the Oxford Movement* (Cambridge: Cambridge University Press, 1990), p. 157. I originally came across this quotation in T. Dudley-Smith, *John Stott: The Making of a Leader* (Leicester: IVP, 1999), p. 14. Cf. the comments of David Killingray, 'Black Christian Biography', *Christianity and History Forum Newsletter* (Autumn, 2002), p. 21: 'In a close study of an individual…it is possible to become closely attached; familiarity should not lead to suspension of critical faculties, to either excessive warmth or hostility. Walk a middle path is, I suppose, good advice.'

18   Cf. the similar comment by Dudley-Smith, *John Stott*, p. 17.

CHAPTER ONE

Andrew Fuller in Context

The Christian profession had sunk into contempt amongst us

Andrew Fuller was born on 6 February 1754 at Wicken, a village near Ely in Cambridgeshire, the youngest son of Robert Fuller (d. 1781) and Philippa Gunton (d. 1816).[1] Robert was a tenant farmer working a succession of small dairy farms, and in 1761 he took over a farm in the village of Soham, also in Cambridgeshire. Both his parents were Dissenters and Baptists, although Robert appears to have been less committed than his wife. Philippa became a member of the small and isolated Particular Baptist church at Soham, and the whole family attended. Her own mother, also called Philippa, had actually been one of the founding members of the church. In 1775 her son Andrew, despite having little by way of formal education, would become its pastor.

Numerical and Spiritual Decline in Particular Baptist Life

The struggling church at Soham was not untypical of the denomination as whole, and for most Calvinistic Baptists the greater part of the eighteenth century was characterized by both insularity and decline. There is compelling evidence that the Particular Baptists were in numerical decline during the first half of the century. The best source of statistical evidence for the number of dissenting congregations is a list largely drawn up between 1715 and 1718 by Dr John Evans, a London Presbyterian minister. Probably the list is fairly accurate with regard to

---

1   See J. Ryland Jr, *The Work of Faith, the Labour of Love, and the Patience of Hope Illustrated in the Life and Death of the Rev. Andrew Fuller* (London: Button and Son, 2nd edn, 1818), pp. 8-10, for these and other biographical details in this paragraph. I have written a brief biographical sketch of Fuller in M.A.G. Haykin (ed.), *The Apologetic Ministry of Andrew Fuller* (Studies in Baptist History and Thought: 6; Carlisle: Paternoster, forthcoming, 2003).

paedobaptist churches,[2] but W.T. Whitley was able to discover a number of Particular Baptist churches not on the Evans list. Whitley suggested there were approximately 220 Calvinistic Baptist congregations in England and Wales in the years between 1715 and 1718, statistics accepted by Watts.[3] Figures for the mid-eighteenth century are largely based on a survey by John Collett Ryland (1723-1792), although as with the Evans list, the survey is incomplete.[4] Nevertheless, it is clear that the number of congregations had fallen drastically, probably to about 150.[5] Over a period of less than fifty years therefore, the number of churches had decreased by approximately one-third. Many of those that remained were, like Soham, small and experiencing serious difficulties.

To speak of a parallel spiritual decline is more subjective, but this was certainly what many at the time thought was happening. In 1746 Benjamin Wallin, a prominent London pastor, spoke of 'the universal complaints of the decay of practical and vital godliness'. Writing again in 1752, Wallin stated his belief that they were living in a 'melancholy day' of 'present declensions' amongst Particular Baptist churches.[6] In the west of England there was more cause for optimism, particularly due to the work of the Bristol Baptist Academy, but the annual Western Association newsletters still regularly bemoaned the low spiritual temperature in the churches. The letter for 1740 urged readers to acknowledge the prevailing situation and set aside four days in the year ahead for fasting and prayer, at which what had been said could be 'read publicly and pondered by the members'. But twenty years later it appeared that little had changed. In the 1761 letter Isaac Hann wrote that he and other concerned ministers were 'almost at a loss to know what

---

2   See the comprehensive discussion in M.R. Watts, *The Dissenters*. I: *From the Reformation to the French Revolution* (Oxford: Clarenden Press, 1978), pp. 267-71, 491-510. Watt's conclusion, p. 504, is 'that the Evans list is a largely reliable base from which to estimate the numerical strength of Dissent in the years 1715-18'. Cf. the comments in Haykin, 'A Habitation of God Through the Spirit', p. 305. The MS of the Evans list is held in Dr Williams' Library, London.

3   W.T. Whitley, 'The Baptist Interest under George I', *Transactions of the Baptist Historical Society*, 2 (1910-11), pp. 95-109; Watts, *Dissenters*, I, p. 498. The figures for Wales are most suspect.

4   For J.C. Ryland, the father of John Ryland Jr, see 'John Collett Ryland (1723-1792)', in Haykin (ed.), *British Particular Baptists*, I, pp. 183-201.

5   See A.S. Langley, 'Baptist Ministers in England About 1750 A.D.', *Transactions of the Baptist Historical Society*, 6 (1910-11), pp. 138-57; cf. W.T. Whitley, *A History of English Baptists* (London: Charles Griffin, 1923), p. 108.

6   B. Wallin, *The Christian Life, In Divers of its Branches Described and Recommended* (2 vols; London, 1746), II, p. ix; and also his *Exhortations, Relating to Prayer and the Lord's Supper* (London, 1752), pp. viii, x.

we can say further for the stirring up of sleepy professors'. Those who read Hann's words were exhorted to take heed 'lest they sleep the sleep of death'. He went on to plead with his readers: 'Look over the letters which of late years you have had from us...hearken to the counsel and advice of those who would not cease to warn every one with tears.'[7] Certainly there seemed to have been few ministers who would have disagreed with Daniel Turner of Abingdon in Oxfordshire, who, writing in 1769, expressed his view that the spiritual life of the Particular Baptists was markedly 'on the decline'.[8]

This picture does need to be qualified. As Roger Hayden has shown, throughout the first half of the eighteenth century, through the work of successive tutors at the Bristol Academy, a significant number of educated and evangelistically minded ministers entered Particular Baptist life. Hayden also highlights what he terms the 'inspirational fellowship' provided by the Western Association during this period.[9] Undoubtedly some Baptist historians have been prone to overstatement when describing the so called 'dark ages' of the mid-eighteenth century, and Hayden does a thorough and welcome job in correcting this strain of historiography.[10] Nevertheless, this does not alter the *overall* picture of numerical and spiritual decline, a picture for which there is overwhelming evidence. This decline certainly extended to the churches in the Western Association, and well into the second half of the century. One further piece of evidence can be cited. In 1765 Benjamin Francis had the task of writing the association's annual letter, and in it he sounded a note that was by now typical, commenting on 'the lukewarm and careless' people in the churches, who had grown 'formal in worship, and indolent in the service of God'.[11] Certainly this shows a

---

7   J.G. Fuller, *A Brief History of the Western Association* (Bristol, I. Hemmans, 1843), pp. 40, 44-45.

8   D. Turner to S. Stennett, cited in E.A. Payne, *Baptists of Berkshire: Through Three Centuries* (London: Carey Kingsgate Press, 1951), p. 79. See also R. Brown, *The English Baptists of the Eighteenth Century* (A History of the English Baptists, 2; London: Baptist Historical Society, 1986), p. 78.

9   R. Hayden, 'Evangelical Calvinism Among Eighteenth Century Particular Baptists with Particular Reference to Bernard Foskett, Hugh and Caleb Evans and the Bristol Baptist Academy 1690-1791' (PhD thesis, Keele University, 1991). See e.g. pp. 305-306, 360. Cf. the comments of J.H.Y. Briggs, *English Baptists of the Nineteenth Century* (A History of the English Baptists, 3; Didcot, Baptist Historical Society, 1994), pp. 98, 160.

10   Whitley, *History of the English Baptists*, p. 258: 'In the dark ages of the [mid-] eighteenth century there were not ten learned men by whose reputation the [Baptist] denomination might be redeemed.' See also A.H.J. Baines, 'The Pre-History of Regents Park College', *BQ* 36.4 (October, 1995), p. 191.

11   J.G. Fuller, *Western Association*, pp. 46-47.

deep concern for spiritual growth amongst the churches on the part of some of the Western Association's leading figures. But it is also evidence that this growth was not taking place. Hayden also tends to overestimate the influence of Bristol, and underestimate that of the London ministers, which in some parts of the country was all pervasive.[12] It is hard to disagree greatly with Fuller's own assessment of Particular Baptist life up until the late-eighteenth century. 'Had matters gone on but a few years longer', he wrote, 'the Baptists would have become a perfect dunghill in society.'[13]

Causes of Decline

For the mature Fuller, his early biographers and most Baptist historians, particularly those writing in the nineteenth and early- twentieth centuries, there was little doubt as to the reasons for this decline. The theology known as 'High' or 'Hyper' Calvinism was to blame.[14] More recently E.F. Clipsham has followed this line by stating: 'historians have rightly blamed the Hyper Calvinism which was all but universal among Particular Baptists of the period, for the spiritual deadness of their churches.'[15] This view is undoubtedly an over-simplification, and recent studies have rightly emphasized that the causes of decline were more varied and complex than have often been supposed.[16] There was, in fact, a general decline in dissenting denominations in the first half of the eighteenth century, denominations which together encompassed a broad theological spectrum.[17] There were a number of factors other than

---

12   For London's influence in much of the North of England, see J. Fawcett Jr, *An Account of the Life, Ministry and Writings of the late Rev John Fawcett, DD* (London: Baldwin, Craddock and Joy, 1818), pp. 97-102, and also the discussion in Young, 'Fuller and the Developing Modern Missions Movement', pp. 79-89. In Norfolk and Suffolk the predominance of High Calvinism was even greater. For the minutes of the London Board see W.T. Whitley, 'Baptist Board Minutes, 1750-1820', *Transactions of the Baptist Historical Society* 7 (1918-19), pp. 72-127.

13   J.W. Morris, *Memoirs of the Life and Death of the Rev Andrew Fuller*, 1st edn. (High Wycombe, 1816), p. 267.

14   See, for example, H.C. Vedder, *A Short History of the English Baptists* (Valley Forge: Judson Press, 1907), p. 240; W.T. Whitley, *Calvinism and Evangelism in England and Especially Among Baptists* (London: Kingsgate Press, 1933), p. 28.

15   E.F. Clipsham, 'Andrew Fuller and Fullerism: A Study in Evangelical Calvinism. 1. The Development of a Doctrine', *BQ* 20.1 (1963) , p. 101.

16   Haykin, 'A Habitation of God, Through the Spirit', pp. 304-305, surveys a number of recent works.

17   D.W. Lovegrove, *Established Church, Sectarian People: Itinerancy and the*

theology that contributed to the weakness of much of Calvinistic Baptist life, and some of these can be considered briefly.

One of the problems was the continuing legal and social discrimination that all Dissenters faced, even after the 1689 Act of Toleration. Certainly, and in common with all Nonconformists, Baptists were given a real measure of freedom by this act. Particularly important was the promise of freedom of worship. Watts comments that this in itself may have contributed to decline, as toleration 'brought material benefits that sapped the spiritual zeal of Dissent'.[18] But there were still severe restrictions. Dissenters did not enjoy anything like full civil rights, and even in the area of worship constraints remained. Only buildings registered as meeting houses with the local bishop or justice of the peace could be used for worship, and even then the door had to be kept propped open as a safeguard against seditious activity. Meetings could still be disrupted, and often were.[19] Socially, as well as legally, Dissenters continued to encounter significant discrimination, contributing to insularity and discouraging potential new members.[20] Haykin observes that 'by and large, the Baptists accepted the restrictions placed upon them and for much of the eighteenth century limited their horizons to the maintenance of congregational life'.[21]

A further cause of decline was the geographical isolation of many churches, situated as they were in small villages, with communication between them difficult. This isolation was compounded, not only by the poor transport infrastructure, but also by the traditional Baptist stress on the autonomy and independence of the gathered congregation.[22] With association life generally either weak or non-existent, and no national denominational structure, there was often little or no support for struggling causes and a lack of common purpose. Where there was life and growth, opportunities for this to permeate across to other churches were limited. Fuller's church at Soham can be seen as a prime example

---

Transformation of English Dissent, 1780-1830 (Cambridge: Cambridge University Press, 1988), p. 7; Watts, *Dissenters*, I, p. 385, who speaks of the 'decay of the Dissenting interest'.

18   Watts, *The Dissenters*, I, p. 385.

19   For numerous examples of discrimination after the Act of Toleration, see P. Naylor, *Picking up a Pin for the Lord: English Particular Baptists from 1688 to the Early Nineteenth Century* (Durham: Grace Publications Trust, 1992), pp. 33-39.

20   E.g. Soham Baptist Church Book, 1770-1833 [with records before 1840 transcribed from the 'old church book'] (NC/B - Soham), p. 9, where it is recorded that baptism was administered as 'early as 2 or 3 o'clock in the morning' or late at night, because 'the local populace behaved so ill'.

21   Haykin, *One Heart and Soul*, p. 20.

22   Cf. Lovegrove, *Established Church, Sectarian People*, p. 7.

of one such isolated, struggling cause. It is not difficult to see how the factors we have noted in the last two paragraphs contributed to the prevailing insularity and weakness.

High Calvinism as a Cause of Decline

It is important though, to return to consider the effect of High or 'Hyper' Calvinism on the life of the denomination.[23] Fundamental to High Calvinism was the belief that 'unconverted sinners were under no moral obligation to repent and believe the gospel, since they were rendered incapable of doing so by total depravity, and could not justly be held accountable for failing to do what they were unable to do'.[24] The logical outworking of this position was that what were termed 'indiscriminate exhortations to faith and repentance' could not be addressed to the unconverted. To do so would be a nonsense, because it could not be the 'duty' of the unregenerate to do 'anything spiritually good'.[25] Reflecting back on High Calvinism later in life, Fuller himself summed up its practical effect: nothing was to be said to 'sinners…inviting them to apply to Christ for salvation.'[26] The first systematic exposition of High Calvinism was published in 1707 by Joseph Hussey, appropriately titled *God's Operations of Grace, but no Offers of Grace.*[27] But in mid-eighteenth century Particular Baptist circles it was strongly associated with the views of two London pastors, John Brine (1703-65) and John Gill (1697-1771).

---

23   Following G.F. Nuttall, 'Northamptonshire and *The Modern Question*: A Turning Point in Eighteenth-Century Dissent', *JTS* 16.1 (April, 1965), p. 101, this study uses the term High Calvinism rather than 'Hyper Calvinism' to describe the theology of John Gill and his followers. Fuller used both interchangeably, also referring to 'false' and 'pseudo' Calvinism. P. Toon, *The Emergence of Hyper Calvinism in English Nonconformity 1689-1765* (London: Olive Tree, 1967), p. 144, refers to Gill and Brine as 'Hyper Calvinists' and reserves the term 'High Calvinism' for the developed Puritanism of men like William Ames and John Owen. But to call Owen a High Calvinist in this context is misleading.

24   B. Stanley, *The History of the Baptist Missionary Society, 1792-1992* (Edinburgh: T. & T. Clark, 1992), p. 5.

25   Toon, *Hyper Calvinism*, pp. 144-45 states that 'Hyper' Calvinists 'placed excessive emphasis on the immanent acts of God - eternal justification, eternal adoption and the eternal covenant of grace. In practice this meant that "Christ and him crucified", the central message of the apostles, was obscured. In addition they often made no distinction between the secret and revealed will of God.'

26   Ryland, *Andrew Fuller*, pp. 31-32.

27   For Hussey, see A.P.F. Sell, *The Great Debate: Calvinism, Arminianism and Salvation* (Worthing: H.E. Walter, 1982), pp. 52-54.

Of these two, Gill was the more significant.[28] He was actually born in Kettering, Northamptonshire, the town where Fuller was to become pastor of the Particular Baptist church known as the 'Little Meeting' in 1783. Gill was minister at Carter Lane in Southwark from 1719 until his death, and for most of this time was the leading figure on the London Baptist Board, a group of pastors whose advice on a wide range of matters was sought by Calvinistic Baptist churches from all over the country. But Gill's reputation and influence largely rested on his voluminous works. Best known were perhaps *The Cause of God and Truth*, originally published in four volumes (1735-38) and his nine volume *Exposition of the Holy Scriptures* (1746-66). Self taught, Gill was widely recognized as a skilled Hebraist, and his work was acknowledged with the award of an Aberdeen DD in 1748. Through his writings, later memorably described by Robert Hall Jr as a 'continent of mud',[29] his influence over Particular Baptist life was vast.

Gill has not fared well at the hands of most Baptist historians, who have tended to share Hall Jr's opinion of the London divine. W.T. Whitley in particular has some fun at Gill's expense, saying that he 'drowned in Hebrew except when he woke to fulminate at Wesley' (whilst Brine 'exaggerated hyper-Calvinism till he only had thirty of the elect left' in his congregation).[30] Recently, however, a number of attempts have been made to rehabilitate Gill and to rebut the charge that he was a High Calvinist.[31] A detailed consideration of Gill's position is beyond the scope of this chapter, but the following extract from his collected *Sermons and Tracts* is relevant. In it, Gill made clear his opinion on the 'open offer' of the gospel:

---

28   For biographical details of Gill see J. Rippon, *A Brief Memoir of the Life and Writings of the late Rev. John Gill, DD* (London: John Bennett, 1838); R.W. Oliver, 'John Gill (1697-1771)', in Haykin (ed.), *British Particular Baptists*, I, pp. 145-65; M.A.G. Haykin (ed.), *The Life and Thought of John Gill (1697-1771): A Tercentennial Appreciation* (Leiden: Brill, 1997).

29   See R. Hall Jr, *The Works of Robert Hall* (ed. O. Gregory; 6 vols; London, 1833), VI, pp. 155-56; O.C. Robison, 'The Legacy of John Gill', *BQ* 24.3 (July, 1971), p. 112.

30   W.T. Whitley, *The Baptists of London*, (London: Kingsgate Press, 1928), p. 52. See also the long list of more or less negative assessments in G. Ella, 'John Gill and the Charge of Hyper-Calvinism', *BQ* 36.4 (October, 1995), p. 176 n.1.

31   The best of these is T. George, 'John Gill', in T. George and D.S. Dockery (eds), *Baptist Theologians* (Nashville, TN: Broadman Press, 1990), pp. 77-101. See also G.M. Ella 'John Gill and the Charge of Hyper-Calvinism', *passim*. For a detailed bibliography and survey of the debate, see G.R. Priest, 'Andrew Fuller, Hyper-Calvinism, and the Modern Question', in Haykin (ed.), *Apologetics of Andrew Fuller*.

That there are universal offers of grace and salvation made to all men, I utterly deny; nay I deny that they are made to any; no not to God's elect; grace and salvation are provided for them in the everlasting covenant, procured for them by Christ, published and revealed in the gospel and applied by the Spirit.[32]

George Ella protests that this particular quotation, which is often referred to in the secondary literature on Gill, is taken out of context, although it is not clear how a knowledge of the context alters the basic meaning.[33] Certainly Gill thought that the phrase 'to offer Christ' lacked any biblical foundation. Talk of 'gospel-commands, gospel-threatenings and gospel-duties' were to him a 'contradiction in terms', and smacked of 'loose and unguarded speech'.[34] In 1748 Gill wrote a Preface to the seventh edition of the hymns of Richard Davis, who from 1689 to 1714 had been minister of the Congregational church at Rothwell, Northamptonshire.[35] In it Gill commented on the fact that 'the phrase of offering Christ and grace is sometimes used in these hymns'. He continued:

I can affirm, upon good and sufficient testimony, that Mr Davis, before his death, changed his mind in this matter, and disused the phrase, as being improper, and being too bold and free for a minister of Christ to make use of. And though I have not thought fit to alter any words or phrases in the revision of these hymns, yet in the use of them in public service, those who think proper may substitute another phrase in its room more eligible.[36]

Gill's own views are clear enough from this extract. The entirely negative view of Gill and his ministry expressed by Whitley undoubtedly needed some revision. But attempts to defend him from the

---

32   J. Gill, *Sermons and Tracts* (3 vols; London, 1778), III, pp. 269-70. Cf. John Brine: 'Offers of grace as I conceive, are not made to those who are not under grace...', J. Brine, *The Certain Efficacy of The Death of Christ*, p. 75, cited by Toon, *Hyper Calvinism*, p. 129.

33   Ella, 'John Gill and the Charge of Hyper-Calvinism', p. 167. Gill was writing against Wesley's teaching regarding a universal atonement.

34   J. Gill, *The Doctrines of God's Everlasting Love to His Elect... Stated and Defended. In a Letter to Dr Abraham Taylor* (London, 1752), p. 78. See also Robison, 'John Gill', p. 120. Note in addition comments in Gill's *The Cause of God and Truth* (London, 1855 [1735-38]), pp. 166-67.

35   For Davis, a controversial figure in his own right, see Nuttall, 'Northamptonshire and the Modern Question', pp. 104-108.

36   J. Gill, 'Recommendatory Preface to the Hymns of Richard Davis' (1748), printed in G.T. Streather, *Memorials of the Independent Chapel at Rothwell* (Rothwell: Rothwell United Reformed Church, 1994), p. 63-64.

charge of High Calvinism are ultimately unconvincing.[37]

There is a compelling weight of evidence to suggest that High Calvinism was the prevailing theology amongst many Particular Baptists for much of the eighteenth century. John Fawcett Jr, reflecting back on the situation in the north of England in the 1760s, commented:

> The possession of [Gill's] elaborate performances was, in those days, considered as almost an essential part of the library, not only of ministers, but of private Christians of the Baptist denomination, who could afford to purchase them. They were read almost exclusively, to the neglect of other works on divinity.[38]

Surveying the wider scene, John Ryland Jr stated that, largely through the influence of Gill and Brine, the opinion 'spread pretty much among the ministers of the Baptist denomination [that] it is not the duty of the unregenerate to believe in Christ'. Consequently they were 'too much restrained from imitating our Lord and his apostles, in calling on sinners to repent and believe the gospel'.[39] When Ryland wrote these words, between 1815 and 1816, he was Principal of Bristol Baptist Academy and would hardly have been ignorant of or biased against the Bristol tradition. Ryland, Fuller's official 'tombstone' biographer, was, together with John Sutcliff (1752-1814), Fuller's closest friend and colleague from the early 1780s onwards. He had himself been strongly inclined towards High Calvinism as a young man, but had been weaned away from it through his friendship and correspondence with the Evangelical clergyman John Newton (1725-1807).[40] But there were few who had access to such a mentor. The violent reactions to works which challenged High Calvinism, particularly to Fuller's own *The Gospel Worthy of All Acceptation*, showed how deeply this theology had become embedded in much of Particular Baptist life. John Eve (d. 1782),[41] Fuller's Pastor at Soham until 1771, was representative of the

---

37   Gill's ministry is well discussed by Sell, *Great Debate*, pp. 76-83; Oliver, 'John Gill', pp. 161-2; Priest, 'Andrew Fuller'. The debate turns on whether Gill's theology choked the evangelistic life of the denomination, or whether he helped to keep Particular Baptists orthodox (particularly on the Trinity), in an age where Unitarianism was a very real threat. Probably both these propositions are true to some degree, although the extent to which churches so little involved in evangelism can properly be called 'orthodox' is another question. My own view is that Gill's High Calvinism had a generally adverse effect on Particular Baptist life, as will become clear.

38   Fawcett Jr, *John Fawcett*, p. 97.

39   Ryland, *Andrew Fuller*, p. 8.

40   B. Hindmarsh, *John Newton and the English Evangelical Tradition: Between the Conversions of Wesley and Wilberforce* (Oxford: Clarendon Press, 1996), pp. 142-49.

41   Eve was originally a sieve-maker from Chesterton in Cambridgeshire. A

type of High Calvinist minister Fawcett Jr and Ryland had in mind. Eve was an avid reader of Gill and had, according to Fuller, 'little or nothing to say to the unconverted'. It is no surprise that when Fuller, as the new pastor at Soham, sought to introduce 'open offers' of the gospel into his preaching in the late 1770s, he encountered significant opposition from within the church.[42]

My contention is that High Calvinism contributed to a number of trends in Particular Baptist life during this period, trends with which Fuller was to grapple throughout his ministry. These included a distinct lack of evangelistic impetus, unsurprising given the prevailing theological climate. Once again there were exceptions, which included Andrew Gifford (1700-84), the effective evangelistic pastor of Eagle Street Baptist Church in London from 1735 until his death. Gifford was a friend of George Whitefield and it was estimated that some 600 people were converted under his preaching. Gifford could have been an important influence for good in the capital, but significantly he was kept at arms length by the Baptist ministers of the London Board.[43] The nineteenth-century Baptist historian Joseph Ivimey's (1773-1834) summary of the general situation was probably not unfair: 'Ministers were contending earnestly that they were an elect people, whom God would save through sanctification of the Spirit, and the belief of the truth, but without using the appointed means for bringing the sheep of Christ into his fold by going after the strayed and the lost.'[44] Soham, Fuller's immediate context, was in fact broadly representative of the denomination as a whole. Maintenance rather than mission was the order of the day.

Also worth noting is the tendency towards doctrinal controversy and heresy hunting that both contributed to, and was the result of, the prevailing insularity. One example of this general trend which touched Fuller directly was the work of John Johnson (1706-91). Johnson

---

member of St Andrews Baptist Church in Cambridge, he was ordained pastor at Soham in 1752. See 'Soham Baptist Church Book, 1770-1833', pp. 2-4; K.A.C. Parsons (ed.), *The Book of the Independent Church (Now Pound Lane Baptist), Isleham 1693-1805* (Cambridge: Cambridge Antiquarian Records Society, 1984), p. 255.

42   John Sutcliff had a similar experience when he tried to bring this new note into his own preaching at Olney, also in the late 1770s. See Haykin, *One Heart and Soul*, p. 151. Ryland Jr was accused at Northampton of being a 'linsey-woolsey' preacher. 'Linsey-woolsey' was a material made up of a mix of coarse wool and cotton – neither one thing nor the other. See Naylor, 'John Collett Ryland', in Haykin (ed.), *British Particular Baptists*, I, pp. 192-93.

43   R.W. Oliver, 'George Whitefield and the English Baptists', *Grace Magazine* 5 (October, 1970), pp. 10-11; Brown, *English Baptists*, pp. 80-81.

44   *HEB*, III, p. 280. For Joseph Ivimey see *DEB*, I, p. 597.

became pastor of Byrom Street Baptist Church in Liverpool in 1741, and within a couple of years had caused a split in the congregation. Johnson is described by one historian as 'basically a prickly Hyper Calvinist with a taste for travel, theological hair splitting and provoking strife'. Everything he touched was 'soon seething with controversy'.[45] He wrote a number of pamphlets propagating his own brand of highly speculative theology, on subjects such as the supposed pre-existence of Christ's human soul. Eve was an admirer of Johnson, and Fuller began to read him round about 1774. Fuller found Johnson a 'forceful pamphleteer'. There was, he said, 'something imposing in his manner [of writing] by which a young and inexperienced reader is apt to be carried away'. Although 'perplexed' by Johnson, Fuller concluded that 'his scheme had no foundation in the Scriptures'. Not everyone was so discerning. Johnson's teaching went on to split a number of Baptist causes as well as his own.[46] As we shall see in chapter two, Soham was also to be riven by doctrinal controversy in the early 1770s, although this was not linked with the teaching of Johnson.

It will be clear that during the period between 1700 and 1775, the majority of Calvinistic Baptists had a very insular concept of the church. Many described themselves proudly as 'a garden enclosed', language taken from one of their favourite texts (Song of Songs 4.12). According to Gill, the church, as 'a garden enclosed', is protected and 'encompassed with the power of God as a wall about it... It is so closely surrounded, that it is not to be seen nor known by the world; and indeed is not accessible to any but believers in Christ'.[47] Gill himself recognized that the Particular Baptist cause was in decline; he could hardly do otherwise.[48] But the way to renewal for Gill and those who followed in his tradition was jealously to guard Calvinistic Baptist distinctives of church government and discipline. This insularity was a key contributing factor to the resistance of most Particular Baptists to forces linked with the Evangelical Revival. This resistance merits a more detailed treatment.

---

45   I. Sellers, (ed.), *Our Heritage: The Baptists of Yorkshire, Lancashire and Cheshire* (Leeds: Yorkshire Baptist Association, 1987), p. 13.

46   Ryland, *Andrew Fuller*, pp. 54-55, 63.

47   J. Gill, *An Exposition of the Old* Testament (4 vols; London: Matthews and Leigh, 1810), IV, p. 662. See also Haykin, *One Heart and Soul*, p. 20.

48   See *HEB*, III, p. 277.

The Evangelical Revival and Particular Baptist Life

The Evangelical Revival profoundly affected British religious life, and gave birth to modern Evangelicalism, described by David Bebbington as 'a popular Protestant movement that has existed in Britain since the 1730s'.[49] The Revival's two most important figures in England were George Whitefield (1714-70), who from 1737 began preaching to crowds in the open air, exhorting them to seek the 'new birth', and John Wesley (1703-91). In 1738 Wesley felt his heart 'strangely warmed' as he trusted in 'Christ alone for salvation', and a year later, encouraged by Whitefield, he too famously began 'field preaching' himself. The Revival was a trans-atlantic phenomenon, greatly facilitated by a religious print culture that was both sophisticated and international. Already in 1734 there had been a Revival in Northampton, Massachusetts, where Jonathan Edwards was minister of the Congregational church, and this was a precursor to the American 'Great Awakening' of 1740-42, in which Whitefield, making the first of his six visits to America in 1740, was the major figure.[50] The results of the Evangelical Revival in both Britain and America were dramatic: a substantial increase in the number and intensity of new religious commitments resulted, with a concomitant increase in the 'fervour and intensity' of corporate religious life.[51]

Because Evangelicalism was to become so important, both for Fuller and for Particular Baptist life, an awareness of what it meant to be 'Evangelical' is vital for this study, although arriving at a precise definition of the term is notoriously difficult.[52] Nevertheless the understanding that all subsequent writers have had to reckon with is that proposed by Bebbington in his groundbreaking *Evangelicalism in*

---

49   For information in this paragraph see Bebbington, *Evangelicalism*, pp. 1, 20-1. Throughout this study I have used the term 'Evangelical' with an upper case E to refer to 'modern Evangelicalism'.

50   Of these three key figures in the transatlantic eighteenth-century Evangelical Revival, Edwards is by far the most significant for this study. See S.R. Holmes, *God of Grace and God of Glory: An Account of the Theology of Jonathan Edwards* (Edinburgh: T. & T. Clark, 2000), for a study of his theology. Probably the best book length biography of Edwards available is that by I.H. Murray, *Jonathan Edwards: A New Biography* (Edinburgh: Banner of Truth, 1987). See also *DEB*, I, pp. 345-46.

51   See K.R. Hylson-Smith, *The Churches in England from Elizabeth I to Elizabeth II. II: 1689-1833* (London: SCM Press, 1997), pp. 120-22, for a useful discussion on the distinguishing marks of 'Revival' in its eighteenth-century context.

52   Cf. the comments of A.E. McGrath, *Evangelicalism and the Future of Christianity* (London: Hodder & Stoughton, 1996), p. 49.

Modern Britain. Bebbington argues that the central qualities that have been the 'special marks' uniting Evangelicalism are 'conversionism, crucicentrism, biblicism and activism'. Together these form 'a quadrilateral of priorities that is the basis of Evangelicalism'. In a later work he puts this more simply, speaking of a 'zeal for conversion', 'proclamation of the cross', 'devotion to the Bible' and 'unbounded activism'.[53] Bebbington's understanding of the movement has attracted widespread support, although some criticism too.[54] Nevertheless G.M. Ditchfield is surely right in describing Bebbington's analysis as 'the most convincing summary of evangelical characteristics by a modern historian'.[55] It is Bebbington's 'essentialist' understanding of Evangelicalism that we work with in this study. What is certain is that the Revival and the Evangelicalism it spawned had a powerful impact on eighteenth-century religious life from the 1730s onwards. But up to 1775, the majority of Particular Baptists stood aloof from this powerful revivifying force on the religious scene. The reasons for this are once again linked with insular ecclesiology and the predominance of High Calvinist theology.

Questions of church order were crucial in determining most Particular Baptists' negative attitude towards Evangelicalism. The Revival was initially an Anglican, not a dissenting movement. The Revival leaders (Wesley and his brother Charles, Whitefield and Howell Harris), were all members of the Church of England, which was regarded by Gill as apostate. William Herbert, a Welsh Baptist pastor, wrote to Harris in 1737 asking him whether he did not realize that the scriptures described the church as 'a garden inclosed [sic], a spring shut up, a fountain sealed...separate from ye profane world.'[56] Gill was particularly hard on any concept of a 'national church'. Any such body, he argued, should be regarded as 'carnal'.[57] Given these strictures, it is not surprising that Particular Baptists stood apart from what was happening. Whitefield in particular, who might have been expected to have attracted more

---

53   Bebbington, *Evangelicalism*, pp. 2-3, 5-17, and 'Towards an Evangelical Identity', in S. Brady and H.H. Rowden (eds), *For Such a Time as This* (London: Scripture Union, 1996), p. 44.

54   For support see e.g. Hindmarsh, *John Newton*, p. 9; K.D. Brown, 'Nonconformist Evangelicals and National Politics', in J. Wolfe (ed.), *Evangelical Faith and Public Zeal: Evangelicals in Society in Britain 1780-1980* (London: SPCK, 1995), p. 140. For notable criticism see D.A. Carson, *The Gagging of God: Christianity Confronts Pluralism* (Leicester: IVP, 1996), pp. 449-50.

55   Ditchfield, *Evangelical Revival*, p. 26.

56   Cited by Haykin, *One Heart and Soul*, p. 27.

57   J.W. Brush, 'John Gill's Doctrine of the Church', in W.S. Hudson (ed.), *Baptist Concepts of the Church* (Philadelphia: Judson Press, 1959), p. 59.

support in the light of his Calvinism, was completely uninterested in the questions of church order that were dear to Gill, Brine and their followers. In fact, against the background of High Calvinism, Whitefield's adherence to true Calvinistic principles was considered deeply suspect, and Particular Baptists spoke dismissively about his 'Arminian dialect'.[58] As far as the Wesleys were concerned, their aggressive Arminianism, together with their caustic comments about the 'people called Anabaptists', clearly put them beyond the pale.[59] As long as High Calvinism held sway, many Particular Baptists would remain 'a garden inclosed' from any Revival influences.

Questions of what was termed 'enthusiasm' were also relevant. Whitefield and Wesley were both accused of this in an age which exalted reason. A cartoon by the celebrated eighteenth-century satirist William Hogarth, 'Credulity, Superstitions and Fanaticism' (1762), shows a fanatical Methodist preacher haranguing a hysterical congregation. Dotted around the church building are copies of Wesley's sermons, Whitefield's *Journal* and older works on 'witchcraft, demonology and apparitions'.[60] Hogarth's cartoon captures well the view held by many opponents that Wesley and Whitefield were guilty of 'enthusiasm', however much they might try to rebut the charge. Enthusiasm's 'basic theological meaning in the eighteenth century was a claim to extraordinary revelations or powers from the Holy Spirit; and, more vaguely and abusively, any kind of religious excitement.'[61] Calvinistic Baptists were in general strongly critical of anything that smacked of enthusiasm, and perhaps particularly of the phenomena associated with the Revival, together with the associated emotional style of preaching.[62] Gill in his *A Complete Body of Doctrinal and Practical Divinity* stated that spiritual joy 'is not to be expressed by those who experience it; it is better experienced than expressed.' In its historical context, this remark was almost certainly an implicit criticism of the

---

58   See M.A.G. Haykin, 'The Baptist Identity: A View From the Eighteenth Century', *Evangelical Quarterly* 67.2 (1995), pp. 141-43.

59   Haykin, *One Heart and Soul*, pp. 26-28.

60   H.D. Rack, *Reasonable Enthusiast: John Wesley and the Rise of Methodism* (Epworth Press: London, 1989), p. 277. Cf. the very similar Hogarth engraving, 'Enthusiasm Delineated' (1761), in D.L. Jeffrey (ed.), *English Spirituality in the Age of Wesley* (Grand Rapids: Eerdmans, 1987), p. 14.

61   Rack, *Reasonable Enthusiast*, p. 276. Cf. the definition in Dr Johnson's *Dictionary*, quoted by Rack, p. ix:, '*Enthusiasm*: A vain belief of private revelation; a warm confidence of divine favour or communication.'

62   For Whitefield's extemporaneous, 'dramatic' style of preaching see H.S. Stout, *The Divine Dramatist: George Whitefield and the Rise of Modern Evangelicalism* (Grand Rapids: Eerdmans, 1991), pp. 66-86.

Evangelical Revival.[63] The net result of these concerns was that people were excommunicated from Particular Baptist churches for associating with Methodists. There is no evidence that this happened at Soham – but then there is no evidence that Revival influences ever touched the church during Eve's pastorate.

We have already noted that there were some exceptions to the general trend of resistance to the Revival. As well as Andrew Gifford, there were other Baptist ministers who were on good terms with Whitefield and invited him into their pulpits and encouraged him to engage in field preaching in their areas.[64] But perhaps more importantly, as the century wore on, there were some in Baptist pastoral ministry who owed their conversion and theological formation to Evangelical preaching. Both Robert Robinson (1735-90) and John Fawcett (1740-1817) owed their conversions to Whitefield himself. Robinson first went to Whitefield's Tabernacle in Moorfields, 'pitying the poor deluded Methodists', but at the end of the service 'went away envying their happiness'. He was converted there in 1752.[65] Fawcett's son, John Fawcett Jr, records his father's reaction to Whitefield's preaching:

> The first time our young disciple saw and heard this eminent man of God was at Bradford, in an open part of town, near the waterside (the year was 1755). No place of worship could contain the concourse of people assembled on that occasion. The text was John iii: 14. 'As Moses lifted up the serpent in the wilderness' &c. His own language will best describe what his sensations were on that interesting occasion: 'As long as life remains, I shall remember both the text and the sermon.' He admired, he was astonished with almost every sentence, both in the devotional exercises and the sermon.

Fawcett always kept a picture of Whitefield in his study, and 'the very mention of his name inspired the warmest emotions of grateful remembrance'. Clearly Fawcett never forgot his debt to the Evangelical leader, and when he became a correspondent of Fuller after 1792, bemoaned the fact that the Particular Baptists did not have their own Whitefield.[66] None of this alters the general picture of resistance to

---

63   See Haykin, *One Heart and Soul*, p. 31. Gill's separate works on 'Doctrinal' and 'Practical' Divinity were later combined.

64   This occurred as early as 1739. See Brown, *English Baptists*, p. 81. Gifford was still exceptional in that he was on good terms with so many of the key Revival leaders.

65   For Robinson, see Brown, *English Baptists*, p. 81; G.W. Hughes, *With Freedom Fired: The Story of Robert Robinson, Cambridge Nonconformist* (London: Carey Kingsgate Press, 1955), *passim*. Robinson was unusual amongst Particular Baptists of this period in that he became unorthodox on the Trinity later in life.

66   Fawcett Jr, *John Fawcett*, pp. 15-18; 297.

Revival influences or, indeed, of general decline. But it does indicate that as the eighteenth-century wore on, things were beginning to change. It also suggests from where renewal for the Particular Baptists would come.

Conclusion

In this opening chapter I have sought to briefly outline Fuller's immediate and wider context as essential background to this study. When, in April 1770, he was baptized and joined the church at Soham, Fuller became a member of an isolated, struggling congregation, with an introverted ecclesiology, where the prevailing theology was High Calvinism. Moreover, in displaying these characteristics, Soham was not untypical of many other Particular Baptist churches, and symptomatic of an overall decline in the life of the denomination as a whole. The causes of this malaise were many, varied and interrelated. Clearly there was a complex matrix of factors – social, political and geographical as well as theological – which contributed to decline. While I fully accept this complexity, I have sought to reassert how important it is to consider theological reasons as a major factor leading to decline. Just as Fuller, Ryland Jr and Sutcliff were right to regard Gill as a High Calvinist, they also correctly saw that this theology had greatly contributed to the malaise in denominational life.

It is, of course, true that the whole of the dissenting interest declined during the period under discussion, and that the majority of denominations in retreat were not gripped by High Calvinism. But there were theological reasons for their decline too, with many capitulating to the rationalism of the age by embracing Unitarianism. Watts writes that in its search for a theology Dissent was torn between 'a Calvinism that was rejected by the leading thinkers of the age...and a rationalism which, as Doddridge realized, had no popular appeal.'[67] Other groups that were in decline, such as the old General Baptists, and many Presbyterian churches, would not see theological renewal in the last quarter of the eighteenth century, and all but dwindled away. But for Fuller and the Particular Baptists in 1775, theological renewal was on the horizon, a renewal that would go hand in hand with a major upturn in their fortunes.[68]

---

67   Watts, *Dissenters*, I, p. 385.

68   Cf. L.G. Champion, 'Evangelical Calvinism and the Structures of Baptist Church Life', *BQ*, 28.5 (January, 1980), p. 197, who argues that theological factors led to renewal.

CHAPTER TWO

The Gospel Worthy of All Acceptation and the Development of Fuller's Evangelical Theology

The sentiments usually denominated evangelical

By the beginning of the nineteenth century a new word had entered the theological vocabulary of the Particular Baptists. The term 'Fullerism' began to appear as early as 1804 in pamphlets such as *A Blow at the Root of Fullerism* and *Fullerism Defended.*[1] As Geoffrey Nuttall points out, its coining and subsequent acceptance by friend and foe alike 'points to a remarkable achievement'. He quotes Ernest Payne: 'It was Andrew Fuller's vigorous independent mind which first broke out of the trammels of Hyper-Calvinism and produced in *The Gospel Worthy of All Acceptation*…a little book destined to effect a theological and practical revolution in most of the Calvinist [i.e. Calvinistic Baptist] churches.'[2] For once Payne, normally such a careful historian, overstates his case. As noted in chapter one, there were a number of Particular Baptists who had never accepted the High Calvinism typified in the works of Gill and Brine, and by the time *The Gospel Worthy of All Acceptation* was first published in 1785, there were many others who were already embracing the Evangelical Calvinism it contained.

But there is no doubt that for the Particular Baptists, *The Gospel Worthy of All Acceptation* (henceforth *The Gospel Worthy*), *was* a seminal book. Not only did it help crystallize the thinking of some who were moving in the same direction as Fuller, but it influenced many more who were as yet uncertain. Consequently it was both illustrative of the changes taking place in denominational life, and a key text in

---

1   Morris, *Andrew Fuller*, 2nd edn, pp. 238-39; Nuttall, 'Northamptonshire and the Modern Question', p. 101. Unsurprisingly, Fuller protested against the use of the term.

2   E.A. Payne, *College Street Church, Northampton, 1697-1947* (London: Kingsgate Press, 1947), p. 22. Cf. Young, 'Fuller and the Developing Modern Missions Movement', who states, in p. 2 of his Abstract, that Fuller 'almost single-handedly turned the theological tide from hyper-Calvinism to a moderate Calvinism that demanded vigorous evangelism'.

spreading those changes still further. *The Gospel Worthy* was also warmly received by many Evangelicals who were not Particular Baptists. In the words of E.F. Clipsham, it 'provided a theology such as thinking men were seeking'.[3] 'Fullerism' was destined to become a potent force – in Particular Baptist life and beyond.

In *The Gospel Worthy* Fuller sought to stress the importance of human responsibility alongside divine sovereignty. There were two main thrusts to his work. Firstly it was the responsibility of all who heard the gospel to believe in Christ. Everyone, including those who were not part of the 'elect', had a 'duty' to respond. The second point was the logical corollary of the first. Preachers could, indeed should, exhort all their hearers to believe in Christ. In saying this he was arguing for the universal, indiscriminate 'offers' of the gospel that Gill and Brine had rejected. Already it should be clear that Fuller had travelled far from the High Calvinist views he had initially inherited. This chapter begins with a summary of the central points of Fuller's argument in *The Gospel Worthy*, and then goes on to examine the reasons behind the development of his thought.

The Gospel Worthy of All Acceptation: Summary of the First Edition[4]

Fuller began *The Gospel Worthy* by challenging the prevailing High Calvinist definition of faith. High Calvinists understood faith as being analogous to a person having an 'inner persuasion' of their 'interest' in Christ, something given to them by the Holy Spirit. This gave the person concerned a so-called 'warrant of faith', encouraging them that they were part of the elect, so enabling them to come to Christ. This effectively made faith into a person's subjective, conscious feeling that the Holy Spirit was beginning to work savingly in their life, and that the gospel was therefore for them. But this, asserted Fuller, was not biblical

---

3   E.F. Clipsham, 'Andrew Fuller's Doctrine of Salvation' (BD thesis, Oxford University, 1961), p. 281, cited by R.W. Oliver, 'The Emergence of a Strict and Particular Baptist Community Among the English Calvinistic Baptists, 1770-1850' (DPhil thesis, CNAA [London Bible College], 1986), p. 85.

4   A. Fuller, *The Gospel Worthy of All Acceptation* (Northampton: T. Dicey, 1st edn, 1785). Several copies are held in the Angus library, Oxford (21/6/2). The 2nd edn is printed in *Fuller's Works*, II, pp. 328-416, where the date of publication for the 1st edn is wrongly given as 1786. See Haykin, *One Heart and Soul*, pp. 142-47, for a recent summary of the 2nd edn, which appeared in 1801. There are significant differences between the two editions, some of which are commented on by Oliver, 'Emergence of a Strict and Particular Baptist Community', pp. 82-87.

faith. The scriptures represented true faith as being fixed, not on something subjective or 'within' the person concerned, but on something objective or 'without', namely Christ himself. To establish this was extremely important to Fuller, because if faith was someone's belief that they were 'interested' in Christ, then it could not be the 'duty' of the unconverted to believe. Indeed, he stated '[t]hat if this be faith...the controversy is, or ought to be, at an end...none but real Christians have any warrant to believe; for it cannot be any man's duty to believe a lie.'[5] Fuller, however, was able to show that faith should be defined differently, as a 'cordial belief of the truth' (i.e. the truth of Christ and his gospel).[6] Because the focus of biblical faith was on something objective it *could*, he argued, be a person's duty to believe. Indeed it *was* a duty, for 'the least thing we can be obliged unto upon any declaration of God is the belief of it'.[7]

Having established this foundation, Fuller marshalled further arguments to show that faith in Christ was the 'incumbent duty' of all who heard the gospel. Central among these was that in the scriptures unconverted sinners were *commanded* to have faith. Indeed, in the New Testament, 'true saving faith [was] enjoined upon unregenerate sinners, as plain as words can express it'. Fuller brought forward a whole series of texts to support this contention, just one example being John 12.36: 'While ye have the light, believe in the light, that ye may be the children of light,' which he went on to expound:

> The persons to whom this was addressed were such, who though [Christ] had done so many miracles among them, yet believed not on him. Yet it seems they were given over to judicial blindness, and were finally lost. By the light they were commanded to believe in he undoubtedly meant himself...and what kind of faith it was that they were called upon to exercise is very plain, for that on their believing they would not have abode in darkness, but would have been the children of light, which is a character never bestowed on any but true believers.[8]

In other words, those who were not believers (and in Fuller's view never became so), were commanded to have saving faith – by Christ himself. Surely to such a command it had been their 'duty' to respond, although in fact they had never done so.

A number of possible objections to Fuller's views, with a focus on

---

5   Fuller, *The Gospel Worthy*, 1st edn, p. 6.

6   Fuller, *The Gospel Worthy*, 1st edn, pp. 29, 10, where Fuller refers to 2 Thess. 2.13. Cf. the Preface to *The Gospel Worthy*, in *Fuller's Works*, II, p. 329.

7   Fuller, *The Gospel Worthy*, 1st edn, p. 33. Fuller was citing from the Puritan, Stephen Charnock.

8   Fuller, *The Gospel Worthy*, 1st edn, p. 40, Fuller's italics.

those which might be raised by Particular Baptists, were stated and then demolished. The arguments Fuller was putting forward were not inconsistent with, for example, the decrees of God (God's commands, not his secret purposes, are our 'rule of conduct'),[9] or particular redemption (even if not one of the elect, it was still a person's duty to believe what God had revealed).[10] None of the central tenets of Calvinism were in dispute, as Fuller had immediately made clear in his Preface.[11] He saw himself standing in the tradition of older writers, particularly the sixteenth-century Puritans, from whom he quoted liberally. His was not a 'new scheme', rather a return to the 'good old way'.[12] It was because of this (in addition to natural modesty), that he was later unhappy when the views he expressed in *The Gospel Worthy* came to be dubbed as 'Fullerism' (why not 'Owenism' or 'Bunyanism' he protested?).[13] But there *was* a distinctive eighteenth-century dimension to his argument. As Fuller dealt with further objections he responded to the view that if faith really was the duty of all, it could not, at one and the same time, be a sovereign gift of God given to some and not to others. Fuller was able to maintain that faith was both a duty and a gift by distinguishing between what he called 'natural' and 'moral' inability, a distinction one will look for in vain amongst the Puritans. Fuller's use of these terms, and the basis for them, are explored later on in this chapter.

In his conclusion, Fuller came to the two crucial, practical outworkings of his thesis. The first was that there was 'free and full encouragement for any poor sinner to...venture his soul on the Lord Jesus Christ.' No one need hold back from coming to Christ because they lacked a strong enough 'inner persuasion' that God was at work in

---

9   Fuller could even quote John Brine to buttress his argument, see *The Gospel Worthy*, 1st edn, p. 126: 'God's word and not his secret purpose, is the rule of our conduct.' There are a number of further quotations from Gill and Brine in *The Gospel Worthy*, 1st edn, e.g. pp. 34-35 (Brine) and 44-45, 98-99 (Gill), but almost always in relation to minor details not central to the main argument. On the substantive points at issue Fuller was, of course, aware that both Gill and Brine were against him.

10   Fuller's arguments relating to particular redemption he would later regard as inadequate, and substantially alter. See chapters three and four below.

11   The Preface to the first edition is included in *Fuller's Works*, II, pp. 328-32.

12   Fuller, *The Gospel Worthy*, 1st edn, p. 138: 'A great outcry has been raised of late respecting a *new scheme* which some ministers have adopted, and many insinuations thrown out as if they had forsaken the *good old way*. 'Tis wonderful indeed, to think how some things of modern date can lay claim to antiquity. The truth is, they have only returned to the good old way which all the servants of Christ walked in from age to age, till the present century.'

13   Morris, *Andrew Fuller*, 2nd edn, pp. 238-39.

their lives. The gospel itself was all the 'warrant' that was needed. Fuller's second conclusion flowed naturally from the first. Christians, especially gospel ministers, should exhort everyone, indiscriminately, to believe in Christ. The New Testament was full of such open 'offers' of the gospel. 'Calls, warnings, invitations, expostulations, threatenings and exhortations, *even to the unregenerate*', were perfectly consistent with Calvinistic belief.[14] Thus Fuller struck, quite deliberately, at the two pillars of High Calvinist 'orthodoxy', contending that it was the duty of all to believe, and the duty of ministers to offer the gospel to all. This was the argument which was to have such far reaching consequences, both for Fuller himself and for the Particular Baptist denomination. What had led to this sea-change in Fuller's thinking? A range of points need to be considered.

Fuller's Conversion Experience

As noted in chapter one, the little Particular Baptist church at Soham which Fuller attended with his family was a bastion of High Calvinism, with an insular ecclesiology and a pastor, John Eve, who had 'little or nothing to say to the unconverted'. Later in life Fuller would state that: 'The preaching upon which I attended was not adapted to awaken my conscience, as the minister seldom had anything to say except to believers, and what believing was I neither knew, nor was I greatly concerned to know.'[15] It was not that Eve, and ministers like him, did not believe in conversion. But those who were among the 'elect' would eventually be brought to realize their position by having the all-important 'inner persuasion', thus giving the required 'warrant of faith' enabling them to trust in Christ. In 1766 Fuller began, by his own account, to see himself as a 'poor sinner'. But he believed that this did not constitute a sufficient warrant to believe, and therefore that he was not 'qualified' to come to Christ. In the years following 1766 he came under increasing conviction, but simply did not know what to do. In

---

14   Fuller, *The Gospel Worthy*, 1st edn, pp. 162-63, 166, italics added.

15   Unless otherwise stated, the details and quotations describing Fuller's conversion, in this and the following two paragraphs, are taken from Ryland, *Andrew Fuller*, pp. 12-20. Ryland reproduces a series of letters written by Fuller to Dr Stuart of Edinburgh, the first two of which were originally published, anonymously, in the *Evangelical Magazine* in 1798. Ryland has taken these and another similar set of letters and, whilst preserving entirely Fuller's words, used them to produce a uniform account. They are extremely helpful in tracing the origins of Fuller's change of thought. For background on Charles Stuart, who had met Fuller in Scotland through the latter's tours on behalf of the BMS, see Haykin (ed.), *Armies of the Lamb*, p. 65, n. 1.

popular High Calvinist teaching the 'warrant' often took the form of a particular text of scripture suggesting itself forcibly on a person's mind. Fuller thought he had experienced this in 1767, when the verse 'Sin shall not have dominion over you, for ye are not under the law, but under grace' (Rom. 6.14), came strongly to him. But despite this and further 'impressions', he found that the 'bias of his heart' was not changed.

But Fuller's sense of conviction and unhappiness remained and, after a period of 'wickedness' (Fuller specifically mentions, amongst other things, 'playing idle tricks' with one of the servants on a Sunday), this became increasingly intense: 'The fire and brimstone of the bottomless pit seemed to burn within my bosom... I saw that God would be perfectly just in sending me to hell, and that to hell I must go, unless I were saved of mere grace.' But what was Fuller to do without a sufficiently strong warrant of faith? Eventually he was encouraged by the Old Testament examples of Esther, who went in to see the King without being invited (Esth. 4.11; 5.1-2), and Job, who threw himself on God's mercy with the words: 'Though He slay me, yet will I trust him' (Job 13.15). Through these rather unlikely texts, Fuller found release from the agonies of conviction. Gunton Fuller described his father's conversion experience:

> He...came to this resolve, 'I must, I will – yes, I will – trust my soul, my sinful, lost soul, in his hands; if I perish, I perish.' As he looked away from self, and fixed his eyes upon a crucified Saviour, his guilt and fears began to dissolve...and he found how true were the words of Christ, 'Come unto me all ye that labour and are heavy laden, and I will give thee rest'.[16]

By his own reckoning, Fuller had been struggling with 'guilt' and 'fears' for at least three years previous to this. It was not until the autumn of 1769, when he was sixteen years old, that 'his troubled soul' finally found this 'rest'. Eve at least accepted Fuller as a genuine convert and he was baptized in April 1770, joining the church at Soham.

Fuller's conversion experience, as he and his biographers would later relate it, was in the classic Evangelical pattern of 'agony, guilt and intense relief'.[17] It resulted in serious theological reflection on what he described as the 'erroneous views of the gospel', which had kept him in 'darkness and despondency for so long'. He was clear, for example, that he would have committed himself to Christ sooner if he had not 'entertained the notion of...having no warrant to come to Christ without some previous qualification,' despite his felt moral failure and intense

---

16   A.G. Fuller, *Men Worth Remembering*, p. 28.
17   Bebbington, *Evangelicalism*, p. 5.

mental distress.[18] The delay had been extremely painful and, as he now saw it, quite unnecessary. Fuller's Evangelical conversion, the struggles which accompanied it, and his desire for others coming to Christ to have a somewhat smoother path, were all highly significant as he developed his theology of salvation.

Controversy at Soham

Gunton Fuller, commenting on the 'straitness' and 'sluggishness' of the Soham church, nevertheless noted one 'redeeming feature'. There was, he believed, a good family spirit of 'brotherly affection' amongst the small membership.[19] But in 1771 even this was lost as the small church was split by a dispute which Fuller was later to refer to as the 'wormwood and gall of my youth'. By his own admission it was to have a formative influence on his thought.[20]

The conflict began in the autumn of 1770, when Fuller himself discovered that a fellow member at Soham (identified in the church book as James Levit),[21] had been guilty of excessive drinking. Fuller saw Levit and, with newly converted zeal, challenged him on 'the evils of his conduct'. Levit answered in a way that suggests that antinomianism,[22] which often went hand in hand with High Calvinism (at least in practice if not in theory), was certainly present at Soham. To Fuller's consternation, Levit explained that he could not help his drinking and did not have the power to keep himself from sin. Fuller considered this a 'base excuse'. Levit was told that 'he *could* keep himself from sins such as these, and that his way of talking was merely to excuse what was 'inexcusable'. The errant member's behaviour was promptly reported to the church (by Fuller himself) and the result was that Eve commended Fuller, whilst Levit was excluded from membership. In the course of the dispute, however, Eve appears to have made a comment to the effect that although people had no power in and of themselves to do anything spiritually good, they did have the power

---

18   Ryland, *Andrew Fuller*, p. 30; A.G. Fuller, *Men Worth Remembering*, p. 28.

19   A.G. Fuller, *Men Worth Remembering*, pp. 32-33.

20   See Ryland, *Andrew Fuller*, pp. 23-28, for quotations from Fuller and other details in the next three paragraphs, unless otherwise stated.

21   'Soham Baptist Church Book, 1770-1833', p. 16.

22   Antinomianism: the belief that those chosen by God are exempt from the need to observe the moral law. See Sell, *Great Debate*, pp. 67-84, for antinomianism in its eighteenth-century context. Sell distinguishes between theoretical or doctrinal antinomianism, which he argues was rare, and practical antinomianism, which was more common.

to obey the will of God 'as to outward acts'. This seemingly innocuous statement was to open up a more general debate and eventually led to Eve's resignation.

Leading members of the church including Joseph Diver (d. 1780), who though an older man was particularly close to Fuller, challenged Eve concerning his assertion about a believer's ability to do God's will. Fuller, who had also taken this view, was readily excused as a 'babe in religion', but the pastor 'should have known better'. Believers did not have the power to keep themselves from evil, but should constantly pray for 'keeping grace'. Scriptures that Eve was referred to included Psalm 19.13 and Jeremiah 10.23: 'The way of man is not in himself: it is not in him that walketh to direct his steps'. Fuller initially agreed with his pastor, but as the dispute continued he found it increasingly difficult to see how Eve's opponents could be answered. With obvious pain and great reluctance he switched sides. The dispute was never properly resolved and Eve was eventually forced to resign from Soham in 1771, leaving for a church in Wisbech. Eve's High Calvinism had not been consistent enough for the majority of his church members.[23]

The dispute is clearly revealing of the type of theology, attitudes and concerns prevalent at Soham. It clearly caused Fuller deep pain: 'our plowhares was [sic] converted into swords, and our pruning hooks into spears,' he lamented.[24] But it also left Fuller himself with a major theological problem. To what extent, and in what sense, was it a person's 'duty' to do the will of God? Fuller was increasingly dissatisfied with High Calvinism, particularly its practical effects, but was unable to articulate clearly what was wrong. As he said: 'Our late disputes had furnished me with some few principles inconsistent with [High Calvinism], yet I did not perceive their bearings at first.' These tensions would only ultimately be resolved by Fuller recasting his whole theological system, and writing *The Gospel Worthy*.

Early Reading and the Influence of the Puritans

Fuller was also influenced by some of his reading as a new convert. Before his resignation in 1771, Eve had encouraged the young believer to read the ubiquitous Gill and Brine, and the text of *The Gospel Worthy* reveals a good working knowledge of both men.[25] But Fuller had also

---

23   Cf. the comment of Watts, *Dissenters*, I, pp. 459-60.

24   A. Fuller 'A Narration of the dealings of God in a way of Providence with the Baptist Church at Soham from the year 1770', Cambridge County Records Office (NC/B - Soham R70/20), p. 11.

25   See Ryland, *Andrew Fuller*, p. 36, and Fuller's comment, 'I had read pretty

got hold of books by the sixteenth-century dissenter John Bunyan (in fact he had read *Grace Abounding to the Chief of Sinners* and *Pilgrim's Progress* in the late 1760s). He began to compare these works with those of Gill: 'I perceived...that the system of Bunyan was not the same as [Gill's]; for while he maintained the doctrines of election and predestination, he nevertheless held with the free offer of salvation to sinners without distinction.'[26] Fuller's initial thought was that Bunyan was not as consistent in his Calvinism as Gill, but he began to change his mind as a result of further reading. In particular he found that all the sixteenth- and seventeenth-century Calvinist writers he was able to check agreed with Bunyan. Morris commented that as Fuller became 'better acquainted' with the Puritans, 'particularly Dr Owen', he 'found them to harmonize much more with [Bunyan] than with Dr Gill or Mr Brine'.[27]

When he came to write *The Gospel Worthy*, Fuller would include quotations from a number of Puritan authors, for example Stephen Charnock and Thomas Goodwin.[28] But a close examination of the text suggests that John Owen (1616-83) was the most important, and that Morris was right to highlight him. The son of a Puritan vicar, Owen rose to prominence when he was appointed Dean of Christ Church, Oxford, in 1651, and a Vice-Chancellor of the University the following year. He became a convinced Congregationalist and after 1660 was a leader of the Independent churches.[29] Known for his astonishing written output, he was arguably the greatest systematic thinker of all the Puritans. Owen's works were quoted extensively and with approval by Fuller in the first edition of *The Gospel Worthy*.[30] When Fuller was later accused by an opponent, who had seen the manuscript of *The Gospel Worthy*

---

much of Dr Gill's *Body of Divinity*'.

26   Ryland, *Andrew Fuller*, p. 36.

27   J. Bennett and D. Bogue, *A History of the Dissenters during the last 30 years* (London, 1839), p. 472, echoed Morris when they stated that: 'By reading the works of Dr John Owen [Fuller] found that there was one who harmonized with Bunyan in invitations to sinners, rather than with Gill and Brine.'

28   See Fuller, *The Gospel Worthy*, 1st edn, e.g. p. 9 n., for a reference to 'the great Charnock', and p. 161, for a quote from Thomas Goodwin.

29   For these and further details of the life of the man dubbed, in his own lifetime, 'the Calvin of England', see S.B. Ferguson, *John Owen on the Christian Life* (Edinburgh: Banner of Truth, 1987), pp. 1-19. See J.I. Packer, *Among God's Giants: The Puritan Vision of the Christian Life* (Eastbourne: Kingsway, 1991), for an appreciative introduction to aspects of Puritan thought, including much material on Owen.

30   See Fuller, *The Gospel Worthy*, 1st edn, pp. 86-88 and 127, for lengthy quotations from Owen.

before publication, of 'disrespect to Drs Gill and Owen', Fuller replied concerning Owen '[t]hat I know of no writer for whom I have so great an esteem; it would be a faint expression for me to say I approve his principles – I admire them.'[31] Fuller's response was unsurprising, as he was convinced that on the main points at issue, the seventeenth-century divine was on his side.

A balanced assessment of the importance of Puritan writers for the development of Fuller's thought needs to take into account a number of factors. Bunyan (although not strictly a Puritan as he was a Nonconformist), was clearly significant at a particular stage in Fuller's life. But he was hardly referred to in the text of *The Gospel Worthy* itself, and leaves little clear or lasting imprint on Fuller's theology of salvation.[32] In assessing the importance of Owen (and others), the key issue is the extent to which they were *formative* for Fuller. Certainly the Puritans are cited often in *The Gospel Worthy*, and sometimes at key points in the argument.[33] But the evidence tends to suggest that Fuller's reading of them was important primarily in confirming his growing convictions, rather than shaping them directly. In *The Gospel Worthy*, with its target readership of Particular Baptists, they were especially useful in buttressing the main points of the argument and showing that Fuller had indeed not left 'the good old way'. Rather it was the High Calvinists who were the innovators. This to a degree explains the frequency of quotation (and as already noted, Fuller could also quote from Gill and Brine where they were in agreement with him). Owen was not mentioned in the Preface of *The Gospel Worthy*, where Fuller noted a range of different authors who had been important to him, nor in the letters reprinted by Ryland where he described his early religious experience and subsequent theological formation.[34]

My conviction is that Owen and other Puritans were not as crucial for the development of Fuller's thought as has sometimes been suggested, and that he often deployed quotations from them to support positions he had already arrived at by another route. But if their role should not be over-emphasized, neither should it be discounted. Fuller's use of Owen, Charnock and others emphasizes, together with a wealth of material

---

31   A.G. Fuller, *Andrew Fuller*, in *Fuller's Works*, I, p. 39.

32   Although there is a reference in *The Gospel Worthy*, 2nd edn, *Fuller's Works*, II, p. 388. For the influence of Bunyan on Fuller, see R.W.F. Archer, 'The Evangelistic Ministry of John Bunyan 1655-1688' (MPhil thesis, University of Wales, 1995), pp. 51-52.

33   Fuller, *The Gospel Worthy*, 1st edn, p. 138, where Fuller showed that Owen held that it was the duty of sinners to believe.

34   Note too the fact that Fuller quoted more from Owen in the 2nd edn of *The Gospel Worthy* than in the 1st edn. See *Fuller's Works*, II, p. 353, for a quotation from Owen in the 2nd edn not included in the 1st.

from elsewhere, the degree of continuity between eighteenth-century Evangelicals and their Puritan (and sixteenth-century Reformation) forebears. As the Methodists did, Fuller owed the Puritans a substantial debt.[35]

The Possible Influence of John Calvin

If Fuller was influenced by the works of sixteenth- and seventeenth-century English Calvinists, it is reasonable to ask whether his changing views were shaped by a reading of John Calvin himself. A.H. Kirkby has contended that they were and has gone so far as to suggest that Fuller rejected High Calvinism because it did not correspond with the teachings of the Genevan Reformer.[36] At first sight Kirkby appears to have amassed a considerable body of evidence to support this claim, consisting of a number of suggested similarities between Fuller's work and Calvin's, together with a few direct quotations. The centrepiece of this evidence is an alleged 'remarkable parallel' between the first article of the personal confession of faith Fuller made on his induction as minister at Kettering in 1783, and a much longer passage in Calvin's commentary on Psalm 19. Kirkby states that 'almost every word' of Fuller's statement can be found in Calvin's commentary. The two relevant passages are quoted together, with 'words and phrases common to both' in italics.[37]

Fuller

When I consider the heavens and the earth, with their vast variety, it gives me to believe the existence of a God of infinite wisdom, power and goodness, that made and upholds them all. Had there been no written revelation of God given to us, I should have been without excuse if I had denied or refused to glorify him as God.

---

35   Indeed, Methodism could be described as 'A new species of Puritanism', see Rack, *Reasonable Enthusiast*, p. 183; Bebbington, *Evangelicalism*, p. 35. Fuller, *The Gospel Worthy*, 1st edn, p. 178, also believed that in advocating the need for 'direct addresses' to 'unconverted sinners' he was standing in the tradition of 'Luther, Calvin, Latimer, Knox…and numerous others of our reformation champions.'

36   Kirkby, 'Theology of Andrew Fuller', and his 'Andrew Fuller - Evangelical Calvinist', *passim.*

37   Kirkby, 'Andrew Fuller - Evangelical Calvinist', p. 199. Cf. Clipsham, 'Fuller and John Calvin', pp. 150-51. Kirkby is quoting from Ryland, *Andrew Fuller*, p. 99, and Calvin, *Commentary on the Psalms*, I, pp. 308-309.

Calvin

When a man, from *beholding and contemplating the heavens* has been *brought to acknowledge God* he will learn also to reflect on and to admire His *wisdom and power*... In the first verse, the Psalmist repeats one thing twice, according to his usual manner. He introduces the heavens as witnesses and preachers to the glory of God, attributing to the dumb creatures a quality which, strictly speaking does not belong to it, in order the more severely to upbraid men for their *ingratitude, if they should pass over so clear a testimony* with unheeding ears...

When we behold the heavens we cannot be but elevated by the contemplation of them, to him who is their great Creator; and the beautiful arrangement, and *wonderful variety*...cannot but furnish us with an *evident proof of His providence. Scripture, indeed, makes known to us the time and manner of creation; but the heavens themselves, although God should say nothing on the subject, proclaims loudly and distinctly enough* that they have been *fashioned by his hands*: and this in itself abundantly suffices to bear testimony to men of His glory. As soon as we acknowledge God to be the Supreme Architect who has erected the beauteous fabric of the universe, our minds must necessarily be ravished with wonder at His *infinite goodness, wisdom and power*.

Although God should not speak a single word to men yet the orderly and useful succession of days and nights eloquently proclaims the glory of God and that there is *now left to men no pretext for ignorance*.

The first thing to note is that the similarities between the two quotations are in fact far from remarkable. Much of the passage from Calvin (which would have been even longer if Kirkby had cited it in full), has no parallel in the Fuller paragraph at all. Even the words and phrases highlighted as 'common to both' are often only vaguely alike, conveying comparable ideas but frequently in very different language. One of E.F. Clipsham's four articles on Fuller's theology of salvation for the *Baptist Quarterly* is written specifically to challenge Kirkby's views. He is being generous when he describes the two passages Kirkby cites as being 'no more than generally similar'. Moreover, as Clipsham goes on to state, 'both the ideas and vocabulary used to express them were...part and parcel of the current coinage of Calvinist theology'.[38] There is certainly no need to posit a direct reading of John Calvin as the reason for Fuller writing in this way. Perhaps most tellingly, even if some sort of dependence had been shown it would have proved little

---

38   Clipsham, 'Fuller and John Calvin', pp. 151-52.

because the paragraph in question does not deal with the distinctive doctrines of 'Fullerism' at all. The article in his personal confession which was most relevant to Fuller's central concerns was article XV, where he made a statement concerning people's inability to do 'spiritual things'. This inability, he considered, was 'wholly of the moral, and therefore of the criminal kind'.[39] For this Kirkby was unable to find any parallel in Calvin although, as we shall see, there is a clear one in Jonathan Edwards.

Kirkby's argument clearly fails at this point, and the rest of his evidence is no stronger. Even where Fuller directly quoted Calvin (and it was not very often), it was in support of a view that he had already come to by another route, as Clipsham, in his article tackling Kirkby's views, is able to show.[40] In fact Fuller only quotes from Calvin once in the first edition of *The Gospel Worthy* itself, on the necessity of the work of the Holy Spirit in conversion, something that was hardly in dispute.[41] Overall, Clipsham does a thorough job in refuting Kirkby's thesis. But in respect of the development of Fuller's doctrine of salvation, which is my particular concern here, his case could have been made even stronger. The simple point is that in all the key sources for tracing the origins of Fuller's thought – the early biographies, the letters and private diaries reproduced by Ryland, the Preface and the text of *The Gospel Worthy* itself – there are no references suggesting that a direct dependence on Calvin was at all important to him. Indeed there is no firm evidence that he directly read Calvin during the 1770s, and it is not impossible that the quotation he deployed in the 1785 edition of *The Gospel Worthy* was passed on to him by someone else.[42] Kirkby ignores this and concentrates on looking for parallels and echoes of Calvin's thought in Fuller's writing, but where these exist they can be adequately explained in terms of his Calvinistic Baptist heritage. Kirkby's conclusions fly in the face of the plain evidence. There is no direct link between Calvin's writing and *The Gospel Worthy*.

---

39   Ryland, *Andrew Fuller*, 1st edn, pp. 99, 106.

40   Clipsham, 'Fuller and John Calvin', p. 148.

41   Fuller, *The Gospel Worthy*, 1st edn, p. 145.

42   Morris, *Andrew Fuller*, 2nd edn, p. 359, described Fuller's library, during this period and for many years after, as being small, 'consisting chiefly of a scanty collection of the writings of the Puritans, and those of the New England school'. Calvin's works are not mentioned. Calvin's *Institutes* are included, however, in Fuller's own list of his books which he made on 28 August 1798. See 'Book of Miscellaneous Writings', Bristol Baptist College Library (G 95 B), where the *Institutes* are number 15 on Fuller's main list.

Biblicism

It is important to return to what Fuller was actually reading, not only in the 1770s but for the rest of his life. If data suggesting the direct influence of John Calvin is negligible, that pointing to the formative importance of the Bible itself is everywhere. Fuller's biblicism, during the period of his life when the views he was to express in *The Gospel Worthy* were taking shape, can be shown in a number of ways. In 1775 he visited London, where he read a pamphlet which he was later to refer to as crucial in the development of his thought.[43] The tract was entitled *The Modern Question*, and it was written by Abraham Taylor, a London Congregational minister and tutor at a dissenting academy for training Independent ministers, although when it first appeared in 1742 it was published anonymously. The 'Modern Question' which concerned Taylor was 'whether the unconverted have a duty to believe the gospel'.[44] Clearly relevant to Fuller's concerns, literature on the 'Modern Question' had begun to appear in 1739 with the publication of a pamphlet by Matthias Maurice, *A Modern Question Mostly Answer'd*. According to Fuller, however, before coming across Taylor's tract 'he had never seen anything relative to this controversy before'.[45] Later, in the text of *The Gospel Worthy* itself, he would engage with one of the High Calvinist protagonists in the debate, Lewis Wayman of Kimbolton.[46]

Fuller read Taylor's tract carefully. The Congregationalist's style (Philip Doddridge had accused him of 'bigotry'),[47] was unlikely to endear Taylor to Fuller. Indeed, by his own account Fuller was 'but little impressed with [Taylor's] reasonings'. That was until he came to a passage where Taylor cited a string of biblical texts, specifically some of those where John the Baptist, the apostles and Christ himself directly addressed the unconverted. Taylor was able to show, in a way that Fuller was unable to answer, that New Testament figures repeatedly challenged the 'ungodly' to spiritual repentance and faith. The impact this had on Fuller was clearly great. In the following months he read and

---

43   Ryland, *Andrew Fuller*, pp. 34, 37.

44   Toon, *Hyper Calvinism*, pp. 131-39, and especially Nuttall, 'Northamptonshire and the Modern Question', pp. 101-23, cover this dispute, and the main protagonists, in some detail. Taylor was theological tutor at the dissenting academy which met in the 'Great House' in Union Street in London, and pastor of the Congregational church in Deptford.

45   Ryland, *Andrew Fuller*, 1st edn, p. 55.

46   Fuller, *The Gospel Worthy*, 1st edn. See e.g. pp. 101, 134-35.

47   Nuttall, 'Northamptonshire and the Modern Question', p. 115, who speaks of Taylor's 'tart manner' and 'somewhat obtrusive scholarship'.

reflected theologically on the relevant scripture passages. 'The more I read and thought', he said, 'the more I doubted the justice of my former views'. Fuller could not forget these texts, nor help feeling that they exposed his preaching as 'anti-scriptural and defective in many respects'.[48] The point is not so much that Taylor influenced Fuller, but that the passages Taylor cited did. These were the same texts that Fuller himself would later quote and painstakingly expound in *The Gospel Worthy*.

There is more evidence that the scriptures themselves were formative for Fuller's theological shift. In the Preface of the first edition of *The Gospel Worthy*, Fuller, in describing the process that led to his change of views, emphasized reflection on passages of scripture as crucial. He referred in particular to Psalm 2, 'where Kings who set themselves against the Lord and against his anointed are positively commanded to kiss the Son'.[49] He went on to expound the Psalm, focusing on the way that it was used in Acts 2, in the main body of the text.[50] Fuller's resolve, in the 1770s and indeed throughout his life, to search the scriptures before accepting that something was true, was also commented on by a number of his biographers.[51] But perhaps most significantly this commitment also appears in Fuller's private papers, particularly in a solemn and private 'covenant' with God discovered by Ryland after his subject's death.[52] This is worth considering in more detail.

The 'covenant' was clearly not intended for publication, or indeed to be seen by anyone but the author. It is dated by Fuller as being written on 10 January 1780, and Ryland believed it was occasioned by Fuller's having read a piece 'written at the time of the controversy between the Calvinistic and Arminian Methodists'.[53] Having read tracts written by both sides, with texts thrown back and forth in support of diametrically opposing views, Fuller was acutely aware of how difficult a thoroughgoing biblicism is in practice. He reflected how there were many who professed 'to be searching after truth [and] to have Christ and the inspired writers on their side', and he was fully conscious that he

---

48   Ryland, *Andrew Fuller*, pp. 34, 37.

49   Fuller, Preface to *The Gospel Worthy*, in *Fuller's Works*, II, p. 328.

50   Fuller, *The Gospel Worthy*, 1st edn, pp. 37-38. This section is headed 'Faith in Christ is Commanded in the Scriptures to Unconverted Sinners'.

51   E.g. Ryland, *Andrew Fuller*, p. 43.

52   A. Fuller, 'Sermons…in shorthand, with occasional meditations in longhand [Books 1-5 bound in 1 vol.]', Bristol Baptist College library (G 95 A). Book 3, pp. 2-3, contains the 'covenant'.

53   See Rack, *Reasonable Enthusiast*, pp. 198-202, for some of the details of this ongoing dispute.

was 'as liable to err as other men'. But he was determined to go back to the scriptures, which he regarded as the very 'oracles of God'. At the heart of his 'covenant' was the following passage:

> Let not the sleight of wicked men, who lie in wait to deceive, nor even the pious character of good men (who yet may be under great mistakes), draw me aside. Nor do thou suffer my own fancy to guide me. Lord, thou hast given me a determination to take up no principle at second hand; but to search for everything at the pure fountain of thy word.[54]

This is especially valuable for being heartfelt and private, and also because of the humility before God that it reveals. And there is good evidence to suggest that what was resolved in secret was worked out in public. Of course an approach to scripture that is free of cultural 'presuppositions' is not possible, and I am not suggesting that Fuller achieved this. His reading of scripture was influenced by his temperament, his background and his times. But the writing and subsequent publication of *The Gospel Worthy* itself shows that Fuller was able to submit his theological system to a rigorous biblical critique and revise it accordingly, at great personal cost. In this he displays a characteristic that was one of the hallmarks of the Evangelical Revival. My own conviction is that Fuller's biblicism was thoroughgoing and central to him, and we will need to return to it on a regular basis throughout this study. Certainly the process which led to the writing of *The Gospel Worthy* cannot be understood if what Haykin terms Fuller's 'transparent desire to be true to the Scriptures' is forgotten.[55] As we look further at the development of Fuller's thought, the decisive influence of the Evangelical Revival becomes even more clear.

The Northamptonshire Association

Early in 1775, before his trip to London, Fuller had accepted the call from his own church at Soham to be Eve's replacement as their pastor.[56] Robert Hall Sr (1728-91) of Arnesby came seventy miles to deliver the ordination 'charge', and continued to be the younger man's 'father and friend' until his death.[57] That year, on 8 June, the Soham congregation

---

54   Ryland, *Andrew Fuller*, 1st edn, pp. 203-204, Fuller's italics.

55   Haykin (ed.), *Armies of the Lamb*, p. 17.

56   Fuller, 'Narration', pp. 20-24. The church officially requested that Fuller accept the Soham pastorate four times before he eventually did so. The first approach was made on 17 July 1774.

57   For Hall Sr, see *HEB*, IV, pp. 603-609; M.A.G. Haykin, 'Robert Hall, Sr.

applied to join the Northamptonshire Association of Particular Baptist churches by 'unanimous consent'.[58] The new association had been formed in 1764 and was, according to John Briggs, the 'archetype of the new associations, born out of the Evangelical Revival'.[59] This brought Fuller into contact with John Sutcliff, who had recently settled at the Baptist church at Olney, and with his future biographer, John Ryland Jr, who was then at Northampton.[60] Fuller wrote that in them he found 'familiar and faithful brethren' who, 'partly by reflection, and partly by reading the writings of Edwards, Bellamy, Brainerd, &c', had rejected High Calvinism as a system.[61] Fuller would continue to be active in the Northamptonshire Association until his death.

Clearly this was highly significant. Both Sutcliff and Ryland had trained for the ministry at Bristol Baptist Academy, the college which had largely remained committed to an older Calvinism, more expansive and less dependant on High Calvinist theology.[62] Sutcliff and Ryland shared what they had learnt from Bristol with Fuller, as revealed by a long quotation from the Bristol Principal, Caleb Evans (1737-91), in the first edition of *The Gospel Worthy* (and this on the crucial distinction between natural and moral inability).[63] Fuller's initial contact with Sutcliff and Ryland blossomed into a friendship which would become one of the bulwarks of his life. The improved transport and communication links of the late-eighteenth century made regular, meaningful contact with these men possible. But it is important not to

---

(1728-1791)', in (ed.), Haykin, *British Particular Baptists*, I, pp. 202-10.

58   Fuller, 'Narration', p. 25; Morris, *Andrew Fuller*, 1st edn, p. 31. Soham was of course in Cambridgeshire, but the Northamptonshire Association accepted churches from neighbouring counties. Hall Sr's church at Arnesby was in Leicestershire. For this, and further information about the association, see T.S.H. Elwyn, *The Northamptonshire Baptist Association* (London: Carey Kingsgate Press, 1964), *passim*.

59   Briggs, *English Baptists*, p. 203.

60   Both Sutcliff and Ryland are significant figures for this study, and references to them occur regularly. For their lives see Haykin, *One Heart and Soul* (for Sutcliff); G. Gordon, 'John Ryland, Jr. (1753-1825),' in Haykin (ed.), *British Particular Baptists*, II, pp. 76-95 (for Ryland). All subsequent references to 'Ryland' in this book are to Ryland Jr, as distinct from his father, John Collett Ryland. Fuller appears to have first met Sutcliff on 28 May 1776, at an association meeting at Olney. See Morris, *Andrew Fuller*, 1st edn, p. 34.

61   Ryland, *Andrew Fuller*, 1st edn, p. 56.

62   Hayden, 'Evangelical Calvinism and the Bristol Baptist Academy', *passim*; Bebbington, *Evangelicalism*, p. 34.

63   Fuller, *The Gospel Worthy*, 1st edn, pp. 183-85. Evans is introduced as a 'judicious writer of the present age'. See also Hayden, 'Evangelical Calvinism and the Bristol Baptist Academy', pp. 218-21.

exaggerate either the extent to which the transport infrastructure improved or the degree of influence men like Sutcliff and Ryland had over Fuller's theological formation. Fuller wrote: 'As I lived sixty or seventy miles from them, I seldom saw them, and did not correspond upon the subject. I therefore pursued my enquiries by myself, and wrote out the substance of what I afterwards published under the title of *The Gospel Worthy of all Acceptation*.'[64]

The direct influence of Sutcliff and Ryland on the development of Fuller's thought is therefore difficult to evaluate. Certainly the knowledge that there were others who were thinking along the same lines as him would have been important as he hammered out his own ideas. And yet, as the above quotation indicates, he pursued his detailed studies independently, geographically isolated as he was from his new friends. Their main significance was in helping Fuller to revise his manuscript after it had been largely written and then encouraging him to publish.[65] This was important, but not formative, and their direct influence on his theological development was probably small. It *was* through Hall Sr, Ryland and Sutcliff, however, that Fuller was able to read works from Evangelicals from America, most importantly those of Jonathan Edwards. This was crucial and merits a more detailed treatment.

The Northamptonshire Association, Jonathan Edwards and the Transatlantic Evangelical Network

Jonathan Edwards was born on 5 October 1703 in Windsor, Connecticut. Following a period as tutor at Yale, he accepted a post as assistant to his grandfather, Solomon Stoddard, at the Congregational church at Northampton, Massachusetts, in 1726.[66] Edwards became the sole pastor when Stoddard died in 1726. In 1734 and 1735 he was involved in a remarkable 'Revival' at Northampton, with over 300 people apparently converted over a six month period. Edwards subsequently described what had happened in *A Faithful Narrative of Surprising Conversions*, originally published in 1737. From 1740-42 he was also involved in the so-called 'Great Awakening', although the

---

64   Ryland, *Andrew Fuller*, p. 35; Morris, *Andrew Fuller*, 2nd edn, p. 41: 'He [Fuller] had to explore his path...unaided and alone.'

65   Both Sutcliff and Ryland saw Fuller's manuscript on the 'Modern Question' [i.e. *The Gospel Worthy*] as early as 1782. See Hayden, 'Evangelical Calvinism and the Bristol Baptist Academy', p. 354.

66   For these and other biographical details of Edwards see *DEB*, I, pp. 345-46; Holmes, *God of Grace*, pp. 1-9.

name that would always be primarily associated with this remarkable period in American religious and cultural history would be that of George Whitefield.[67]

After a controversy regarding the conditions for communicant church membership, Edwards was dismissed from the pastorate at Northampton in 1750, later accepting a call to a small frontier church at Stockbridge, Massachusetts. He died in 1758 following an unsuccessful smallpox vaccination, shortly after having accepted the presidency of the College of New Jersey (Princeton). Edwards was a philosopher and theologian of the very first rank. Particularly fruitful in terms of writing was his period at Stockbridge, where he had lighter pastoral duties. There he was able to produce a number of highly significant works, including *A Careful and Strict Enquiry into the Modern Prevailing Notions of the Freedom of the Will*, which was first published in 1754. This work in particular would have a profound affect on Fuller's theological formation.

Fuller's discovery of Edwards and other New England writers needs to be seen in context. The eighteenth century had seen the establishment of strong links between Evangelicals on different sides of the Atlantic (the friendship between Edwards and Whitefield being a prime example). Susan O'Brien states that 'through an exchange of ideas and materials Calvinist revivalists...built a "community of saints" that cut across physical barriers.'[68] In addition to the regular exchange of letters there was, from the 1740s onwards, a shared literature which included Revival narratives and theological works. A central figure in this transatlantic network was John Erskine (1721-1803) of Edinburgh,[69] and, certainly by the early 1770s, Ryland and Sutcliff were in contact with him. It was via this route that Fuller started to receive Evangelical works that originated in America, although many were now in the form of British editions, published in Scotland. These included Edwards' *Life of David Brainerd* and other biographies of those who had been missionaries amongst the Native Americans.[70] In the Preface of *The*

---

67   Cf. the details on the Evangelical Revival given in the previous chapter.

68   Susan [Durden] O'Brien, 'A Transatlantic Community of Saints: The Great Awakening and the First Evangelical Network, 1735-1755', *American Historical Review* 91 (1986), p. 813.

69   M.A. Noll, 'Revival, Enlightenment, Civic Humanism, and the Evolution of Calvinism in Scotland and America 1735-1843', in G.A. Rawlyk and M.A. Noll (eds), *Amazing Grace: Evangelicalism in Australia, Britain, Canada and the United States* (Grand Rapids: Baker, 1993), p. 77.

70   J. Edwards, *The Life of David Brainerd*, in *The Works of Jonathan Edwards*, vol. VII, ed. N. Pettit (New Haven: Yale University Press, 1985 [1749]). In *The Gospel Worthy*, 1st edn, Fuller also mentions the New England minister Gilbert Tennant. For Brainerd and

Gospel Worthy, Fuller, referring to himself in the third person, commented directly on the influence these works had on him:

> Reading the lives of such men as Elliot, Brainerd, and several others, who preached Christ with so much success to the American Indians, had an effect on him. Their work, like that of the apostles, seemed to be plain before them. They appeared to him, in their addresses to those poor benighted heathens, to have none of those difficulties with which he felt himself encumbered. These things led him to the throne of grace, to implore instruction and resolution.[71]

Fuller had access to these works, at least by the early 1780s and probably earlier.[72] Clearly he was impressed by the practical vitality of what he was reading, indeed he was deeply moved by the sacrificial efforts of these pioneers. Further reflection convinced him that what men like Eliot and Brainerd had done was biblical, that they were indeed standing in the tradition of the apostles by freely offering the gospel whilst he himself was 'encumbered' in his own preaching. Thus his changing theological stance was influenced by works that were descriptive of Evangelical action.

Probably the crucial link between Ryland, Sutcliff and John Erskine was established through the Evangelical clergyman John Newton, who was friends with both the Northamptonshire men. Newton was himself a fruitful source of Evangelical literature, and it was directly from him that Ryland received two printed sermons by a New England minister, John Smalley (1734-1820), in 1776.[73] These were passed on to Robert Hall Sr, but not before Ryland had carefully transcribed them.[74]

Tennant, see Murray, *Jonathan Edwards*, especially pp. 132-33; 300-309.

71   *Fullers Works*, II, p. 329; cf. Ryland, *Andrew Fuller*, p. 90. For a summary of John Eliot's missionary work amongst native Americans in seventeenth-century New England, see Pettit's introduction to Edwards, *David Brainerd*, pp. 26-28. Eliot's efforts were celebrated by a later generation because they were exceptional, not because they were the norm.

72   Clearly Fuller had read of Eliot's life by late 1780, and he probably read Edwards' *Life of Brainerd* in early to mid-1781. See Fuller to J. Sutcliff, 28 January 1781, Fuller Letters (4/5/1): 'I cannot tell how you come to think of my having had Brainerd's life. I have never seen it.' Hayden's comment on this, 'Evangelical Calvinism and the Bristol Baptist Academy', p. 363, that 'no doubt Sutcliff remedied' the situation, is surely reasonable. In 1780, there was a note in the Northamptonshire Baptist Association Circular Letter recommending Edwards' *Life of Brainerd* to 'all that love evangelical, experimental and practical religion'.

73   See Hindmarsh, *John Newton*, pp. 149-55 for Newton's friendship with Ryland, including the loan of Smalley's book.

74   See Ryland's preface to *Help to Zion's Travellers*, in R. Hall Sr, *The Complete*

Smalley's pamphlet was essentially a distillation, in more popular form, of Edwards' *Freedom of the Will*.[75] This was a work that Hall Sr had received some years earlier, probably from the same source.

The elder Robert Hall is significant here because it was he who initially suggested, at their first meeting in 1775, that Fuller read 'Edwards on the Will'. After asking about the reasons for Eve's resignation from Soham, he recommended Edwards' work as an antidote to the young pastor's confusion regarding the ability of people to do what is spiritually good. Initially this confusion was compounded as Fuller obtained the wrong book: *Veritus Redux* by an 'Episcopalian Calvinist', Dr John Edwards. Although Fuller appreciated this work, he was puzzled that it seemed to have nothing to say relevant to 'the power of man to do the will of God'. It is yet further evidence that Fuller had to pursue his studies alone, that it was not until 1777 that he discovered his mistake and obtained the right book, possibly from Ryland, although he does not say.[76]

As noted earlier, the first edition of Edwards' work, *A Careful and Strict Enquiry into the Modern Prevailing Notions of the Freedom of Will*, was published in 1754.[77] The treatise (which was written to combat Arminian views), was largely philosophical rather than theological (the first reference to Jesus Christ does not occur for 175 pages, taking the text from the Yale edition).[78] Doubtless in part because of this, Edwards' publishers thought it necessary to raise subscriptions for the work prior to printing, so to insure themselves against serious loss. Significantly, forty-two of the original 298 subscribers were from Scotland.[79] Edwards' argument was that 'the freedom human beings possess, when properly understood, is not inconsistent with our actions being predictable or indeed necessitated – not incompatible

---

Works of the Late Robert Hall (ed. J.W. Morris, London, 1828) p. 48; Ryland, *Andrew Fuller*, 1st edn, pp. 9-10 n.

75   Smalley's book was *The Consistency of the Sinner's Inability to comply with the Gospel; with his inexcusable guilt in not complying with it, illustrated and confirmed in two discourses, on John VIth, 44th* (1769). See Hindmarsh, *John Newton*, pp. 153-54. Smalley was actually converted by reading Edwards' *Freedom of the Will*. See *DEB*, II, p. 1021.

76   Ryland, *Andrew Fuller*, p. 36.

77   For the text see J. Edwards, *Freedom of the Will*, in *The Works of Jonathan Edwards*, vol. I, ed. P. Ramsey (New Haven: Yale University Press, 1985 [1754]), pp. 135-440; J. Edwards, *The Works of Jonathan Edwards*, (ed. E. Hickman; 2 vols; Edinburgh: Banner of Truth, 1974 [1834]), I, pp. 1-93. I have cited the text from the Yale Edition.

78   As noted by Holmes, *God of Grace*, p. 153. The distinction between theology and philosophy was less sharply drawn in Edwards' day.

79   Murray, *Jonathan Edwards*, p. 425.

fundamentally with predestination.'[80] The will 'is simply that by which the mind chooses anything', and these choices are always determined by the strongest motive 'in view of the mind'.[81] Holmes uses an image of some traditional balancing scales. We have a series of inducements to act one way or another, and what we judge to be the strongest set of inducements will *inevitably* determine which way the scales will tip (i.e. what choices we make). The will itself, therefore, is not free, because (contrary to what Arminians believed or implied), it had no self-determining power. Put another way, although a person may correctly be described as 'free' because they possess a will, the will itself is not free because it does not possess a 'will' of its own. Something always causes an act of the will.

It was in expanding on his notion of cause that Edwards developed a distinction between what he termed natural and moral inability, a distinction which was to be absolutely crucial to Fuller. The most relevant section was Part 1, Section 4, headed 'Of the distinction of Natural and Moral Necessity and Inability'.[82] No one could respond to the gospel without the electing grace of God and the regenerating work of the Holy Spirit. But this helplessness was not because of a lack of any 'natural' powers. Rather a person's inability was wholly of the 'moral' or 'criminal' kind. They could not respond because they did not have a 'mind' to. To return to the image of the scales, there were not enough inducements (as far as the unregenerate mind was concerned), to tip the balance in favour of a positive response. Put simply, such a person could not come because they would not come. Anyone who did not respond was, therefore, criminally culpable. All had the natural powers to respond, but they refused to do so.

The significance of Edwards' work for Robert Hall Sr himself is clear. In 1779 he would preach to the Northamptonshire Association a sermon which was later published in expanded form with the title *Help to Zion's Travellers*.[83] Hall Sr's concern was to attempt to remove 'various stumbling blocks' from the path of those who wanted to follow Christ. In a wide-ranging address, he contended, amongst other things 'that the way to Jesus is graciously open for everyone who chooses to come to him'. As he expanded this point, Hall Sr was clearly making

---

80   Holmes, *God of Grace*, p. 151. See pp. 151-54 for Holmes' reading of Edwards' work, from which I have drawn. Cf. his 'Edwards on the Will', *International Journal of Systematic Theology* 1.3 (1999), pp. 266-85.

81   Edwards, *Freedom of the Will*, p. 137.

82   Edwards, *Freedom of the Will*, pp. 156-62.

83   Hall Sr, *Complete Works*, pp. 47-199, contains the second edition, with Ryland's 'Recommendatory Preface'. The sermon was originally preached in Ryland's father's pulpit at Northampton.

use of arguments derived from Edwards' *Freedom of the Will*. This is particularly clear in the section 'Natural and Moral Ability Distinguished' but also in many other places throughout his work. To quote just one sentence: 'Scriptural exhortations to repentance and faith appear quite consistent, which could never be defended if criminality arose from natural, and not moral inability.'[84] Ryland made it clear in his Preface to the published work, that Hall Sr 'took a particular delight in the writings of President Edwards'.[85] There is little evidence that *Help to Zion's Travellers*, or the sermon that preceded it, were particularly formative for Fuller in themselves, although he does refer to Hall Sr's book once in the first edition of *The Gospel Worthy*.[86] However, the way that Edwards had influenced his friend would certainly be paralleled in Fuller's own work.

In pointing out the influence ministers from the Northamptonshire Association had over Fuller, both directly and indirectly, it is worthwhile also noting that the revitalization of association life was in itself evidence of the growth of Evangelicalism amongst the Particular Baptists. The prevalence of High Calvinism had led not only to a refusal to 'offer Christ' but also to a general suspicion of all human 'means', such as ministerial training and associating. Consequently High Calvinists were 'classic non-joiners',[87] a description that could never be applied to Hall, Ryland, Sutcliff or Fuller. The influence of Jonathan Edwards, so important to Fuller, was mediated to him through the revitalization of association life.

An Assessment of the Influence of Jonathan Edwards

That Edwards was a central figure for Fuller and the Particular Baptists in his circle is certain. Indeed they appeared to give him an almost iconic status, and there is evidence that other Evangelicals thought that the Northamptonshire ministers were over-dependent on him.[88]

---

84   Hall Sr, *Complete Works*, p. 200. See pp. 183-87, for the section on 'Natural and Moral Inability Distinguished'.

85   Hall Sr, *Complete Works*, p. 48.

86   Fuller, *The Gospel Worthy*, 1st edn, p. 163.

87   See S. James, 'Revival and Renewal in Baptist Life: The Contribution of William Steadman (1764-1837)', *BQ* 37.6 (April, 1998), p. 266, 281 n. James notes that this suspicion of associating continued with William Gadsby, who took up a pastorate in Manchester in 1804, and remained 'aloof' from the association life which Steadman so fervently supported.

88   For example John Newton. See Hindmarsh, *John Newton*, p. 154 n. Hindmarsh comments: 'Edwardsean New England divinity was never revered as highly by Newton as

Edwards, through his writings, certainly played a key role in shaping Fuller's life and work. On 28 April 1815, as he lay dying, Fuller dictated a letter to Ryland which included the following:

> We have heard some, who have been giving out of late that 'if Sutcliff and some others had preached more of Christ and less of Jonathan Edwards, they would have been more useful'. If those who talk thus, preached Christ half as much as Jonathan Edwards did, and were half as useful as he was, their usefulness would be double what it is.[89]

The vital importance of Edwards for Fuller will be clear throughout this study.

As far as writing *The Gospel Worthy* is concerned there is a broad consensus in the historiography of the period that Edwards was of great importance to Fuller. This is true both in studies that are specifically focused on Particular Baptist life,[90] and in more general works.[91] The major exception is the study of Fuller's theology by Kirkby, although his thesis has some modern support.[92] Much of what Kirkby says is unfounded. For example, in referring to Fuller's letter to Ryland already quoted above, he seeks to diminish the importance of Edwards for Fuller by stating: 'It should not be overlooked that in this criticism [i.e. the one Fuller was quoting], Andrew Fuller is not specifically named. Only Sutcliff is mentioned by name, as if he were the chief disciple of Edwards.'[93] This ignores the welter of other evidence that conclusively shows the importance of Edwards for Ryland and Fuller (Ryland named one of his sons Jonathan Edwards Ryland!).[94] But even if Fuller's

---

by the Fuller-Ryland circle.'

89   Ryland, *Andrew Fuller*, 1st edn, pp. 545-46. Fuller was responding to criticism from William Hawkins who was one of the supply preachers at Olney following Sutcliff's death (ironically on Fuller's recommendation). Hawkins' views left 'the entire town in an uproar'. See Haykin, *One Heart and Soul*, pp. 346-51.

90   See e.g. Haykin, *One Heart and Soul*, pp. 145-46; Clipsham, 'Development of a Doctrine', pp. 110-13. Oliver 'Emergence of a Strict and Particular Baptist Community', p. 85, is slightly more cautious: 'Some help from the writings of Jonathan Edwards helped him to work out his system.'

91   Watts, *Dissenters*, I, pp. 459-60; Hylson-Smith, *Churches in England*, II, p. 109.

92   The most relevant pages of Kirkby, 'Theology of Andrew Fuller', are pp. 54-63. See also G.M. Ella, *Law and Gospel in the Theology of Andrew Fuller* (Durham: Go Publications, 1996), pp. 23-24, 168. Ella states that 'convincing evidence for a direct influence by Edwards on Fuller has still to be produced, and this author is very sceptical whether such material will ever be produced'. He adds nothing to Kirkby's case, however.

93   Kirkby, 'Theology of Andrew Fuller', p. 55.

94   Jonathan Edwards Ryland was born on 5 May 1798. See J. Culross, *The Three*

deathbed letter were to be taken in isolation, Kirkby's comments are strained, seeing that the reference to 'others' was clearly shorthand for Fuller and his correspondent.

Kirkby is right, however, to point out that Fuller did not read 'Edwards on the Will' until 1777. This was six years after Fuller, by his own admission, began to reflect on the theological problems he would eventually resolve in the pages of *The Gospel Worthy*. Kirkby makes an important point when he calls attention to the critical and formative nature of these early years. His conclusion that 'Edwards and his writings played no part in determining [Fuller's] theology'[95] is still unwarranted, though Kirkby could have made his case stronger if he had cited a passage from Gunton Fuller's biography of his father, *Men Worth Remembering*. Fuller's Preface to *The Gospel Worthy* stated that, although not published until 1785, the work was actually written in 1781. But Gunton Fuller claimed to have found amongst his father's papers a manuscript of sorts, 'neither designed nor adapted for publication', which contained the 'elements' of *The Gospel Worthy*. The paper was 'endorsed with the date of 1776'.[96]

I will return to this extra piece of evidence in a moment, but first of all it should be clear that Kirkby's conclusion regarding Edwards' lack of importance for Fuller flies in the face of the plain evidence of *The Gospel Worthy* itself. To begin with there is Fuller's own acknowledgement of the importance of Edwards for him in the Preface to *The Gospel Worthy*. Fuller makes the following comments, continuing to write in the third person:

> He had read and considered, as well as he was able, President Edwards's Inquiry into the Freedom of the Will, with some other performances on the difference between natural and moral inability. He found much satisfaction in the distinction; as it appeared to him to carry with it its own evidence – to be clearly and fully contained in the Scriptures... The more he examined the Scriptures, the more he was convinced that all the inability ascribed to man, with respect to believing, arises from the aversion of his heart.[97]

The pattern is one typical of Fuller – reading a particular work and then reflecting on it in the light of the scriptures. The 'other performances' he mentioned almost certainly included John Smalley's

---

Rylands (London: Elliot Stock, 1897), p. 95.

95   Kirkby, 'Theology of Andrew Fuller', p. 62.

96   A.G. Fuller, *Men Worth Remembering*, p. 168. Gunton Fuller's comments, which I believe are significant, are often missed in the secondary literature on Fuller, although Naylor, *Calvinism, Communion and the Baptists*, has noted them.

97   *Fuller's Works*, II, p. 330.

Two Discourses referred to earlier, which was definitely circulating amongst the Northamptonshire men. In 1794, the *Evangelical Magazine* would carry an anonymous, appreciative review of a new 1793 edition of Smalley's book, almost certainly written by Fuller himself, although not included in his *Works*. This of course does not prove that Fuller had read Smalley in the 1770s, although it must be likely. Probably Smalley was significant for Fuller, although direct evidence is lacking.[98]

Also worth noting is Joseph Bellamy (1719-90), another New England theologian mentioned by name in the text of *The Gospel Worthy*, and one who would become increasingly important for Fuller in the years following 1785, the period covered in chapters three and four of this study. At some stage Fuller also read Caleb Evans' *An Address to Serious and Candid Professors of Christianity*, from which he quoted in *The Gospel Worthy*. [99] But in the Preface to *The Gospel Worthy* it was Edwards and his *Freedom of the Will* that Fuller directly referred to, and with good reason. It was from Edwards that the distinction between natural and moral ability derived, and all the other writers who made it, such as Smalley and Evans,[100] were leaning on him. Just how crucial this distinction was for Fuller is shown by an examination of the text of *The Gospel Worthy* itself.

In the main body of his work, Fuller regularly showed his debt to Edwards. This is not just true in the chapter, 'General Observations on Natural and Moral Inability', but at many other points too. For example, in the section where Fuller drives home his main practical conclusions, he makes heavy use of this key distinction.[101] In an earlier passage he deals with one objection to his view of 'duty faith', that people have 'no power to believe', by saying that

> Men want power to do this [i.e. believe in Christ] no more than they want power
> to do everything else that is really good, even so much as to think a good thought.
> But if this be not the duty of men, then the Almighty had no reason to complain as
> he did, when he looked down upon the children of men, that none of them did

---

98   For the text of the review and comments see Kirkby, 'Theology of Andrew Fuller', Appendix C, pp. 279-84.

99   Published in Bristol, 1772. See Hayden, 'Evangelical Calvinism and the Bristol Baptist Academy', p. 217.

100   Hayden, 'Evangelical Calvinism and the Bristol Baptist Academy', p. 217, exaggerates the importance of Evans for Fuller, however (the quotation, on pp. 183-85 of *The Gospel Worthy*, was dropped from the second edition). For the regard Evans had for Edwards, see Fuller Chapel Letters [Letters to Andrew Fuller], vol. 1 (1-34), vol. 2 (35-71), Fuller Baptist Church, Kettering; 35, C. Evans to Fuller, Bristol, 7 November 1787: 'I have just been reading Edwards on virtue…what precision, what modesty, what sublimity!'

101   Fuller, *The Gospel Worthy*, 1st edn, pp. 172-84, especially p. 186.

good, no not one. Moreover, I wish what has, or may be said on the subject of natural and moral inability, to be taken as an answer to this objection.[102]

As far as the necessity of the work of the Holy Spirit in conversion was concerned, Fuller believed that rather than opening the door to Arminianism, Edwards' work was actually the saviour of Calvinism. Towards the end of the treatise he wrote:

> For want of knowing better, some people have suspected this distinction [i.e. between natural and moral inability] to be friendly to Arminianism, a sort of fragment, as they suppose, of the old idol free will, whereas nothing is better calculated to destroy that system. It is abundantly improved for this purpose by PRESIDENT EDWARDS, in his Inquiry into the Freedom of the Will.[103]

Once again Fuller made his dependence on Edwards quite explicit. Edwards allowed Fuller to hold together strict Calvinism (no one would come without the regenerating work of the Holy Spirit) and evangelistic preaching (all had the *natural* powers to come, even though because of *moral* or criminal inability they would not, apart from the Spirit's work). Because their inability was not natural, therefore it was their duty to believe and consequently Fuller's duty to preach. This line of argument is absolutely fundamental to *The Gospel Worthy*. If Fuller had not been reading 'Edwards on the Will', together with other writers who derived their arguments from this work, it is hard to see how *The Gospel Worthy* could have been published. I agree, therefore, with E.F. Clipsham who believes that Edwards was 'probably the most powerful and important extra biblical influence' on Fuller. Indeed, the distinction between natural and moral ability 'became one of the foundation stones' of his doctrine.[104]

As Bebbington states, Jonathan Edwards 'stands at the headwaters' of eighteenth-century Evangelicalism.[105] The evidence that he shaped Fuller's argument so decisively is just one factor clearly defining *The Gospel Worthy* as an Evangelical tract. Edwards was also an Enlightenment figure. Influenced by the English philosopher John Locke (1632-1704), his attention to epistemology, that is the theory of knowledge, was typical of the spirit of the age.[106] Crucial to his

---

102 Fuller, *The Gospel Worthy*, 1st edn, pp. 152-53.

103 Fuller, *The Gospel Worthy*, 1st edn, p. 192. Morris, *Andrew Fuller*, 2nd edn, p. 383, was reflecting his subject's own views when he described 'Edwards on the Will' as 'that bulwark of the Calvinistic system'.

104 Clipsham, 'Development of a Doctrine', pp. 110-11.

105 Bebbington, *Evangelicalism*, p. 6.

106 See Rack, *Reasonable Enthusiast*, p. 163; Bebbington, *Evangelicalism*, p. 48. The

argument in the *Freedom of the Will* is that God does not compel people to behave in a manner contrary to their wills. Bebbington summarizes: 'Free acts are not forced though they are caused. This was to contend that human beings are part of an ordered universe, but to hold that nevertheless they are responsible for what they do. Edwards was reinterpreting the sovereignty of God as an expression of the law of cause and effect.'[107] Consequently *The Gospel Worthy*, leaning as it did on these ideas, was also marked by aspects of the cultural mood and intellectual climate of the age.[108]

To conclude this section, however, it is worthwhile returning to Gunton Fuller's statement which was highlighted earlier in this chapter. If we accept his assertion as reliable, the comment that Fuller's 1776 paper 'was neither designed nor adapted for publication' is significant. What state this 'paper' was in can only be guessed at. It is worth noting, too, that it is probable that at least some of Edwards' central ideas had already been mediated to Fuller through his association contacts by this date. The comments in *Men Worth Remembering* remain tantalizing. But this cannot overturn the great weight of evidence, particularly that of *The Gospel Worthy* itself, that points to the crucial importance of Edwards to Fuller.

Nevertheless, the existence of some of Fuller's ideas in written form, probably (the paper to which Gunton Fuller referred is now lost) before he had had the chance to read Edwards directly, is significant. It reminds us that there were other factors that were crucial in Fuller's theological formation. It is too simplistic to infer, as some general works doubtless inadvertently do, that Fuller read Edwards and because of this came to the views he expressed in *The Gospel Worthy*.[109] Neither is it true to say that Fuller was merely a popularizer of Edwards, or that he took on board the New England theologian's views uncritically. Certainly, Fuller used Edwards' ideas and applied them to his own context. But many of the longer quotations we have included in this chapter show that whether different theological works or personal experience was in question, Fuller's method of evaluation was the same: prolonged theological reflection with the scriptures as the 'final arbiter of the truth'. Once again this underscores his thoroughgoing biblicism. It also shows him as an independent thinker and a theologian of some

---

degree to which Edwards was or was not influenced by Locke is discussed by Ramsey in his introduction to Edwards, *Freedom of the Will*, pp. 47-64.

107   Bebbington, *Evangelicalism*, p. 64.

108   One might add, albeit tentatively, that Fuller's careful and even-handed weighing of evidence, suggests that he was influenced by certain characteristics associated with the English Enlightenment, particularly empiricism.

109   See e.g. Hylson-Smith, *Churches in England*, II, p. 109.

considerable ability (and he was only twenty-seven years old in 1781, by which time *The Gospel Worthy* had been substantially written). In the words of Underwood, he was 'A self taught man, with no gifts of style and little technical learning, [yet] he had real power as a thinker, and with a terrier like tenacity, he kept hold of what he deemed the error of his opponent and shook it to death.' Underwood's conclusion is that Fuller was perhaps 'the soundest and most creatively useful theologian the Particular Baptists have ever had'.[110]

Conclusion

What then were the reasons leading to the formation of Fuller's theology of salvation, as expressed in *The Gospel Worthy*? Clearly there were a complex variety of factors, but also a common theme which emerges. The variety of factors include Fuller's conversion, his other early experiences at Soham (all of which were interpreted through the lens of a growing Evangelicalism), together with his reading of older Puritan works. Also important was the influence of the Northamptonshire Association and its leading figures, which, as well as exerting a direct influence on Fuller's development, brought him into contact with various new works, particularly important being those from New England. Jonathan Edwards and his distinction between natural and moral inability deserves special mention, crucial as it was to Fuller's overall argument in *The Gospel Worthy*. But as important was his commitment to reflect on everything (with an extremely able mind) and submit everything to scripture, a commitment the evidence suggests he carried through in practice. The common theme is that Fuller's theology was being shaped by forces associated with the Evangelical Revival. The following two chapters show how Fuller's theology of salvation developed after 1785. There were significant modifications but already it should be clear that, as Fuller stood on the verge of taking his manuscript to the press at the end of 1784, the decisive change had already taken place. It is no exaggeration to say that Fuller had become an Evangelical.

---

110   A.C. Underwood, *A History of the English Baptists* (London: Kingsgate Press, 1947), p. 166.

CHAPTER THREE

The Disputes with High Calvinists and Arminians regarding *The Gospel Worthy of All Acceptation*

I feel reluctant in being asked to attend to controversy

Towards the end of 1784, Fuller at last felt ready to submit *The Gospel Worthy of All Acceptation* for publication. On 21 October he wrote in his diary:

> I feel some pain in the thought of being about to publish on *the obligations of men to believe in Christ*, fearing I shall hereby expose myself to a good deal of abuse... Had I not the satisfaction that it is the cause of *God and truth*, I would drop all thoughts of printing. The Lord keep me meek and lowly of heart.

A month later he was to walk with some trepidation the short distance from Kettering, where he had been pastor since October 1783, to a printers in Northampton. As he did so he offered up prayer 'that God would bless that about which I am going; namely, the printing of my manuscript on the duty of sinners to believe in Christ.'[1] Fuller's use of the phrase 'the cause of God and truth' in the first extract was almost certainly a conscious echo of Gill's major treatise of the same name, hugely influential in Particular Baptist life earlier in the century. Fuller was clearly apprehensive about publishing, but *The Gospel Worthy* would in fact outstrip even Gill's work in terms of importance and influence, and Fuller would come to believe that his prayers for God's 'blessing' had indeed been answered.

Yet Fuller had correctly foreseen the negative way *The Gospel Worthy* would be received by some. In the wake of publication, Ryland recorded that Fuller had to contend with many 'ignorant people' who 'began to raise an outcry against the book and its author; charging him and his friends with having forsaken the doctrines of grace, and left the

---

1   See Ryland, *Andrew Fuller*, pp. 131-32, for quotations in the first three paragraphs.

good old way.' This comment refers in the main to High Calvinist opponents from within Fuller and Ryland's own denomination. But there were also others in the wider Christian world who thought that Fuller had not gone far enough in modifying his theology. As a result of his decision to go to print, Fuller would be engaged in controversy for the rest of his life.

Both this chapter and the next seek to examine some of the main disputes in which he became involved. Here the focus is on the period from 1785 to 1801, the year a thoroughly revised second edition of *The Gospel Worthy* appeared. As Oliver states, Fuller's theology of salvation 'did not remain static' after 1785,[2] and this chapter charts the key developments and shifts of emphasis that occurred in a period that often receives little treatment in the secondary literature on Fuller.[3] His debates with High Calvinists help clarify Fuller's central concerns, and show how his Evangelical convictions continued to develop. But an analysis of his dispute with the Arminian General Baptist Dan Taylor (1738-1816) reveals something more, namely that Fuller significantly modified his position on the atonement during the period under consideration. Fuller was now being shaped by Evangelical forces and driven by Evangelical concerns. He was leaving High Calvinism far behind.

High Calvinist Opposition to *The Gospel Worthy*

Much of the opposition to *The Gospel Worthy* came from High Calvinists, and much of it was both petty and personal. Pride of place goes to Rushden Baptist Church, ten miles to the south of Kettering, and its pastor William Knowles. One of the Rushden members, a Mrs Wright, had moved to Weekly, a village immediately to the north of Kettering, and she started to attend Fuller's church. But when she asked to come into membership in 1785, Rushden refused to provide the normal letter of transfer because, as Knowles informed her, 'the church at Kettering had gone off from their former principles'.[4] The deacons at

---

2   Oliver, 'Emergence of a Strict and Particular Baptist Community', p. 101.

3   Clipsham, 'Andrew Fuller and Fullerism', and Haykin, *One Heart and Soul* spend little time on these developments, as their focus lies elsewhere. Young, 'Fuller and the Developing Modern Missions Movement', pp. 158-169, covers one aspect of the dispute with Taylor briefly.

4   See 'The Church Book of Kettering Baptist Church (The 'Little Meeting'), 1773-1815', Fuller Baptist Church, Kettering, pp. 84-95, 106, for information and quotations in this paragraph. The relevant entries are for 28 July, 17 August, 6 November, 22 December 1785 and 26 February 1796. Cf. the use made of some of the

Kettering wrote to Rushden on 7 August 1785, protesting 'that we know of no one principle relating to the doctrines of grace which we feel in the least inclined to give up'. They asked the church at Rushden to 'consider the matter again'. Two months later they had received no reply, prompting them to write again, in stronger terms. The Rushden Baptists eventually responded in December, again refusing to provide a letter of 'dismission' for Mrs Wright, and accusing the Kettering church of 'lording it' over them. The real root of the problem was freely acknowledged in the church book at Kettering:

> That there are differences in sentiment between us and the church at Rushden, is true. We consider the doctrines of grace as entirely consistent with a free address to every sinner, and with an universal obligation on all men where the gospel is preached to repent of their sins, and turn to God through Jesus Christ. They think otherwise, and it is simply on account of this difference that they have disowned communion with us.

Described as 'a timid character', Mrs Wright was reluctant to transfer membership without a formal dismissal from Rushden, despite the Kettering church now being ready to receive her without a letter of transfer. It was not until 1796, two years after the death of Knowles, that such a letter was provided. Morris mentioned a congregation close to Kettering which refused to have any dealings with Fuller, or 'allow any of their members to have fellowship with his church' for seven years. Probably he was referring to Rushden, although doubtless there were other candidates.[5]

Some of the published replies to *The Gospel Worthy* were replete with personal abuse of the Kettering pastor. Fuller was clearly anxious when he read advertisements concerning a forthcoming work by a certain Dr Withers, who promised to reduce *The Gospel Worthy* to 'dust'. When he received a copy of Withers' work he was deeply shocked by its violent language: 'What horrid sentiments does he advance!', Fuller wrote in his diary. According to Ryland, Withers was a man 'deeply tinged with antinomianism' whose work was full of 'extravagant crudities'. He appears to have accused Fuller of, amongst other things, 'tremendous deformity of thought'. Despite this work evidently gaining a wide circulation, Fuller was not prepared to respond in any detailed way in print.[6] The incident with the Rushden church and

---

same material by Haykin, *One Heart and Soul*, pp. 150-51.

5   Morris, *Andrew Fuller*, 2nd edn, p. 271.

6   Ryland, *Andrew Fuller*, pp. 132-34. The entry was for 29 January 1786. Withers' treatise was entitled *Philanthropos, or a Letter to the Revd. Fuller in reply to his Treatise on Damnation* (London, 1786). A copy of this work has not been traced, but

Withers' pamphlet are illustrative of the sort of opposition that would dog Fuller for the rest of his life. This was clearly painful for him, but of greater significance were some of the other pamphlet replies to *The Gospel Worthy*. Two in particular, both written from a High Calvinist perspective by Particular Baptists, merit a more detailed treatment. These were by William Button (1754-1821) and John Martin (1741-1820), both of whom were London pastors.

The Response of Button and Martin

These responses to *The Gospel Worthy* were significant in that both Button and Martin were respected figures within the Particular Baptist denomination (although in Martin's case this would later change) and because Fuller responded in print to both. Button was pastor at Dean Street, Southwark, from 1774 until his resignation in 1813 due to financial difficulties. He was, in the words of Oliver, 'a representative of those London churches which still revered the memory of John Gill'.[7] Dean Street was in fact an offshoot from Gill's old church in Carter Lane, where Button's father had been a deacon. It was created by a minority of members who opposed the appointment of the Bristol Academy student John Rippon (1750-1836) as Gill's successor in 1773. Button's *Remarks on a Treatise entitled The Gospel Worthy of All Acceptation* appeared in London in 1785, prompting a reply from Fuller two years later.[8] Personal relations between Button and Fuller remained reasonably good, and Button later became a supporter of the Baptist Missionary Society.[9]

John Martin, pastor at Grafton Street, Westminster, from 1773, was

---

there are quotations from it in *Fuller's Works*, II, pp. 418-19. Withers was not a Particular Baptist.

7   Oliver, 'Emergence of a Strict and Particular Baptist Community', p. 87. The financial difficulties Button experienced were in connection with a bookselling business he had set up for his two sons.

8   A. Fuller, *A Defence of a Treatise, entitled, The Gospel of Christ Worthy of All Acceptation: Containing a Reply to Mr Button's Remarks and the Observations of Philanthropos* (Clipstone: J.W. Morris, 1787). See *Fuller's Works*, II, pp. 421-511. The 'Philanthropos' in question was not Withers but, as we shall see, the New Connexion General Baptist Dan Taylor.

9   As Fuller was later to write, Fuller to W.R. Ward, 7 Jan 1813, Fuller Letters (4/5/1): 'Our High Calvinist Brethren are coming nearer; the mission attracts them, as well as the General Baptists; and we endeavour not to counteract its salutary influence by our behaviour in either case.' For biographical details of Button see *HEB*, IV, pp. 335-37.

one of the ministers listed as being present at Button's ordination. Martin had been the supply preacher at Carter Lane in the weeks immediately following Gill's death in 1771, but his history was more complex than Button's. He was actually the author of the often quoted Northamptonshire Association circular letter of 1770, which stated: 'Every soul that comes to Christ to be saved from hell and sin by Him is to be encouraged... The coming soul need not fear that he is not elected, for none but such will be willing to come and submit to Christ.' The letter went on to declare that if people coming to Christ were being 'drawn by the bands of [God's] love', then pastors should not scruple to draw them 'with the cords of man'.[10] Fuller actually referred Martin's comments as having an influence on him when he had read them in 1775, at about the same time he studied the tract by Abraham Taylor on the 'Modern Question'.[11] At the time he wrote the circular letter, Martin had been pastor of Shepshed Baptist Church, which was in the Northamptonshire Association, but after moving to Grafton Street he was drawn into the London Particular Baptist scene and became an implacable High Calvinist. He published a series of intemperate attacks against Fuller between the years 1788 and 1791,[12] colourfully dismissed by Morris as a 'ponderous load of polemics'.[13] Not surprisingly, in Fuller's reply to Martin's first pamphlet he frequently drew attention to the Grafton Street pastor's change of views. Martin, a political conservative, became estranged from the majority of Particular Baptists when in 1798, to their horror, he accused them of being sympathetic to the prospect of a French invasion.[14] But at the time of his disputes with Fuller, he was still a figure of standing in the London Particular Baptist community. A number of significant points arise from the dispute between Fuller and his two opponents.

---

10   'The Circular Letter from the Ministers and Messengers assembled at Kettering, May 22-23, 1770', cited by, amongst others, Brown, *English Baptists*, p. 90.

11   Ryland, *Andrew Fuller*, p. 37.

12   J. Martin, *Thoughts On The Duty Of Man Relative To Faith In Jesus Christ, In Which Mr Andrew Fuller's Leading Propositions On This Subject Are Considered* (London, 1788-91). Copies of both Button and Martin's works are held in the Angus Library, Regents Park College, Oxford.

13   Morris, *Andrew Fuller*, 1st edn, p. 269.

14   A. Fuller, *Letters Relative to Mr Martin's Publication on The Duty of Faith in Christ* (Clipstone: J.W. Morris, 1788), in *Fuller's Works*, II, pp. 716-36. For biographical details of Martin see E.A. Payne, 'Abraham Booth, 1734-1806', *BQ* 26.1 (January, 1975), pp. 39-40; *HEB*, IV, pp. 77-82, 342-50.

The Arguments of Button and Martin

Predictably, both Button and Martin attacked Fuller's leading premise, that faith in Christ was the duty of all who heard the gospel. According to them, because no one could respond without the electing grace of God, saving faith could not be the duty of all. It was just as absurd to talk of someone who was unregenerate having a 'duty' to believe as it was to call the blind to look, the deaf to hear or the dead to rise. Neither of the London men were afraid to take these principles to their logical conclusion. In the words of Button: 'As to calls, invitations and exhortations to special faith and spiritual acts [it] appears surely, after what has been said, to be inconsistent with Scripture and with common sense.'[15] How then were ministers to address their congregations? Martin, in Part III of his Treatise, spoke of the sort of preaching he wanted to encourage:

> Sinners in my opinion, are more frequently converted, and believers more commonly edified, by a narrative of facts concerning Jesus Christ, and by a clear, and connected statement of the doctrines of grace, and blessings of the gospel, than by all the exhortations and expostulations that were ever invented.[16]

This, for Martin and other High Calvinists, was gospel preaching. The gospel could be presented, but indiscriminate 'exhortations' to believe were inappropriate. This was the approach famously described by Ivimey (not unfairly), as the 'non-invitation, non-application scheme'.[17] Sinners could be encouraged to 'attend the means of grace', a traditional High Calvinist stress, but evangelistic preaching where the gospel was 'offered' to all was, it was declared, utterly inconsistent with true Calvinistic principles.[18]

Fuller's Response and the Differences between him and his High Calvinist Opponents

These were broadly the arguments that Fuller had ventured into print to counter, and whilst interacting with his opponents needed to do little more than restate his main themes again, something he did with vigour. As he did this he strongly attacked the High Calvinist emphasis to which

---

15   Button, *Remarks*, p. 99.

16   Martin, *Thoughts*, Part III, pp. 62-63.

17   *HEB*, III, pp. 272-73.

18   Martin, *Thoughts*, Part I, p. 18.

Martin in particular had referred, namely that of encouraging 'sinners' to 'attend the means of grace'. He did so with a direct appeal to the scriptures. The language of the Bible, he contended, was not 'use such and such a means to get those dispositions of which you are present destitute'. Rather than using this sort of vague and indefinite language, the Bible dealt in direct commands. Those which Fuller cited, stressing the definite words of command, included: 'BE YE HOLY for I am holy... Be NOT wise in your own conceits' and 'Let that mind BE IN YOU that was in Christ Jesus'. If the Bible dealt with people in these terms, gospel ministers should do no less.[19] But this debate has wider significance than merely showing that some High Calvinists remained resolutely opposed to the Edwardsean Evangelical Calvinism of *The Gospel Worthy* and that Fuller, although under fire, remained true to what he had written. Although there was little that was new in these disputes, they were nevertheless extremely revealing of the gulf there now was between Fuller and his High Calvinist critics, and the key points which divided them.

The first point worth highlighting is that Button and Martin's works betray a fundamental and overriding commitment to High Calvinism *as a system*. That is to say, an *a priori* commitment to the principles of High Calvinism, over and against Arminianism, exercised a controlling influence over their work. Button complained that Arminians had been saying that Fuller's work would 'cure some of their Gillism and Brineism', and that for this reason alone it was suspect.[20] Fuller had admitted in *The Gospel Worthy* that some Calvinistic ministers who had preached in an invitational manner had subsequently gone on to 'to dabble in Arminianism'. Both Button and Martin quoted this passage, seizing on it as evidence that Fuller was wrong to argue as he did.[21] 'Offering Christ' in preaching might be the slippery slope to Arminianism; therefore, on this basis alone, it should be avoided.

This way of arguing might have seemed sound to Button and Martin, but it was completely unacceptable to Fuller. He rejected the charge that offering the gospel to sinners necessarily led to Arminianism, any more than Calvinism necessarily led to Antinomianism. But more importantly, although Fuller had a high opinion of Gill and Brine (perhaps higher in public than in private), he was adamant that they should not be set up as infallible 'standards of orthodoxy'. Rather, he urged, people should be free to examine the scriptures and think for themselves. When arguing a particular point in reply to Button, who had

---

19   Fuller, *Reply to Martin*, in *Fuller's Works*, II, p. 732.

20   Button, *Remarks*, p. v.

21   Button, *Remarks*, pp. i-ii & 100; Martin, *Thoughts*, p. 77. The quotation is from *The Gospel Worthy*, 1st edn, p. 167.

cited Gill, Fuller stated: 'What was Dr Gill's meaning I cannot tell, nor is it worth while to dispute about it, as the opinion of the greatest uninspired writer is not decisive.'[22] For Fuller, adherence to a system or a human author was far less important than a commitment to the Bible and a spirit of free enquiry. Scriptures were none the less true for having been quoted by Arminians.

A further difference between Fuller and his opponents was revealed in Martin's charge that Fuller was over dependant on certain American theologians. 'America is his market' he declared, asserting 'that what our author has imported from America, he has mixed with his own manufacture, but not to his own advantage'. Martin attacked the views of Jonathan Edwards without always naming him in Part I of his treatise, although there was little doubt as to who his target was. In Part II, Martin was to be more specific, commenting that Edwards' style was 'frequently coarse and often quaint', and that 'his sentiments [were] sometimes difficult to understand and sometimes not worth understanding'. Although the Grafton Street pastor was prepared to admit Edwards' works had 'some good in them', they would all be better off thoroughly abridged.[23] For Martin, Fuller was clearly over reliant on Edwards and his disciples to the detriment of his own work.

Fuller only ever responded publicly to Part I of Martin's work, believing there was nothing new in Parts II and III to lead him to venture into print again. But there was enough insinuated about Edwards and other New England writers in Martin's first pamphlet to lead Fuller to respond with some heat. Morris spoke of the contempt that Fuller expressed in private for 'such a writer', and it is hard to see how Haykin can say that relations between the two men remained on 'friendly' terms.[24] On the particular charge being levelled, Fuller replied:

> Much is said of my having read Edwards, Bellamy and other American writers. Mr M. seems as if he would have his readers think he has made a great discovery here, though it is no more than I had freely acknowledged. It is true I have received instruction in reading the authors above mentioned; nor do I know of any sin or shame either in the thing itself, or in openly acknowledging it.

But Fuller also wanted to make it clear that he had not read these theologians uncritically. He continued:

---

22 *Fuller's Works*, pp. 442, 456-57, 421.

23 Martin, *Thoughts*, Part I, pp. 81, 84; Part II, p. 70. See pp. 73-74, for further strictures on Edwards.

24 Morris, *Andrew Fuller*, 1st edn, p. 303; Haykin, *One Heart and Soul*, p. 149.

Mr M. may wish to insinuate that I have taken matters upon trust from these writers without examining them; but in answer to such insinuations it is sufficient to say, that is more than he can prove. All he knows or can know of the matter is, that I have read them, and approve of some of their sentiments.[25]

The significance of Edwards for Fuller is underlined once again in this exchange, as is the influence of other New England theologians (The importance of Bellamy and 'other American writers' for his thought is something that will be dealt with more fully in chapter four). Martin's largely negative assessment of Edwards himself is also worth highlighting. There was a clear division between the High Calvinists and Fuller (together with the other Northamptonshire pastors), on this point.

But even more strikingly both Button and Martin not only reject, but also in large measure fail to understand, the key Edwardsean distinction between natural and moral inability. Button appeared especially perplexed and it is hard to avoid the conclusion that encountering Fuller's use of Edwards' work was, for him, like entering a completely different world. He repeatedly confused Fuller's use of the term 'natural' with the 'natural man', accusing him of obvious 'inconsistency'. What he was quite unable to grasp was how it was possible to maintain on the one hand that someone's inability to believe was total, and on the other say that that inability was not 'natural', but moral or 'criminal'. 'All I contend for' he complained, 'is for the total inability of man to believe. Mr F says this is what he never denied, and yet fills up 196 pages which tend to the contrary. How he can clear up this inconsistency I am at a loss to determine. I must leave it to himself.'[26]

Martin too failed to grasp the difference between natural and moral inability. He also accused Fuller of 'inconsistency', together with obscurity and error, and charged him of 'magnifying man' through his concept of duty faith. Martin represented Fuller as saying that it was the duty of every man to 'produce and possess' faith 'by an act of his own, unassisted and prior to regeneration'.[27] Of course Fuller was saying no such thing. Indeed, it was precisely this sort of argument against faith being a duty that the distinction between natural and moral inability was meant to undercut. As we have seen, if Edwards' distinction was maintained it was possible to hold both on the one hand that people were totally unable to respond to the gospel without God's electing

---

25   Fuller, *Reply to Martin*, in *Fuller's Works*, II, p. 719.

26   Button, *Remarks*, pp. 56-58.

27   Martin, *Thoughts*, pp. 56-59, 142. See also Fuller's *Reply to Martin*, in *Fuller's Works*, II, p. 719.

grace, and on the other that their inability was not natural but criminal, leaving them culpable and responsible. That this reasoning cut no ice with men like Martin was clearly frustrating for Fuller. But this was only symptomatic of the great divide that had opened up between them.

The Overall Significance of the Disputes with High Calvinists

The main fault lines dividing Fuller from this sort of opponent should now be clear enough. Button and Martin, as representative High Calvinists, were wedded to a system in a way that Fuller, although he never repudiated Calvinism, was not. For him, an overriding Evangelical commitment to scripture was key. The High Calvinists were suspicious of the New England theologians, whilst Fuller was prepared to look to them for instruction, thus giving his theology a trans-atlantic dimension. Button and Martin failed to understand the distinction between natural and moral ability, derived from Edwards' *Freedom of the Will*. To the extent that they did understand the distinction, or perhaps thought they did, they rejected it.

As a parenthesis, this might be the point to note that the Edwardsean distinction between natural and moral inability has been criticized by some theologians in the Reformed tradition, often because it appeared to undercut the doctrine of total depravity (a doctrine which Fuller, and of course Edwards, always held to).[28] Recently Holmes has critiqued the philosophical basis for Edwards' arguments, before going on to argue that the *Freedom of the Will* contains *theological* resources (in a short discussion on the holiness of Christ), for arguing similar conclusions to the ones that Edwards did in fact reach.[29] Nevertheless, it is fair to say that very few would want to defend the distinction between natural and moral inability today without some modification or qualification. But the merits of Fuller's work do not rest on the Edwardsean distinction being watertight in every respect, although in the context of the eighteenth century it was quite coherent. What Fuller saw was the need to restore the concept of human responsibility alongside that of divine responsibility, and that this was thoroughly biblical. The *Freedom of the Will* was vital to Fuller as he pursued that task, but his conclusions do not fall if Edwards' arguments would be better off being recast and having different foundations today. The narrow point about Button and

---

28   See e.g. L. Berkhof, *Systematic Theology* (Edinburgh: Banner of Truth, 1981 [1949]), pp. 247-48; cf. the brief discussion in Haykin, *One Heart and Soul*, p. 146.

29   Holmes, *God of Grace*, pp. 153-57; cf. his 'Edwards on the Will', *International Journal of Systematic Theology*, 1.3 (1999), pp. 266-85. Priest, 'Andrew Fuller', is more negative.

Martin's works is that they completely failed to understand and engage with the distinction in *any* meaningful way. They were not offering a reasoned critique; they just found it incomprehensible from their standpoint as implacable High Calvinists who were wedded to that system.

Olin C. Robison, writes perceptively concerning the differences between Gill and 'those in his tradition', and the eighteenth-century Evangelical Particular Baptists. Gill was a 'scholastic' and a 'systematizer'.[30] 'He felt that God's laws...could be put down in orderly statements and in this effort he spent the major part of his time, both in pulpit and study.' He and his followers were interested in 'truth for its own sake' and the reasons for God's actions. But the moderate 'evangelical' Calvinists were far more concerned with 'practical piety', the call to repentance and 'with truth primarily as an instrument to lead men to God'. It was not so much the 'reasons for God's actions' but 'what God did in the lives of men' that was important. Moreover, if Gill 'had moved in a theological world which owed more than it realized to the medieval scholastics', the eighteenth-century Evangelicals, with their conception of religious truths as 'few, simple in their form and essentially practical in their application', owed more 'than perhaps they cared to concede' to the Enlightenment.[31]

To sum up, not only was there a difference between the two different groups in terms of content, but also in terms of presuppositions, aims and method. Speaking of Fuller, Morris summed up his approach:

> He burst asunder the enslaving fetters of human dogmas, emancipated himself
> from their paralysing influence on his researches after truth, and taking the word
> of God alone for his guide, he determined to call no man master upon earth, but to

---

30   Quotations from this paragraph, unless otherwise stated, are from O.C. Robison, 'The Particular Baptists in England: 1760-1820' (DPhil thesis, University of Oxford, 1963), pp. 35-36. See also the use made of Robison's work at this point by Hayden, 'Evangelical Calvinism and the Bristol Baptist Academy', pp. 333-34.

31   In this study I have referred to the 'Enlightenment' with an upper case E, knowing how controversial and unsatisfactory this is. See 'The Enlightenment' in D.J. Atkinson and D.H. Field (ed.), *New Dictionary of Christian Ethics and Pastoral Theology* (Leicester, IVP, 1995), pp. 347-48; R. Porter, *Enlightenment: Britain and the Creation of the Modern World* (London: Penguin, 2000), pp. xvii-xviii, who surveys the historiography and concludes that it might be better to speak of 'enlightenment' or better still (particularly in an English context), 'enlightenments'. Nevertheless the term is useful shorthand for the social and intellectual trends such as empiricism and rationalism which began to develop in the late-seventeenth century. Bebbington, *Evangelicalism*, pp. 51-74, argues at length that eighteenth-century Evangelicals were influenced by certain Enlightenment traits.

follow, with a firm and cautious step, the dictates of an enlightened understanding.[32]

The language was perhaps overblown, but also perceptive. It is hard to believe that Fuller did not owe a very real debt to Enlightenment empiricism. But this comment must be immediately qualified. As Morris correctly highlighted, for Fuller the authority of scripture remained key. This was an authority that he believed never needed to be established. Rather the scriptures were the 'Oracles of God' and should be accepted as such.[33] It should also be noted that Fuller strongly resisted the rationalizing trends that were part and parcel of the Enlightenment, as evidenced by many of his apologetic works.[34] Thus, although influenced by certain strands of Enlightenment thinking, he strongly contended with others aspects. The 'dictates of an enlightened understanding' were useful in the search for truth. But ultimately nothing could overturn the 'Word of God'.

The Response of Dan Taylor and Arminianism

It was not only the High Calvinists who responded to *The Gospel Worthy*. Fuller also had to defend his work on another, quite different front. In a diary entry for 5 February 1786, he recorded: 'My mind has been generally much engaged in perusing different publications against my treatise on the gospel of Christ. This morning I received another, written by Mr Dan Taylor.' For his next entry he wrote:

> Read the above piece. The author discovers an amiable spirit; and there is a good deal of plausibility in some things he advances. My mind has been much employed, all the week, on this piece. The more I examine it, the more I perceive it is, though ingeniously wrought together, open to a solid and effective reply.[35]

Dan Taylor (1738-1816) was the leader of the New Connexion of General Baptists, formed in 1770 as a result of disillusionment with the 'unevangelical views and outdated traditions' of existing General Baptists.[36] The New Connexion was organized along unashamedly

---

32   Morris, *Andrew Fuller*, 1st edn, pp. 270-71.

33   See M.A.G. Haykin, '"The Oracles of God": Andrew Fuller and the Scriptures', *The Churchman* 103.1 (1989), pp. 60-76, especially p. 64.

34   See especially *The Gospel its Own Witness* (1799) in *Fuller's Works*, II, pp. 3-287.

35   Ryland, *Andrew Fuller*, p. 134.

36   Brown, *English Baptists*, p. 69. See pp. 56-64, for the theological and other

Evangelical lines, but was also Arminian. All the ministers of the Connexion were required to subscribe to six articles of faith (which rejected both Unitarianism and Calvinism) and give an account of their religious experience. There was a strong commitment to churches associating together, and they 'were much more alive to the needs of the time than the old Assembly', engaging in vigorous outreach work in the rapidly expanding towns, for example the lace and hosiery centres of the Midlands.[37] Taylor himself had impeccable Evangelical credentials. Thoroughly indebted to the Revival, as a youth he had walked twenty or thirty miles to hear Whitefield and Wesley when they visited his native Yorkshire. He began preaching in Wesleyan Methodist Societies around Halifax in 1761 but became unhappy with certain features of Methodism as practiced in the West Riding. By 1763, whilst remaining strongly committed to Arminianism, he had become convinced of believer's baptism. No local Particular Baptist minister would baptize him, so together with a colleague he walked to the Nottinghamshire village of Gamston to be baptized by a General Baptist minister in February 1763.[38]

Taylor published his *Observations on the Rev Andrew Fuller's late pamphlet entitled The Gospel of Christ Worthy of All Acceptation*, in 1786, under the pseudonym Philanthropos, and in the form of letters to a friend. Fuller's reply, as has already been noted, was coupled with the one to Button. But the controversy did not end there. Taylor dropped his use of 'Philanthropos' for his two further pamphlets, published under his own name in 1787 and 1790 respectively. Curiously Fuller did the reverse, adopting a pseudonym of his own, 'Agnostos', in replying to Taylor's second tract in 1788.[39] The possible reasons for this will be

---

difficulties (disputes over hymn singing, for example), which dogged The General Baptist Assembly during this period. Nevertheless, to begin with the New Connexion was able to maintain reasonably good relations with the older body.

37   Hylson-Smith, *Churches in England*, II, p. 107.

38   For biographical details of Taylor and the early history of the New Connexion see A. Taylor, *Memoirs of the Rev. Dan Taylor* (London: Baynes and Son, 1820), *passim*.; F. Rinaldi, 'The Tribe of Dan': The New Connexion of General Baptists 1770-1891. A Study in the Transition from Revival Movement to Established Denomination (PhD thesis, Glasgow University, 1996), especially pp. 12-16, and his, *The Tribe of Dan: The New Connexion of General Baptists, 1770-1891* (Carlisle: Paternoster, forthcoming, 2003); Watts, *Dissenters*, I, pp. 454-56.

39   D. Taylor, *Observations on the Rev Andrew Fuller's Reply to Philanthropos* (St Ives, Cambridgeshire, 1788), and *The Friendly Conclusion Occasioned by the Letters of 'Agnostos'* (London, 1790). Oliver was unable to locate a copy of Taylor's first, pseudonymous, work, but one is held in Spurgeon's College Library, bound together with the two later pamphlets. Fuller's *The Reality and Efficacy of Divine Grace*

discussed later in this chapter. By the time this dispute began Taylor was an established and respected leader in the Evangelical world.[40] That respect was certainly shared by Fuller himself, as will become clear.

The Conduct of the Dispute with Taylor

Before looking at Taylor's central arguments, it is well worth considering the manner in which the debate was conducted, particularly if the tone of Fuller's disputes with his High Calvinist opponents is borne in mind. The dispute with Martin was as acrimonious as any Fuller was ever involved in, at least in print. Martin accused Fuller of being 'a very *obscure, inconsistent, erroneous, ignorant, artful, vain, hypocritical* kind of writer'. Fuller replied with some strong invective of his own, including some biting satire.[41] He would come to believe that he overstepped the mark, directing that his *Remarks on Mr Martin's Publication* be omitted from any posthumous collection of his works because of its severity, an instruction later editors chose to ignore.[42] By contrast, one of the most striking aspects of the parallel dispute between Fuller and Taylor is the respectful tone both adopted. 'I love many things contained in Mr F's pamphlet', Taylor stated, 'and I love him for his work's sake'. Taylor, writing as 'Philanthropos', warmly welcomed the main thrust of *The Gospel Worthy*, conceded that Fuller had written with 'perspicuity' (a judgment Fuller himself contrasted with Martin's accusation of 'obscurity').[43] He was further concerned in case anything he had written should give his opponent 'a moment's pain' from a personal point of view.[44] Fuller wrote in a similar vein in return. 'If I have, in any instance, mistaken his meaning', Fuller said, 'I hope he will excuse it', and he was quick to acknowledge that 'Philanthropos' had

---

(originally published as 'by Agnostos') is found in *Fuller's Works*, II, pp. 512-60. Some of Fuller's response to Taylor is considered, alongside other works where Fuller engages with aspects of Arminianism, in C. Sheehan, 'Great and Sovereign Grace: An Exploration of the Defence of the True Gospel of Christ by the Rev. Andrew Fuller Against the Errors of Arminianism' (provisional title), in Haykin (ed.), *Fuller's Apologetics*. Sheehan has not looked at Taylor's works directly, only considering Fuller's responses.

40   Ryland, *Andrew Fuller*, p. 132.

41   *Fuller's Works*, II, p. 716 (and p. 725 for an example of what can only be described as Fuller's anger at Martin).

42   Ryland, *Andrew Fuller*, p. 135.

43   *Fuller's Works*, II, p. 719.

44   Taylor, *Philanthropos*, pp. 6, 63.

treated him 'with candour and respect'.[45] As far as any personal pain was concerned, Fuller was able to reassure Taylor that none had been given. This eirenic tone, in marked contrast to Fuller's clash with Martin and even the more civilized dispute with Button, was maintained by both writers right to the end of the debate. Fuller would continue on good terms with Taylor, and preached for him in London on at least two occasions in 1806 and 1807, to 'convince the world that perfect cordiality subsists between [Taylor] and myself'.[46]

But Taylor and Fuller had far more in common than a mutual respect, and it is worth commenting on some of the presuppositions the two men clearly shared. These included an overriding commitment to scripture. Taylor's comment regarding the use of quotations from 'great men' to prove a point, that 'how great soever they were, their writings are not Scripture', entirely mirrored Fuller's own views. It was, Taylor insisted (and again Fuller would have agreed), the 'infallible book' that counted.[47] Both men wanted to maintain a thoroughgoing biblicism, and comments like the ones cited above pepper both their works. Taylor and Fuller also shared a commitment to a common methodology as they argued their respective cases. Taylor's own commitment to an empiricist weighing of the evidence was clearly stated:

> It is the glory of Christianity, that it imposes nothing upon man, without evidence; but appeals to our reason, understanding and conscience, for the truth and importance of what it recommends to our faith and practice... One excellency of [Fuller's] performance is the unreservedness with which he declares his sentiments, and intimates his desire to have them sincerely examined; and that one reason why his friends advised the publication of it was 'to invite a spirit of impartial enquiry'. This is speaking and acting like a man who wishes truth to be discovered.[48]

---

45   Fuller, *Reply to Philanthropos*, in *Fuller's Works*, II, pp. 510, 459.

46   A. Taylor, *Dan Taylor*, p. 177 n. Morris asserted that Taylor's final pamphlet in the dispute was 'disgusting' to Fuller, but it appears that any bad feeling was quickly cleared up. Morris was not at his best in surveying this dispute, and some of Adam Taylor's strictures (pp. 178-82), on Morris's summary of it carry weight. Fuller's friend, Samuel Pearce, also preached at least once for Taylor in London in the late summer of 1795. See E.A. Payne, 'Some Samuel Pearce Documents', *BQ* 18.1 (January, 1959), p. 30.

47   Taylor, *Philanthropos*, p. 35. Compare the comments of Fuller, *Reply to Philanthropos*, in *Fuller's Works*, II, pp. 421, 442, 456-57 on how Gill and Brine should not be set up as 'standards of orthodoxy'.

48   Taylor, *Philanthropos*, p. 8, cf. p. 12: 'The pious and candid spirit with which he appears to submit his performance to public examination, greatly endears him to me.'

From this beginning, Taylor then proceeded to examine and carefully weigh all the evidence relative to the dispute. For his part, Fuller was able to respond in kind once again, stating in his reply: 'He has examined with freedom what I have advanced [and] I respect him for so doing. I can, with the less fear of offence, use a like freedom in return.'[49] Both Fuller and Taylor must, at least in some sense, be described as 'enlightened', although the qualifications already noted should be borne in mind. Nevertheless, their shared commitment was to the pursuit of truth through impartial enquiry ('let us remember, truth itself is of the greatest importance') and their approach was a 'scientific' one, in which 'hypotheses' could be exposed to all sorts of tests to examine their truthfulness ('neither of us ought to take his own hypothesis for granted').[50] Fuller's own commitment to this way of arguing is shown by contrast in his disputes with Button and Martin. It is also highlighted by the similarities in method between himself and Taylor.[51]

Finally, Fuller and Taylor displayed a common concern for what we can term 'practical' religion. Their mutual hatred of controversy for its own sake, and their commitment to gospel ministry and to invitational evangelistic preaching regularly surfaced. These emphases were allied with a significant degree of pragmatism in religious matters. Taylor argued that the 'success...which has generally attended [the] free manner of addressing sinners' was a sure sign that this was the right approach. Indeed, it was 'a proof in fact, which nothing in theory [could] withstand, that God approves of, and owns this method of preaching; and is glorified by it'.[52] In other words, because 'gospel invitations' worked, that was sure evidence they were right. Fuller had already argued along broadly similar lines in the first edition of *The Gospel Worthy*. In his reply to 'Philanthropos' he stated that he did not believe that success on its own could be proof 'of the goodness of a doctrine',

---

49   Fuller, *Reply to Philanthropos*, in *Fuller's Works*, II, p. 459.

50   Both these quotations are from Fuller, *Reply to Philanthropos*, in *Fuller's Works*, II, pp. 481, 511. With reference to Taylor, Rinaldi, 'Tribe of Dan', pp. 28-29, writes: 'The influence of the Enlightenment may be detected in terms of the role that reason had to play in interpreting the scriptures… The adoption of a scientific approach resulted in a rejection of metaphysical discussion in favour of a concentration on observation.' Rinaldi does not deal directly with these disputes between Fuller and Taylor, and his comments are made with respect to Taylor's general approach.

51   Fuller's twin commitments to scripture and a 'spirit of free and impartial enquiry' in pursuit of the truth are also exemplified in his *Dialogues and Letters between Crispus and Gaius*, in *Fuller's Works*, II, pp. 647-80. See especially p. 665 for an illustration of Fuller's method.

52   Taylor, *Philanthropos*, pp. 4-5.

although he allowed that it should be given considerable weight. He then proceeded to argue that those Taylor termed 'inconsistent Calvinists' (i.e. Calvinists who 'offered Christ' in their preaching), were at least as successful in gospel ministry, if not more so, than Arminians![53] It hardly needs stating that this line of argument would have been anathema to both Button and Martin, indeed to all High Calvinists. In surveying all this data, it is hard to avoid the conclusion that Fuller had more in common with this Arminian Evangelical, steeped in the experience of the Revival, than with either of his High Calvinist opponents from his own denomination.

Fuller's Response and Change of View on the Extent of the Atonement

Throughout the dispute, which spanned the years 1786-90, Taylor maintained that 'the universal calls and invitations' of the gospel could only be based on the 'universality of Divine love, and the death of Jesus Christ, as the propitiation for the sins of the *whole world*'.[54] That universal offers of the gospel should be made, in preaching and other evangelistic work, was of course not a matter of dispute between Taylor and Fuller. It was the grounds upon which such invitations to believe could be made which was the area of debate. The distinction between natural and moral inability was again important as the arguments unfolded, although this time the issues were different. Taylor clearly had a more optimistic view of human nature than Fuller, believing that people are perfectly able to respond to the gospel. There was no inability of any kind standing in their way. Taylor believed that if Fuller's definition of moral inability was allowed to stand, then men would be blameless and God would be unjust in punishing any who did not embrace the gospel. He stated 'that if men could never avoid [moral inability], and cannot deliver themselves from it, and the blessed God will not deliver them, surely they ought not to be punished for it, or for any of its necessary effects'.[55]

In engaging with Evangelical Arminianism Fuller reasserted his Calvinistic orthodoxy, once again leaning heavily on Edwards, who was explicitly cited.[56] People were morally incapable of believing, and

---

53   Fuller, *Reply to Philanthropos*, in *Fuller's Works*, II, p. 509

54   See title pages of both Taylor, *Philanthropos*, and *Observations on the Reply to Philanthropos*, italics added.

55   Words actually quoted by Fuller, *Reply to Philanthropos*, in *Fuller's Works*, II, p. 472.

56   See e.g., Fuller, *Reply to Philanthropos*, in *Fuller's Works*, II, pp. 477-78.

God's electing grace was needed for anyone to come to Christ. But Fuller took care to point out that he defended these principles, not because of any prior commitment to Calvinism as a system. Rather he believed the tenets he was defending to be scriptural, and therefore true. He stated:

> For my own part, though I never mean to set up any man as a standard of faith, and though in some things I think differently from Calvin, yet, as I agree with him in the main, particularly in the leading sentiments advanced in the former treatise... I have used the term Calvinist, and have no objection to being so called by others.[57]

Fuller continued to maintain most of the 'leading sentiments' of *The Gospel Worthy*. But the dispute was especially noteworthy because during it Fuller *did* shift his position on a number of issues relative to the atonement. It is in this that the major significance of the debate consists.

As will be clear, Taylor argued that Christ died, not for the elect only, but for the whole world.[58] In saying this, he was not espousing universalism, for only those who responded to the gospel would be saved. But he was clear that the atonement was general and not particular, and that there was potential provision in the death of Christ for all mankind, irrespective of whether they believed and were saved eventually. The scriptures he asserted, 'never give us any intimation...that Christ died for some and not for others.'[59] Taylor made this an important part of the debate as a whole, because he argued that universal invitations for sinners to believe the gospel could only be properly grounded in a universal provision in the death of Christ. It was quite inconsistent to hold to a limited provision and plead for universal offers, because the preacher would be commanding something that, for many, would be not only morally impossible (to use Edwards' terms), but naturally impossible as well. Fuller and Taylor were both in agreement that no one could be saved unless Christ had died for them. Yet Taylor was able to argue that in Fuller's scheme, although no one could perhaps say with certainty that he was excluded from Christ's death, 'yet he must, in the exercise of reason say, that if he be excluded, his salvation is utterly impossible'. And, Taylor continued, 'It is certain

---

57   Fuller, *Reply to Philanthropos*, in *Fuller's Works*, II, pp. 472-83, especially p. 477.

58   Taylor, *Philanthropos*, pp. 70-88.

59   Taylor, *Philanthropos*, p. 29, cf. pp. 29-30, 'Christ died for all men, as the Scripture positively asserts'. Texts that Taylor cited include 2 Cor. 5.14-15 and 1 Tim. 2.6, 'Christ Jesus...gave himself as a ransom for all.'

that God could never command a thing which is naturally impossible'. In short, Fuller's view was both unscriptural and unreasonable.[60]

Fuller considered these arguments carefully, and clearly felt the force of them. Taylor's tightly argued appeal, particularly his assertions that it was 'naturally impossible' for some to believe if Christ did not in some sense die for them, almost certainly carried great weight with Fuller.[61] Elsewhere he was unimpressed with Taylor's comments on natural and moral inability, believing that his opponent's strictures lacked clarity and consistency.[62] But here, it seemed, the leader of the New Connexion had an unanswerable point. If Fuller continued to hold that the atonement was limited, how could he also maintain that the inability of at least some was only criminal and not natural too, since there was no provision for them in the atonement? Fuller later confessed: 'I tried to answer my opponent...but I could not. I found not merely his reasonings, but the Scriptures themselves, standing in my way.'[63] By the time he published his reply to 'Philanthropos', a significant change in his views had taken place.

In his reply, Fuller stated his revised position on the atonement clearly and openly. The particularity of redemption consisted 'not in the degree of Christ's suffering (as though he must have suffered more if more had been finally saved)...but in the sovereign purpose and design of the Father and the Son.' The sufferings of Christ, he continued, 'are of infinite value, sufficient to have saved all the world, and a thousand worlds, if it had pleased God...to have made them effectual to this end.'[64] Fuller was now locating the particularity of redemption in the application of the atonement, or more precisely 'in the design of the Father and the Son, respecting the persons to whom it shall be applied'.[65] This enabled Fuller to continue to speak of a 'special design' in the death of Christ, because those to whom the atonement would be applied had been decided in the purposes of God 'before time'. Nevertheless, his view of the atonement could now properly be called 'general'. As he stated: 'if all the inhabitants of the globe could be

---

60   Taylor, *Philanthropos*, p. 31.

61   Taylor, *Philanthropos*, pp. 31-32, further commented 'that it appears to be naturally impossible for any man to trust in one whom he does not know or believe to be his friend. Christ is not the friend of any for whom he did not die. How then can any man rationally trust in him, as a Saviour, before he understand that he died for him?'

62   Fuller, *Reply to Philanthropos*, in *Fuller's Works*, II, p. 472.

63   A. Fuller, *Six Letters to Dr Ryland respecting the Controversy with the Rev. A. Booth* (1803), in *Fuller's Works*, II, pp. 709-10.

64   Fuller, *Reply to Philanthropos*, in *Fuller's Works*, II, pp. 488-89.

65   From a 'Conversation with a friend at Edinburgh, on the subject of Particular Redemption, in 1805', recorded by Morris, *Andrew Fuller*, 2nd edn, p. 311.

persuaded to return to God in Christ's name, they would undoubtedly be accepted by him.'[66]

Fuller had come to this view as a result of the dispute with Taylor, surely his most able theological critic, and through reflection on his opponent's central arguments and the scriptures. But he may, once again, have had some help from the writings of Jonathan Edwards. Certainly the view that Fuller was now espousing was basically Edwards' own. Moreover Edwards' views were clearly set out in the all important *Freedom of the Will*. The relevant passage stated:

> However Christ in some sense might be said to die for all, and to redeem all visible Christians, yea, the whole world by his death; yet there must be something particular in the design of his death with respect to such as be saved thereby. God has the actual salvation or redemption of a certain number in his proper absolute design, and of a certain number only; and, therefore, such a design can only be prosecuted in any thing God does in order to the salvation of men.[67]

Edwards clearly held that that atonement was at least in some sense universal (cf. the comments of Holmes who cites other similar quotations from Edwards' *Miscellanies* and notebooks),[68] whilst still speaking of a particular design in the death of Christ. Almost all of this passage from the *Freedom of the Will* would later be cited by Fuller, in his own preface to the English edition of Joseph Bellamy's *True Religion Delineated*. It is hard not to believe that it was relevant to his change of views.[69]

Not surprisingly, Taylor was unimpressed with this modification, believing that the same inconsistencies he had highlighted in Fuller's earlier position still remained.[70] Nevertheless it represented a significant shift for Fuller; a change from his earlier published stance that must have taken not a little courage. In the first edition of *The Gospel Worthy* he had stated that Christ only died 'for some of the human race'.[71] This was now no longer his view. Particular Redemption he now considered

---

66   Fuller, *Reply to Philanthropos*, in *Fuller's Works*, II, p. 506. See also *The Reality and Efficacy of Divine Grace*, p. 541.

67   Edwards, *Freedom of the Will* (ed.), Ramsey, p. 435.

68   Holmes, *God of Grace*, p. 158.

69   Fuller's 'Recommendatory Preface' to J. Bellamy, *True Religion Delineated; or, Experimental Religion... Set in a Scriptural and Rational Light* (London: T. Hamilton, 3rd edn, 1809), p. viii.

70   Taylor, *Observations on Fuller's reply to Philanthropos*, pp. 78-134, especially pp. 78-89.

71   Fuller, *The Gospel Worthy*, 1st edn, p. 106. This comment was quoted by Taylor, *Philanthropos*, p. 30.

to be 'merely a branch of election'.[72] Granted that people were still unable to respond to the gospel without the electing, regenerating grace of God. But there was an objective provision for everyone, whether they believed or not, in the atonement. Fuller believed that in saying this, he had safeguarded the basis upon which the all-important universal calls to repentance and faith could be made. In terms of natural ability everyone could respond, because not only did they have the natural powers enabling them to do so, but there was, potentially, provision for them in the death of Christ. Their inability to respond was entirely criminal. Their 'cannot', as Fuller had always expressed it, was still nothing more than a 'will not'.

He was to make yet further modifications to his views in the course of debate. In his reply to Philanthropos he stated his belief that terms such as ransom and propitiation were only ever applied to those who were finally saved.[73] But in the *Reality and Efficacy of Divine Grace*, his pseudonymous reply to Taylor's second work, he wrote that he believed he had been mistaken. These terms, he now admitted, were 'applicable to all mankind in general...conveying an indefinite, but not universal idea'.[74] That the *Reality and Efficacy of Divine Grace* was by Fuller is confirmed by comments in his biographies, and especially by its inclusion in his *Works* with an explanatory 'Advertisement'.[75] To publish anonymously when engaged in controversy was, as Ivimey noted, unlike his usual 'manly daring'.[76] Ryland may have been right when he stated that this was because of a desire on Fuller's part not to prolong the dispute,[77] but it is also possible that the Kettering pastor was becoming a little uncomfortable with the modifications he was having to make to his views on the atonement. In the context of the Calvinism of his denomination, those changes were certainly significant.

---

72   'Conversation with a friend at Edinburgh', in Morris, *Andrew Fuller*, 2nd edn, p. 311.

73   Fuller, *Reply to Philanthropos*, in *Fuller's Works*, II, p. 496.

74   Fuller, *Reality and Efficacy of Divine Grace*, in *Fuller's Works*, II, p. 550.

75   *Fuller's Works*, II, p. 512.

76   *HEB*, IV, p. 87 n. Cf. the comments of A. Taylor, *Dan Taylor*, pp. 175-76: 'It was a little singular, that Mr. T. who entered the lists in disguise, should acquire courage, in the course of the contest, to throw it aside and avow himself to the world; and that Mr. F. who had commenced the combat in open day, should see it prudent, in the last action, to warp himself in a veil that only death could remove.'

77   Ryland, *Andrew Fuller*, p. 134.

The Second Edition of *The Gospel Worthy*

1801 saw the publication of the second edition of *The Gospel Worthy*. In his 'Advertisement' to this new edition Fuller made it clear he had made a number of significant changes to the book. Indeed: 'the corrections and additions form a considerable part of this edition...it would be inexcusable to have lived all this time without gaining any additional light...upon the subject.'[78] In fact, although the essential argument remained the same, it was a thoroughly revised and expanded work (in terms of style alone there were numerous changes) and the extent of the differences between the two editions has not always been recognized.[79] Focusing on two of the most important changes helps summarize the movement of Fuller's thought which had taken place since 1785.

First of all, it should be noted that Fuller by now felt confident enough to incorporate into his major work all the 'concessions' (as Adam Taylor called them), that he had made on the atonement. Indeed, he completely rewrote the section on particular redemption.[80] In the first edition of *The Gospel Worthy* he had written that there was 'no necessity' for someone to have a 'particular interest in Christ's death, in order to make trusting him his duty'. Fuller used an illustration of a man condemned for treason. Was it not right, Fuller reasoned, for the man to admit his guilt and ask 'his prince' for mercy, not knowing how that plea might be received? There would be no other course of action he could take. Similarly, it was the duty of the sinner to 'cast his soul on Christ for mercy, determined either to be saved by him or to perish at his feet'.[81] This echoed Fuller's own conversion experience, and he supported his argument with quotations from the Calvinist writers Coles, Ridgely, Witsius and Owen.

In the second edition, this line of reasoning was abandoned completely, together with most of the quotations (which Taylor had attacked as proving nothing). The atonement, he now argued, was not 'a literal payment of a debt'. If it was then it would be inconsistent, not only with 'indefinite invitations' but also with 'free forgiveness of sin', for sinners in the scriptures were directed to apply for forgiveness as

---

78   From the 'Advertisement to the Second Edition', *The Gospel Worthy*, in *Fuller's Works*, II, p. 328.

79   Although Oliver, 'Emergence of a Strict and Particular Baptist Community', pp. 115-16, is helpful in tracing the development of Fuller's thought on the atonement.

80   See Fuller, *The Gospel Worthy*, 1st edn, pp. 132-39; *The Gospel Worthy*, 2nd edn, pp. 373-75 in *Fuller's Works*, II, for the relevant sections.

81   Fuller, *The Gospel Worthy*, 1st edn, pp. 132-33.

'supplicants rather than claimants'.[82] Christ's sacrifice was applied, by God's sovereign wisdom, to some and not to others and so there was still, a 'peculiarity of design in the death of Christ'. But there was no inconsistency between maintaining both that there was this special design and also that there was a universal obligation to believe, an inconsistency which would have been present if Christ's death had not been, in some sense, for all.

Taylor had continued to press him in this area, even after he had made his modifications, but Fuller now felt sure of his ground:

> If God, through the death of his Son, has promised salvation to all who comply with the gospel; and if there be no natural impossibility as to a compliance, nor any obstruction but that which arises from aversion of heart; exhortations and invitations to believe are consistent; and our duty, as ministers of the gospel, is to administer them.[83]

The distinction between natural and moral inability, as the ground for asserting that saving faith was the duty of all, had been maintained. Even more crucially, so had the ground on which the gospel could be offered indiscriminately to all.

Practical considerations to do with gospel preaching were never far from the surface in Fuller's theology, and the second important difference between the two editions was a new note of boldness, indeed of urgency, as he pressed the practical consequences of his thesis on his readers. In the first edition, there were several notes of caution sounded in the main concluding section, 'Inferences from the Whole'.[84] One example in particular can be cited. Fuller made it clear that

> It is not intended here to vindicate all the language that has been addressed to unconverted sinners, nor all the principles of those whose practice it has been to address them. Doubtless there have been extremes in these as in other things, and many who have used them have been very wide of the truth as to sentiments on other subjects; but a sober use of such means is nevertheless to be retained.

Fuller followed this up with some detailed comments on what he termed the 'order' of addressing exhortations to the unconverted. Concerned to guard against careless evangelistic preaching, he urged

---

82   This of course reflects Fuller's own conversion experience. Cf. the comments of M.A.G. Haykin, 'Particular Redemption in the Writings of Andrew Fuller (1754-1815)' in D.W Bebbington (ed.), *The Gospel in the World: International Baptist Studies* (Studies in Baptist History and Thought, 1; Carlisle: Paternoster, 2002), p. 117.

83   Fuller, *The Gospel Worthy*, 2nd edn, *Fuller's Works*, II, pp. 373-74.

84   Fuller, *The Gospel Worthy*, 1st edn, pp. 163-84.

that a gospel minister should, amongst other things, first 'labour to convince them of the evil of their sin', together with 'the awfulness and equity of their condemnation'. Hearers should also be exhorted to 'pray to God for an interest in his salvation'.[85] But, as with the section on Particular Redemption, in the second edition these pages were to be completely rewritten.

Fuller's approach in 1801 was to jettison the paragraph quoted above and drastically shorten and alter his comments about the order of addressing the unconverted. In fact none of the sentences cited above from 'Inferences from the Whole' survive in the corresponding chapter in the second edition, entitled 'Concluding Reflections'. Fuller quickly listed the need to preach about subjects such as 'the just requirements of the law' and the 'impossibility of being justified by works' as a preface to gospel preaching. But the central point he wanted to make was that although 'these representations [were] proper and necessary', there was a danger that ministers would be too reticent in preaching the gospel to their hearers. The truth was that it was 'never unsafe' to introduce the gospel. He continued by using an illustration from the Napoleonic wars that were then currently raging: 'Divine truths are like chain shot, they go to together, and we need not perplex ourselves which should enter first; if anyone enter, it will draw the rest after it.'[86]

The reference to 'chain shot' was to the practice of connecting two cannon balls with a chain before firing both at the enemy with the aim of causing maximum damage. The image may have been alarming, but Fuller's point was clear enough. It was not necessarily that Fuller was repudiating everything that he now left out of *The Gospel Worthy*, as he made clear in his 'Advertisement' to the second edition. Rather there were other things which appeared to be more 'immediate'. Fuller had experienced much in the years 1785 to 1801, in addition to the theological disputes we have dealt with here. These years saw the development of his own thoroughly evangelistic pastoral ministry, and the formation of the BMS, with Fuller as the very active secretary (I shall deal with these developments in chapters five and six). By 1801 he was clear that the need of the hour was not caution – rather it was committed gospel preaching.

Conclusion

The material in this chapter has highlighted how Fuller both clarified and modified his theology of salvation between the years 1785 and

---

85 Fuller, *The Gospel Worthy*, 1st edn, p. 164.

86 Fuller, *The Gospel Worthy*, 2nd edn, *Fuller's Works*, II, pp. 391-92.

1801, years in which this theology was a crucial motor for change in the life of the Particular Baptist denomination. The most important change was his shift from a limited to a general view of the atonement during his dispute with the Evangelical Arminian Dan Taylor. Throughout this period Fuller's views were shaped by Evangelical forces (e.g. Edwards), and driven by Evangelical concerns (a desire to safeguard the theological basis for offering the gospel to all). Bebbington speaks of those whose 'eagerness for converts had the effect of modifying the theology of a section of Evangelicalism'.[87] Fuller certainly fits this pattern. His overriding concern now was that Christ should be offered to all.

---

87   Bebbington, *Evangelicalism*, p. 9.

CHAPTER FOUR

The Disputes with Abraham Booth

*There are few...thinking men but what see reason to change their sentiments
in some particulars*

The disputes with High Calvinists and Arminians were not the only ones
in which Fuller became involved as a result of writing *The Gospel
Worthy*. Most important were two separate controversies with the
London based Particular Baptist pastor, Abraham Booth (1734-1806).
Booth was certainly not an Arminian, but neither was he a High
Calvinist, despite being a leading figure in the group of London
ministers who made up the London Baptist Board, which met regularly
at the Jamaica Coffee House. In fact, by the time of his disputes with
Fuller, he had probably taken on Gill's mantle as the most significant
Particular Baptist minister in the capital. Partly because of this, Fuller
found his public falling out with the ·'aged and respected' Booth
extremely difficult.[1]

The disputes began in 1796 (thus overlapping with the controversies
considered in the previous chapter), and continued until 1806, the year
of Booth's death. This chapter seeks to survey the main areas of debate.
The principal controversy centres, once again, on issues relating to the
atonement. Booth was particularly unhappy with some further changes
Fuller had made to his theology of the atonement in the 1801 edition of
The Gospel Worthy, changes not covered in chapter three. But an earlier
dispute between the two men concerning the precise relationship
between regeneration and faith was also significant, and will be dealt
with briefly.

These controversies highlight particularly well not only the
continuing importance of Edwards for Fuller, but also (and especially),
the growing influence other New England theologians had over his
work. Principal among these were Joseph Bellamy and Samuel Hopkins
(1721-1803). Both were former pupils of Edwards, and both had

---

1   This estimate of Booth is Fuller's own. *Fuller's Works*, II, p. 699.

become leading figures in what was known as the 'New Divinity'
movement in America.[2] Booth was highly critical of the effect he
believed Hopkins and other New Divinity men were having on Fuller's
theology, and he was certainly correct in noting that the Kettering pastor
was being influenced from this direction. Their importance for Fuller in
these latter stages of the development of his thought highlight how far
he had travelled from his earlier theological roots. But Fuller was
adamant that he did not take on board their views uncritically. In
particular, where he thought that Hopkins and his followers were
departing either from scripture or from a commitment to the simplicity
of the gospel, he refused to follow them. This final chapter on Fuller's
thought concludes with a brief assessment of his importance and
significance as a theologian, especially for the Particular Baptist
denomination and the wider Christian world of the late-eighteenth and
early-nineteenth centuries.

The Dispute between Booth and Fuller on the Relationship between Regeneration and Faith

As already noted, Abraham Booth was a well known and well respected
London Baptist minister.[3] He had in fact been a General Baptist,
preaching and pastoring in the north of England whilst also working as a
stocking-weaver. But he became convinced of Calvinistic principles,
which he went on to expound in his book the *Reign of Grace*, which
appeared in 1768. It was clear from this work that 'in his rejection of
Arminianism, Booth had not reacted to the extreme of High
Calvinism'.[4] He had actually been encouraged to publish the *Reign of
Grace* by the Evangelical clergyman Henry Venn, who financed the

---

2   For biographical details see *DEB*, I, p. 80, for Bellamy; *DEB*, II, p. 571, for
Hopkins. For the New Divinity movement, also known as 'Hopkinsianism', see J.A.
Conforti, *Samuel Hopkins and the New Divinity Movement* (Grand Rapids: Eerdmans,
1981), especially pp. 3-5, 13-15, 181-89; F.H. Foster, *A Genetic History of the New
England Theology* (Chicago: Univ. Chicago Press, 1907), pp. 107-223.

3   For biographical details see E.A. Payne, 'Abraham Booth, 1734-1806', *BQ* 26.1
(January, 1975), pp. 28-42, especially pp. 28-34; *HEB*, IV, pp. 364-79. Booth's theology has
been surveyed, although not satisfactorily, by R.A. Coppenger, 'Abraham Booth, 1734-
1806: A Study of his Thought and Work' (PhD thesis, Edinburgh University, 1953). Far
more reliable is R.W. Oliver, 'Abraham Booth (1734-1806)' in Haykin (ed.), *British
Particular Baptists*, II, pp. 30-55.

4   Oliver, 'Emergence of a Strict and Particular Baptist Community', p. 101. It is
unclear what led to Booth's own 'theological conversion' from Arminianism to Calvinism,
see Coppenger, 'Abraham Booth', p. 38.

printing himself. Through this work Booth came to the notice of the Particular Baptist church at Prescott Street in London, becoming their pastor in 1769 and remaining there until his death. His reputation grew as he continued to publish works on a variety of subjects, ranging from antinomianism to paedobaptism.[5] Ivimey described him as a 'star of the first magnitude...and one of the brightest ornaments of the Baptist denomination to which he belonged'.[6]

The dispute which focused on the relationship between regeneration and faith began publicly when Booth published *Glad Tidings to Perishing Sinners or The Genuine Gospel a Complete Warrant to Believe in Jesus* in 1796.[7] It seemed from the title and subtitle of *Glad Tidings* that warm support was being given to Fuller's own position, and the first section appeared to confirm this impression. The gospel itself was all the warrant that 'perishing sinners' needed to come to Christ. And yet Fuller was far from happy. The problem was the second half of *Glad Tidings*, where Booth argued that what was termed a 'holy disposition' was not necessary for anyone prior to their believing in Christ.[8] Booth associated the view he was challenging with Samuel Hopkins, but Fuller was not convinced that the New England theologian was the real target. By the mid 1790s Fuller was actually in regular correspondence with Hopkins,[9] and their views on the subject under discussion were basically the same. Fuller's conclusion, which he expressed to William Carey in India, was 'that it was [Booth's] intent to oppose our sentiments, and that he chose to attack us under Hopkins's name.'[10]

Fuller had guessed Booth's intention correctly. The two men met privately in an attempt to solve their differences, but when this was unsuccessful, their disagreement became public. Fuller defended himself in a lengthy appendix to the second edition of *The Gospel Worthy*, where Booth's views were coupled with those of a Scotch

---

5   See A. Booth, *The Collected Works of Abraham Booth, With Some Account of his Life and Writings* (3 vols; London, 1813).

6   *HEB*, IV, p. 375.

7   A. Booth, *Glad Tidings to Perishing Sinners or The Genuine Gospel a Complete Warrant to Believe in Jesus*, 2nd edn, in *Booth's Works*, II, pp. 2-202.

8   Booth, *Glad Tidings*, in *Booth's Works*, II, p. 67.

9   Hopkins was also a correspondent of Ryland. See Conforti, *Hopkins and the New Divinity*, p. 179.

10   Fuller to W. Carey, 6 Sept 1797, Fuller Letters (4/5/1). Fuller had known as early as 1795 that privately Booth was unhappy with some of his statements, see Ryland, *Andrew Fuller*, pp. 227-29. Fuller's views had been set out in *The Gospel Worthy*, 1st edn, p. 15, but especially in his *Reply to Philanthropos*, in *Fuller's Works*, II, pp. 461-71.

Baptist, Archibald MacLean (1733-1812).[11] At one stage, Hopkins himself wrote a reply to Booth, but out of deference to the London pastor, Fuller and Ryland together decided not to publish, although they had permission from the author to do so. They did lend the manuscript to Booth, however. Fuller reported to Carey that since reading it, the pastor of Prescott Street 'was rigidly set against everything from America'.[12]

The Main Points of the Dispute

At the heart of the debate was the relationship between regeneration (inner renewal by the Holy Spirit) and faith. Did regeneration precede faith, or did faith precede regeneration? Fuller had been quite clear on this issue in his dispute with Dan Taylor. Faith was a 'grace of the Holy Spirit', ranked in the scriptures together with hope and love. Therefore biblical faith must be 'holy', and prior regeneration must be necessary for it to be exercised, although only in the sense that 'a cause is prior to an effect that immediately follows'.[13] But Booth did not accept that regeneration was previous to faith in any sense, and for him there was no 'priority or posteriority' with regard to them. For Booth, what Hopkins termed a 'holy disposition' (by which he meant regeneration), was not necessary for someone to exercise saving faith. Booth believed that Hopkins' (and Fuller's) position was tantamount to saying that a subjective 'warrant of faith' was necessary for someone to believe in Christ.[14] If Hopkins' view was allowed to stand then, according to Booth, 'pious affections toward God, and a cordial inclination to keep

---

11   Appendix to *The Gospel Worthy*, 2nd edn, in *Fuller's Works*, II, pp. 393-416. For MacLean see N.M. de S. Cameron, (ed.), *Dictionary of Scottish Church History and Theology* (Edinburgh: T. & T. Clark, 1993), p. 528. MacLean (sometimes M'Lean or McLean) was a Scotch Baptist leader who had been deeply influenced by the views of Robert Sandeman and James Glas. MacLean joined a Glasite church in Glasgow in 1762, and although he left the following year and adopted Baptist views his theological debt to Sandeman and Glas remained. Fuller later published *Strictures on Sandemanianism, in Twelve Letters to a Friend* (London, 1810), to counter MacLean's views, but the two remained on reasonably good terms, as the title to Fuller's book suggests. Sandemanians held to a very passive view of faith, and it was here that MacLean's views were in some respects close enough to Booth's for Fuller to be able to treat them together.

12   Fuller to W. Carey, 22 Aug 1798, Fuller Letters (4/5/1). Hopkins probably wrote his reply late in 1797.

13   *Fuller's Works*, II, pp. 461-71.

14   Fuller, 'Appendix' to *The Gospel Worthy*, 2nd edn, in *Fuller's Works*, II, pp. 397-400.

his commands...must be our state and character before we believe in Jesus!'[15]

This was clearly a misinterpretation, one that Fuller had sought to guard against explicitly,[16] and understandably he was horrified. Both Fuller and Hopkins believed that their position had been badly misunderstood and misrepresented by Booth. Fuller, of course, had written *The Gospel Worthy* precisely in order to show that no subjective warrant was necessary for someone to come to Christ, and this was certainly what Hopkins believed too. As Oliver shows in his survey of this dispute, what had happened was that 'two distinct controversies had become confused'. In England the debate had been whether unbelievers had a duty to believe in Christ. But this had not been a major issue in America. There, 'Edwards and his successors had tried to guard against some careless evangelistic preaching. They had therefore analysed the psychological preparation for conversion.'[17] Part of this involved emphasizing that regeneration must be previous to someone exercising true saving faith. Booth, it seems, had misunderstood Hopkins at least in part because he was not aware of the context in which his remarks were originally made. This was in fact recognized at the time by Thomas Scott (1747-1821), an Evangelical clergyman who entered the controversy, and who Fuller claimed as a supporter.[18]

Scott's book was *The Warrant and Nature of Faith in Christ*, which was published in 1797 and reviewed positively in the *Evangelical Magazine* by Fuller himself.[19] Scott believed that some of Hopkins' comments were unhelpful, particularly when they were read outside their immediate New England context. Booth had been particularly unhappy about a particular statement of Hopkins 'that a hearty submission to, and acquiescence and delight in, the law of God, rightly understood, and so a true hatred of sin, must take place IN ORDER to any degree of true approbation of the Gospel, and FAITH AND TRUST in Christ'.[20] It was language such as this that enabled Booth to represent Hopkins as saying that 'pious affections toward God' were necessary before someone could believe in Christ. Scott also regarded this as unguarded and unhelpful (such comments do not appear in Fuller's

---

15   Booth, *Glad Tidings*, in *Booth's Works*, II, p. 77.

16   See *Fuller's Works*, II, p. 470.

17   Oliver, 'Emergence of a Strict and Particular Baptist Community', pp. 105-106.

18   For Scott see *DEB*, II, pp. 989-90.

19   The *Evangelical Magazine*, VII, 1799, p. 199. The review was anonymous, although Booth was clearly aware of who the writer was. It is included in *Fuller's Works*, III, pp. 749-52. The anonymous review of the 2nd edn of *Glad Tidings* in the *Evangelical Magazine*, VII, 1800, pp. 548-50, was also by Fuller.

20   Booth, *Glad Tidings*, in *Booth's Works*, II, p. 77, Booth's emphases.

writings). But on the main point at issue Scott had no doubt that saving faith was the result of regeneration.[21] Morris would later assert that Booth's view was 'worse than Arminianism itself, which admits at least some kind of divine influence. Here Mr Booth would dissent: but why should he? It is an argument arising from his own principles.'[22]

It is hard to see how Booth could have continued to maintain that Fuller's view of regeneration implied that it was a subjective warrant of faith. Perhaps the refusal of Fuller to distance himself from Hopkins (publicly or privately), enabled him to do so. But the dispute between Booth and Fuller on this issue was never properly resolved although after 1801 it did fizzle out, largely because the two protagonists had moved on to other areas of disagreement. The content of this particular controversy seems obscure and difficult, with little wider interest or significance. But it does highlight some real contrasts between the two men.

Significance of the Dispute

A letter the Kettering pastor wrote to Hopkins in 1798 is particularly helpful in highlighting the differences between Fuller and Booth at this stage. Fuller began by thanking his American friend for his 'remarks on Mr Booth's performance' (the work he and Ryland in the end decided not to publish) and sought to apologize for the London pastor's 'manner of writing', which had clearly irked Hopkins.[23] He then proceeded to make a number of comments about Booth. Firstly, he spoke of Booth's 'seeming contempt for contemporary authors', explaining: 'Mr B...is a generation older than Sutcliff, Pearce, or myself; and perhaps it may be owing to this that he is less attentive to anything we write.' He also believed Booth was guilty of insularity and a certain amount of 'British pride' in his attitude to American writers. Secondly, Fuller commented on the extremely heavy use of quotation in *Glad Tidings*, something which it seems had particularly annoyed Hopkins. The majority of Booth's quotes were from John Owen, often covering whole pages of his work.[24] Fuller wrote that Booth 'is a great admirer of Owen, Vitringa, Verema etc; and seems to suppose that they have gone to the

---

21   See the summary in Oliver, 'Emergence of a Strict and Particular Baptist Community', p. 105.

22   Morris, *Andrew Fuller*, 1st edn, pp. 300-301.

23   Fuller to S. Hopkins, March 17 1798, in Morris, *Andrew Fuller* 1st edn, pp. 381-87. All the quotations that follow from Fuller's letter are taken from these pages.

24   Booth, *Glad Tidings*, in *Booth's Works*, II, e.g. p. 201. In some sections the quotations nearly take over, see e.g. pp. 103-109.

ne plus ultra of discovery.' To this Fuller added that, since Booth's work examining paedobaptism, he 'has got into such a habit of quotation that he seems unable to write half a dozen pages without it'.

These observations are important and based, of course, on personal knowledge of Booth as well as on his published works. Although admittedly made by his opponent, I believe they are astute in their assessment of Booth. The dispute with Fuller had revealed Booth as an older man, less open to new authors (particularly if they were American) and with a reliance on quoting the great Calvinistic divines of the past that was surprisingly reminiscent, at least in style, of the High Calvinist authors considered in chapter three. Booth was certainly not a High Calvinist, as the biographical details given earlier indicate. Yet it is hard to escape the impression that he was here representing not only an older view, but an older *approach*. Holding Fuller and Booth up along side each other, clear differences can be seen between them. Fuller's Evangelicalism (particularly his overriding commitment to scripture) and his approach to controversy influenced by certain aspects of the Enlightenment (his commitment to a spirit of 'free enquiry' in pursuit of the truth), are thrown into yet sharper relief by the comparison with Booth. The London scene was still shot through with High Calvinism, and was certainly a bastion of an older Calvinism, which although not 'High' in the accepted sense of that term, was nevertheless resistant to many of the newer Evangelical emphases. Ivimey commented that Booth 'in some particulars [approached] what is called High-Calvinism'.[25] Had the older man been influenced by over thirty years at the heart of London Particular Baptist life? We saw in chapter two that this was certainly true of one of Fuller's other opponents, John Martin. Booth was a very different character to Martin, but to a degree this seems to have been true of him as well.

Before moving on, it is worth noting that in stressing regeneration in the way that he did, Fuller was emphasizing something that was one of the defining characteristics of Evangelicalism. Eighteenth-century Evangelicals tended to emphasize regeneration more than justification, whereas the sixteenth-century Reformers had tended to stress the latter rather than the former.[26] A direct impression of the Holy Spirit, bringing rebirth and renewal, was a key note of Evangelical preaching and

---

25   *HEB*, IV, p. 375.

26   See e.g. Stout, *Divine Dramatist*, pp. xx, 3, 251-52; M.A. Noll, *Turning Points, Decisive Moments in the History of Christianity* (Leicester: IVP, 1997), p. 232. Cf. S.B. Ferguson and D.F. Wright (eds), *New Dictionary of Theology* (Leicester: IVP, 1988), p. 574: 'It was only with the rise of the Anabaptists, the development of pietism and the Evangelical Awakenings that special emphasis was placed on regeneration as the *starting point* of the Christian life.'

theology. In a private communication to Booth, Fuller contended that 'the powerful motives furnished by the gospel are...no motives to an unrenewed mind. But if the Lord open the heart, we attend to the things that are spoken.' Fuller pleaded, in biblical language, that nothing less than a new heart, a heart not of stone but of flesh, was necessary.[27] Booth may have been giving away more than he realized when he accused Hopkins and Fuller of 'enthusiasm', the epithet so often hurled at Evangelicals for their emphases on experience and 'the new birth'.[28] Morris summarized Fuller's views by saying that only 'the regenerating influences of the Holy Spirit' could lead to faith and the embracing of the gospel. For Fuller, as for eighteenth-century Evangelicals in general, it was vital to stress regeneration.[29]

The Dispute between Booth and Fuller on the Atonement

The 1801 edition of *The Gospel Worthy* was to draw Fuller into even more painful controversy with Booth.[30] As noted in chapter three, Fuller had rewritten the part of the book which dealt with particular redemption, which now bore little resemblance to the corresponding pages in the first edition. In it he spoke of his shift from a 'limited' to a 'general' view of the atonement, and did so in a way that those who had followed his dispute with Dan Taylor would have recognized. But he also sounded a new note. In the same thoroughly reworked section where he had stated that Christ's atonement was 'in itself equal to the salvation of the world, were the world to embrace it', he also argued that this atonement did not proceed on the basis of 'commercial, but of moral justice'. Indeed, its 'grand object [was] to express the Divine displeasure against sin'.[31] In a later publication he was to expand on

---

27   Morris, *Andrew Fuller*, 1st edn, p. 302.

28   Morris, *Andrew Fuller*, 1st edn, p. 302. Booth made this comment in response to the quotations of Jer. 31.33 and of Ezek. 36.26, the 'heart of stone / heart of flesh' passage.

29   Morris, *Andrew Fuller*, 1st edn, p. 321.

30   The theological issues at stake in this dispute between Fuller and Booth are well surveyed by Haykin, 'Particular Redemption in the Writings of Andrew Fuller', in Bebbington (ed.), *Gospel in the World*, pp. 107-128.

31   Fuller, *The Gospel Worthy*, 2nd edn, in *Fuller's Works*, II, p. 372-73. Some of these ideas had appeared in *The Gospel its Own Witness*, see *Fuller's Works*, II, pp. 80-81. Entries in Fuller's 'Commonplace book [first entry 22 June 1798]', Bristol Baptist College Library (95a), indicate that his views had decisively changed by the beginning of 1799, although he was already using governmental language from at least 1796. For examples see the sermons 'The Reception of Christ the Turning Point of Salvation' (n.d.), *Fuller's Works*, I, pp. 273-74, and 'Christianity the Antidote to Presumption and Despair' (n.d.), *Fuller's*

what he meant: 'Sin is a debt only in a metaphorical sense; properly speaking it is a crime, and a satisfaction for it requires to be made, not on pecuniary, but on moral principles.'[32]

Fuller was rejecting what Haykin terms a 'quasi-quantitative' understanding of the atonement, one which made what took place at the cross sound like a commercial transaction, with man as the debtor and God as the creditor.[33] Neither was the cross fundamentally about strict distributive justice. These modifications can be seen as a natural outworking of Fuller's conversion from a limited to a general understanding of the nature of the atonement. He stated that if his former view was to stand, then

> The sufferings of Christ would require to be exactly proportioned to the nature and number of the sins which were laid upon him; and if more sinners had been saved or those who had been saved had been greater sinners than they are, he must have borne a proportional increase in suffering. To correspond with pecuniary satisfactions, this must undoubtedly be the case. I do not know that any writer has so stated things; but am persuaded that such ideas are at the foundation of a large part of the reasonings on that side of the subject.[34]

This view of the atonement, of it proceeding on 'the principle of debtor and creditor', was held by the High Calvinist Tobias Crisp and also by John Gill, and Fuller believed it could not be sustained.[35] Instead he maintained that rather than an offended judge, God should be viewed as the wise and good 'moral governor' of the universe, and rather than Christ 'putting to rest' God's wrath against sin, the cross should be seen as Christ 'putting to right' God's sense of moral justice.[36] It was these views, perhaps especially Fuller's use of terms associated with the 'moral government' theory of the atonement, that led to this further dispute with Booth.

Works, I, p. 322, and cf. Haykin's comments in 'Particular Redemption in the Writings of Andrew Fuller', pp. 121-22.

32   A. Fuller, *Three Conversations on Imputation, Substitution and Particular Redemption* (London, 1806), in *Fuller's Works*, II, pp. 680-98. The quotation is on p. 688. Although this did not appear until 1806, it was probably written three years earlier. See Oliver 'Emergence of a Strict and Particular Baptist Community', p. 109.

33   Haykin, 'Particular Redemption in the Writings of Andrew Fuller', p. 126.

34   Fuller, *Three Conversations*, in *Fuller's Works*, II, p. 690; cf. *The Gospel Worthy*, 2nd edn, in *Fuller's Works*, II, p. 373.

35   Fuller, *Six Letters to Dr Ryland*, in *Fuller's Works*, II, p. 699 (see p. 699 n. for Fuller's comments on Gill).

36   Fuller, *The Gospel Worthy*, 2nd edn, in *Fuller's Works*, II, p. 373-74.

The Course of the Dispute

The conflict followed a pattern similar to the previous one. Fuller, having heard what he regarded as Booth's 'serious and heavy charges' against him, was keen to avoid the private dispute spilling out into public controversy. As in the debate concerning regeneration and faith, Fuller believed he had been misrepresented by the older man. He visited Booth in London, in May 1802, in an attempt to come to an understanding privately. But despite a number of meetings, Booth remained adamant that Fuller was departing from Calvinistic orthodoxy. The situation deteriorated rapidly. From the summer of 1802 reports, presumably emanating from Booth or those close to him, were circulated in London and Northamptonshire, that Fuller had in private admitted that he was now an Arminian. Booth also wrote to Ryland to complain about his friend and so, between 3 and 22 January 1803, Fuller wrote 'Six letters to Dr Ryland' to defend himself, although he decided not to make these public.[37]

It was Booth who was the first to go into print, in 1803, although the dispute between him and Fuller appears to have been widely known in Particular Baptist circles by this time. Booth published a sermon he had originally preached at a ministers' meeting in the capital, entitled *Divine Justice Essential to the Divine Character*, to which he appended various comments where he sought to deal with his opponent's views on the atonement directly, although Booth drew back from actually naming Fuller.[38] It was Fuller, who fired the final shot in what Morris despairingly termed 'this hopeless piece of business',[39] publishing his *Three Conversations on Imputation, Substitution and Particular Redemption* that were quoted from earlier. This was in 1806, the year of Booth's death. The *Three Conversations* take the form of a dialogue between John (Ryland), Peter (Booth) and James (Fuller), and a feature of them is that Peter regularly apologizes to James for having misrepresented him.[40] Evidence from the rest of the dispute does little to suggest that this was any more than wishful thinking on Fuller's part.

---

37   Fuller, *Six Letters to Dr Ryland*, in *Fuller's Works*, II, pp. 699-715. These were not in fact published until 1831, when they appeared in an early edition of *Fuller's Works*. The account of the course of this controversy is largely taken from the first letter (pp. 699-702), where Fuller gives Ryland his own version of the dispute.

38   A. Booth, *Divine Justice Essential to The Divine Character* (London, 1803) in *Booth's Works*, III, pp. 3-95. The appendix, *Relative to the Doctrine of Atonement by Jesus Christ*, is on pp. 78-95.

39   Morris, *Andrew Fuller*, 2nd edn, p. 309.

40   Fuller, *Three Conversations*, in *Fuller's Works*, II, p. 692.

During the course of the controversy Fuller had been drawn out further regarding his views on substitution and imputation (as the title of this last publication indicated). How was a person's sin imputed (i.e. ascribed) to Christ, and how was Christ's righteousness imputed to that person? Fuller was now arguing for a 'figurative' rather than a 'proper' or 'real' imputation. Christ, he wrote, 'was accounted in the Divine Administration AS IF HE WERE, OR HAD BEEN, the sinner; that those who believe on him might be accounted AS IF THEY WERE, OR HAD BEEN, righteous.' Flowing from this, Fuller was now cautious about treating Christ's sufferings as punishment because Jesus was not, in any real sense, criminal. An innocent person could suffer but he could not, properly speaking, be punished. Fuller's view was carefully nuanced. He could still speak of Christ's sufferings being 'penal', just as he could of 'our salvation' being a 'reward'. But, he reasoned, 'as [our salvation] is not a reward to us, so I question whether [his sufferings] can properly said to be a punishment to him'.[41] Christ, as Fuller stated it, was suffering *our* punishment, not his own.

Booth was adamant in rejecting this, insisting that Christ had indeed been *punished* on the cross. Picking up on the words of Paul in Galatians 3.13, where he states that Christ became 'a curse for us', he commented: 'If, therefore Jesus was made a curse, he was PUNISHED – in a REAL and PROPER sense PUNISHED: for scarcely any words can convey the idea of punishment more forcibly than that of the apostle.'[42] One of the reasons Fuller thought he had been unfairly treated in the dispute was that Booth represented him as denying both imputation and substitution, whereas Fuller believed he was merely restating those doctrines in a different way. But that there was a real difference between the two men on these issues should, once again, be clear.

The Reasons for Fuller's Change of View

What were the reasons for these further changes to Fuller's views on the atonement? We noted in chapter two that A.H. Kirkby argues that Fuller's theology, as expressed in *The Gospel Worthy*, was the result of a careful study of John Calvin. He also argues strongly that all the modifications Fuller made in his views on the atonement can be traced to this same source. His strongest case is in regard to Fuller's views on

---

41   Fuller, *Six Letters to Dr Ryland*, in *Fuller's Works*, II, pp. 703-704.

42   Booth, *Divine Justice*, in *Booth's Works*, III, p. 52, Booth's emphases. Oliver, 'Emergence of a Strict and Particular Baptist Community', also cites these passages, pp. 110-11.

imputation.[43] Indeed E.F. Clipsham, who as we saw rejected Kirkby's thesis, allows, albeit tentatively, that imputation may be the exception.[44] This argument rests chiefly on two quotations from Calvin's *Institutes*, which Fuller used during the course of the controversy. In the most significant of these, Calvin stated that Christ was 'smitten of his Father for our crimes and bruised for our iniquities', whilst being clear that at no time was God 'either his enemy or angry with him. For how could he be angry with his beloved son, upon whom his mind rested?' What Calvin believed was that Christ 'sustained the weight of the divine displeasure' in the sense that he felt 'all the tokens of God when he is angry and punisheth'.[45] Unsurprisingly, Fuller was sure that in his terms what Calvin was speaking of was indeed 'figurative' rather than 'real and proper' imputation. He introduced this quotation by stating that it fully expressed his mind.

And yet once again it is far more likely that Fuller had actually reached this conclusion by another route, and was using Calvin to buttress his argument. One of Fuller's letters to Ryland indicates that this was indeed what was happening.[46] Booth had complained, so Fuller noted in his letter, that Fuller no longer held to the doctrine of imputation 'as Calvinists had commonly done, and still continue to do'. If Fuller had derived significant help from Calvin in formulating his views on imputation, it is reasonable to assume that he would have said so now. But what he asserted was as follows: 'It does not appear to me that [Booth's] opinions...are those of Calvin or of Calvinists during the sixteenth century. I do not pretend to have read so much of either as he has; but from what I have seen, so it appears to me.'

---

43   Elsewhere, for example with regards to the modifications Fuller made with regards particular redemption, his argument is unfounded. See Clipsham, 'Fuller and John Calvin', p. 149.

44   Clipsham, 'Fuller and John Calvin', pp. 149-52. We should note that Clipsham offers this conclusion hesitantly and qualifies it immediately, p. 149: 'It is not impossible that Calvin's teaching was a deciding factor, though even here...his chief mentor was Jonathan Edwards.'

45   Extracts from Fuller's quote from the *Institutes, Book II, XVI*, pp. 10-11, see Fuller, *Conversation on Imputation*, in *Fuller's Works*, II, p. 684. For the other quotation, from *Institutes, Book III*, XVI, 23, see p. 682. Fuller was using T. Norton's translation (from the Latin), which was the earliest English translation (1561). See Clipsham, 'Fuller and John Calvin', p. 152 n. As noted in chapter 2, Fuller's own list of his books made on 28 August 1798 and contained in his 'Miscellaneous Writings' includes Calvin's *Institutes*. The list also reveals he possessed three of Calvin's commentaries. As Fuller listed them these were Calvin 'on Acts', 'on the Gospels [Calvin's *Harmony of the Gospels*?]' and 'on the Psalms'.

46   *Fuller's Works*, II, pp. 712-14. The letter is entitled 'Calvinism' and is one of those relative to the dispute that was later published.

Fuller's vague language is striking, and his comments are clearly tentative and provisional. Whatever else they prove, they are hardly the words of someone who has just revised his theological system in the light of a close reading of John Calvin. Clipsham argues that because Fuller was, in his view, 'less clear and more hesitant [on imputation] than on most other subjects', and because the controversy with Booth helped to clarify his thinking, some help from Calvin can be allowed.[47] But even this cautious conclusion has no real evidence to support it, and should be rejected. This is particularly so as there *is* ample and conclusive evidence that Fuller received help from elsewhere in formulating his views, both on imputation and other doctrines relative to the atonement.

The New England Theologians and Fuller's Change of Views

How then had Fuller come to make these significant changes? The evidence suggests that the scriptures were once again central. Fuller was sure that what he repeatedly termed 'the oracles of God' were on his side. Verses that he appealed to included Romans 3.25 and also Romans 8.3, which were relevant because of their implication that it was *sins* that were being punished and condemned rather than Christ himself. Fuller was sure that in the New Testament 'what Christ underwent [was] commonly expressed by the term *sufferings.*' When the terms 'chastisement' or 'punishment' were used the focus was on the fact that he 'bore *our* punishment', not that Christ himself was being punished. Following prolonged reflection on the relevant passages Fuller believed there was 'great accuracy in the scripture phraseology on this subject'.[48] Scripture was vital as it always seemed to be for Fuller. But here perhaps more than anywhere, the influence of the New England theologians can be seen. This is particularly so regarding Fuller's use of the language of 'moral government' to describe the atonement.

Edwards' disciples had taken over the 'governmental' theory of the atonement originally propounded by the Dutch jurist Hugo Grotius (1583-1645) in the seventeenth century,[49] and developed it in a series of works. In speaking of God as 'the infinitely wise and good Governor of the world', they were strongly influenced, according to Mark Noll, by their context in the time of the American Revolution, with its concerns

---

47   Clipsham, 'Fuller and John Calvin', pp. 149 (and p. 153 n.); 152.

48   Fuller, *Six Letters to Dr Ryland*, in *Fuller's Works*, II, p. 705.

49   See Ferguson and Wright, *New Dictionary of Theology*, pp. 284-85, for details on Grotius, the Dutch 'jurist, publicist, statesman and theologian.' Grotius' *Works* were in the library of Yale College by at least 1733. See Foster, *New England Theology*, p. 114.

for 'fairness in government and personal responsibility in citizens'.[50] The key figures were Hopkins himself, Stephen West (1735-1818),[51] and especially Edwards' son, Jonathan Edwards Jr (1745-1801),[52] who among the New England men gave the moral government theory 'it's first elaborate statement'.[53] Hopkins' own views were set out in his *System of Doctrines Contained in Divine Revelation* (1793).[54] But Joseph Bellamy was important too, and can be viewed as a transitional figure, bridging the gap between the older view of Edwards Sr and the newer view of his son. The elder Jonathan Edwards had rejected the idea of the atonement as the literal *quid pro quo* repayment of a debt, but had nevertheless maintained that in the events of the cross God did punish Christ in order to vindicate his own character. Bellamy appeared to believe this too, but stated the Grotian view that 'God acts to uphold His Divine character', alongside it. For example, in his *True Religion Delineated*, (for which Edwards wrote a Preface commending the work), he argued that Christ's death honoured God's moral law, and as a result the benevolent moral governor of the universe could now 'pardon the whole world...consistently with his honour.'[55] Bellamy can therefore be seen as a middleman between the two positions, an 'American precursor for the governmental theory of the atonement'.[56]

---

50   M.A Noll, *A History of Christianity in the United States and Canada* (London: SPCK / Grand Rapids: Eerdmans, 1992), p. 158. Noll continues: 'Hopkins and Bellamy did not repudiate the Calvinistic theology they had inherited from Jonathan Edwards, but the influence of contemporary notions about the imperatives of human happiness and individual rights and the need to justify all intellectual principles at the bar of reason are evident in their work.'

51   West followed Edwards Sr at Stockbridge, Massachusetts, where he was pastor from 1758-1818, see Foster, *New England Theology*, p. 204 n.

52   For brief biographical details of Edwards Jr see Conforti, *Hopkins and the New Divinity*, pp. 38, 73-74, 179, 229; *DEB*, I, pp. 346-47. Edwards Jr studied under Hopkins and Bellamy. While a pastor at Colebrook, Connecticut from 1795-99, he was involved in the 'Second Great Awakening'. Cf. Foster, *New England Theology*, p. 189 n.

53   R.L. Ferm, *Jonathan Edwards the Younger: A Colonial Pastor* (Grand Rapids: Eerdmans, 1976), p. 115 n.

54   Conforti, *Hopkins and the New Divinity*, p. 161.

55   J. Bellamy, *True Religion Delineated* (1750); see Conforti, *Hopkins and the New Divinity*, p. 164. Conforti, pp. 162-63, states that Hopkins was considerably influenced by Bellamy concerning his own views on the atonement: 'Hopkins's *System* borrowed more heavily from Joseph Bellamy than any other of Jonathan Edwards's "improvers".'

56   Ferm, *Jonathan Edwards the Younger*, p. 115-16. See also Conforti, *Hopkins and The New Divinity*, p. 178: 'Within the New Divinity movement Bellamy represented a major link between the First and Second Great Awakenings.'

During the 1790s, when Fuller's views on these matters were forming, he was reading most of the relevant works by these men. Ryland was by 1793 Principal of the Baptist Academy at Bristol, and appears to have been an increasingly fruitful source of a wide range of trans-atlantic publications. Fuller received a copy of Edwards Jr on *Free Grace and Atonement* in 1794 with 'great pleasure'. Writing to thank Ryland he said: 'I suppose I read it some time ago; but I never relished it so well before.' On opening another parcel of pamphlets he was disappointed not to find 'West on the atonement', a work he told Ryland he 'very much longed for'.[57] Presumably his friend was able to satisfy Fuller's wish, as only three weeks later Fuller wrote to Sutcliff describing Stephen West's *The Scripture Doctrine of The Atonement Proposed to Careful Examination* (1785), as a book 'for wh I wd [sic] not take 1/1 [one guinea]'.[58] That Fuller had been reading relevant works by Hopkins for some time is attested by a wide range of sources.[59]

As far as the link with Bellamy was concerned, Fuller actually wrote the Preface to the English edition of *True Religion Delineated*, in which the New England man discussed his views on the death of Christ. In his Preface Fuller stated that the 'leading principles' of Bellamy's work were 'the exceeding sinfulness of sin, the lost state of the sinner, salvation by mere grace through a mediator and acceptance with God by faith in him'. He went on to warmly commend it. 'I do from my heart', he stated, 'wish it may meet with a candid and careful attention from the religious public. Were the doctrines here inculcated to prevail amongst us, I should hope to see more true religion than I have yet seen.'[60] Fuller was clearly leaning on Bellamy and the other New England men as his understanding of the atonement shifted. In particular, it is almost impossible to believe that Fuller would have started using the language

---

57   See Ryland, *Andrew Fuller*, pp. 227-30.

58   Fuller to J. Sutcliff, 22 January 1795, Fuller Letters (4/5/2). Fuller's letter to Ryland was dated 1 January. See Foster, *New England Theology*, pp. 204-205, for West's use of moral government terminology. West's *Scripture Doctrine of the Atonement* helped to popularize the governmental theory of the atonement in New England, see Haykin, 'Particular Redemption in the Writings of Andrew Fuller', p. 121.

59   See e.g. Fuller to J. Sutcliff, 7 January 1801, Fuller Letters (4/5/1). 'Fuller's book list, 28 August 1798', bound in his 'Miscellaneous Writings', has a completely separate section for 'American pieces', although many of what Fuller appeared to consider the major American Works, such as Bellamy's *True Religion Delineated* and Hopkins' *Body of Divinity*, appear in the main list.

60   J. Bellamy, *True Religion Delineated*, with a 'Recommendatory Preface' by Fuller, pp. v-viii. Edwards' Preface to the 1st edn was retained, but printed after Fuller's own.

of 'moral government' without the New England writers.[61] Edwards' followers were probably more significant for Fuller here than at any other point in his theology.

Differences between Fuller and Booth

In his ideas on imputation, Fuller also owed a debt to the New Divinity School. Oliver writes that Fuller's views on imputation 'in particular' seem 'very similar to those developed by Hopkins', whose definition of justification contained no 'real' imputation.[62] Booth had no doubts, again attacking Hopkins in *Divine Justice*.[63] Booth's belief was that Fuller had departed from Calvinistic orthodoxy by importing these ideas, and his fear was that they would be taken over uncritically into the mainstream of Particular Baptist life. This was certainly how Morris viewed Booth's motives. Booth, he stated: 'Suspected that Fuller and his friends were too much attached to the sentiments of President Edwards, and other American Divines of later date, and that by importing their metaphysical refinements, there would be some danger of relaxing that muscular system of theology to which he himself was so ardently devoted.'[64]

For his part, Fuller suspected that Booth had grown 'old', 'peevish' and 'jealous', and that this lay behind some of his opposition. Perhaps it was true that in the final years of his life some of the London man's powers were failing. As with the dispute over regeneration and faith, Booth appears as the older man defending the older view. Booth never rebutted the charge that his views were identical to those of the man often regarded as the father of High Calvinism, Tobias Crisp, and he

---

61   Although it should be noted that some English Evangelicals were using this sort of language to describe the atonement earlier than Fuller. See John Newton's sermon on 'The Lamb of God, the Great Atonement', preached in 1785 and printed the following year, as summarized by B. Hindmarsh, '"I am a Sort of Middle Man": The Politically Correct Evangelicalism of John Newton', in, Rawlyk and Noll (eds), *Amazing Grace*, pp. 45-48. Newton used Grotian or governmental language in this sermon, but also utilized other categories, such as penal substitution, to describe the atonement. Of supreme importance to Newton was 'the free offer of the gospel, graciously extended to all' and in this he strongly resembled Fuller, although Fuller was more precise and rigorous as a theologian. There is no evidence, however, that Fuller had read Newton's sermon, and much that he had derived his use of governmental language directly from the New England men.

62   Foster, *New England Theology*, p. 185. Cf. Oliver, 'Emergence of a Strict and Particular Baptist Community', p. 112.

63   Booth, *Divine Justice*, in *Booth's Works*, III, p. 50.

64   Morris, *Andrew Fuller*, 1st edn, pp. 378-79.

would have found it difficult to do so.[65] I have already suggested that from his settlement in London onwards, Booth became increasingly influenced by the Particular Baptist scene in the capital, a scene which was in general still far from Evangelical. Reading *The Reign of Grace* (which had so delighted not only Henry Venn but also Selina Countess of Huntingdon)[66] and *Divine Justice* alongside each other, it is hard to escape the feeling that Booth had shifted in his emphases. In addition, perhaps Booth's dramatic 'conversion' from Arminianism to Calvinism had left him with a dread of anything that appeared to threaten or deviate from this system, as Morris believed. Whatever the reason, the impression gained from reviewing the disputes between Fuller and Booth is that they were men moving in opposite directions. Fuller had left behind the High Calvinism of his youth; Booth was close to becoming the representative of an older Calvinism over and against the Evangelicalism to which he owed so much.[67]

Differences between Fuller and the New England Theologians

The importance of the New England theologians for Fuller was recognized by his contemporaries, and is brought out in Oliver's recent study. But what Oliver does not highlight so clearly is the way that Fuller read these theologians critically.[68] This is something I have already sought to draw attention to, but it becomes particularly marked as his thinking on the atonement develops. The fact that he engaged critically with the New England theologians can be shown in a number of ways. In his letters to Ryland and Sutcliff, although there was warm appreciation of the Americans, there were also notes of caution. Concerning Edwards Jr on *Free Grace and Atonement*, for example, he wrote to Ryland saying 'I do not coincide with everything it contains'.[69] Fuller was quite prepared to make his caution public, stating in his 'Recommendatory Preface' to Bellamy's *True Religion Delineated* that

---

65   Fuller to W. Carey, 26 November 1802, Fuller Letters (4/5/1): 'I think [Booth's] views of imputation are too much like those of Dr Crisp, as though in the imputation of sin something more was transferred than the penal effect of it.' Cf. *Fuller's Works*, II, pp. 710; 711-14. For Crisp see Toon, *Hyper Calvinism*, p. 49-61; Sell, *Great Debate*, pp. 47-50.

66   See Jeffrey (ed.), *English Spirituality*, p. 15.

67   Interestingly, Oliver, 'Emergence of a Strict and Particular Baptist Community', p. 107 n., notes that Booth was later 'warmly referred to' by Strict Baptists in the Gadsby tradition, including E. Feazey, editor of the *Gospel Standard* from 1899-1905.

68   Oliver, 'Emergence of a Strict and Particular Baptist Community', pp. 101; 111-15. Doubtless this is because the study of Fuller is not his primary purpose.

69   Ryland, *Andrew Fuller*, p. 226.

he did not 'advocate every sentiment' written in the book.[70] Both
Edwards Jr and Bellamy, in their espousal of a general, though not
universal, view of the atonement, had abandoned any thought of a
special design in the death of Christ, and this was undoubtedly one of
the areas of disagreement.[71] Even more revealing was the long letter
Fuller wrote to Hopkins in 1798 at the height of the controversy with
Booth over regeneration, from which I have already quoted. A number
of other passages from this letter are also worthy of extended
comment.[72]

In the letter, Fuller criticized Hopkins over statements that God
should be regarded as being 'the author of sin'. This was also the view
of Edwards Jr and of Stephen West, who asserted 'that it was the
positive design and purpose of God that moral evil should come into
existence'.[73] Fuller was very wary of this way of speaking. He told
Hopkins that to say that God was 'the author of sin' would convey to
most people 'that God is the friend and approver of sin; that we are the
passive instruments, and that he himself, being the grand agent, ought to
be held accountable for it.' He went on to cite James 1.13, and its
statement that 'when tempted, no-one should say "God is tempting
me"'. Fuller believed that to say that God 'was the author of sin' cut
against this teaching. Of course West never meant to convey that God
'was the friend and approver of sin' and Fuller was well aware of this.
But as a man whose context for theology was an everyday pastoral
ministry, he saw the dangers of what was being said on a practical level.
He went on to further criticize the New England men on the basis of
other verses in James chapter one, at some length. On another issue of
disagreement with Hopkins himself, Fuller even contemplated the
possibility of their correspondence being published. Hopkins was a
'mighty reasoner' said Fuller, 'but on this subject I feel my ground'.[74]
Fuller was not afraid of Hopkins. He was willing and more than able to
engage with him.

Also worthy of note are further strictures Fuller offered his friend on
some of the New England men. Very important, in the light of the
preceding discussion on the atonement, were his detailed comments on
Edwards Jr. Fuller objected to the younger Edwards' account of 'public

---

70   Fuller's Preface to Bellamy, *True Religion Delineated*, p. vii.

71   See Foster, *New England Theology*, pp. 116-17, for Bellamy's views.

72   There are detailed extracts from the letter in Morris, *Andrew Fuller*, 1st edn, p.
380-85. The following quotations are all taken from these pages.

73   S. West, *An Essay of Moral Agency* (Salem, 1794), cited by Ferm, *Jonathan
Edwards the Younger*; cf. the following comment by Edwards Jr also cited by Ferm, pp.
124, 132, 'I do not deny, that God is the author of sin'.

74   Morris, *Andrew Fuller*, 2nd edn, p. 386.

justice' as being 'too indefinite', and would never follow Edwards Jr in holding to a general, rather than particular, redemption. He continued to speak of the atonement in substitutionary terms, whilst the majority of moral government men had abandoned substitution.[75] Tom Nettles argues that although Fuller used 'governmental language', his use of their concepts 'did not involve him in the mistakes of the governmentalists'.[76] Whatever judgment is made concerning the value of New Divinity theology (and the verdict has often been harsh),[77] this is certainly a more balanced assessment than to say that Fuller was 'dependent' on these men. His views on the atonement were actually far closer to Edwards Sr and Bellamy than those who followed them. But Fuller never copied. His youthful resolve 'never to be an imitator' had demonstrably not left him.

Fuller's 'independence' is further highlighted by comments to Hopkins about a number of the younger New England men with whom Fuller was particularly unhappy. He confessed to enjoying some of their 'metaphysical pieces', and hoped that those who could 'throw light on evangelical subjects in this way' would continue to write. He nevertheless observed that:

> Wherever an extraordinary man has been raised up, like President Edwards...it is usual for his followers and admirers too much to confine their attention to his doctrines or manner of reasoning, as though all excellence was there concentrated. I allow that your present writers do not explicitly follow Edwards, as to his sentiments, but that you preserve the spirit of free enquiry; yet I must say, it appears to me that several of your younger men possess a rage of imitating his metaphysical manner, till some of them have become metaphysic mad. I am not without some of Mr Scott's apprehensions, lest by such a spirit, the simplicity of

---

75   See e.g. A. Fuller, *The Deity of Christ Essential to Atonement* (London, 1802) in *Fuller's Works*, III, pp. 693-97, especially 693-94.

76   T.J. Nettles, *By His Grace and For His Glory: A Historical, Theological and Practical Study of the Doctrines of Grace in Baptist Life* (Grand Rapids: Baker, 1986), p. 128. Haykin's comment, 'Particular Redemption in the Writings of Andrew Fuller', p. 128, is that: 'Contrary to Booth's impressions, Fuller did not surrender his commitment to particular redemption. Nor did he abandon his conviction that Christ died in the stead of sinners, though, it must be admitted that his fondness for governmental language... hampered rather than helped a clear expression of this conviction.'

77   Perhaps best known are the criticisms of B.B. Warfield, 'Edwards and the New England Theology', in *The Works of Benjamin B Warfield. 9: Studies in Theology* (10 vols; Grand Rapids: Baker, 1991), pp. 515-38; Joseph Haroutunian, *Piety versus Moralism: The Passing of the New England Theology* (New York: Harper and Row, 1932), *passim*. See the bibliographical note in Conforti, *Hopkins and the New Divinity*, pp. 233-36, for more recent comments.

the gospel should be lost, and truth amongst you stand more in the wisdom of man than in the power of God.[78]

Fuller had reached a stage where he was critiquing some of the leading thinkers of his day on their own terms, faulting them for 'imitating' a man to the possible detriment of 'a spirit of free enquiry'. Fuller did not reject the approach of quoting Gill or Owen as authoritative, only to replace it by substituting new human 'authorities' which could be appealed to in order to decide an argument. 'Explicitly following' a man, even a man like Edwards, could not be allowed to get in the way of the pursuit of truth. Also characteristic of Fuller were his concerns for the 'simplicity of the gospel'. Fuller was constantly drawing people back to the 'centre', to those fundamental religious truths that were 'few, simple in their form and essentially practical in their application'.[79] In indulging in rather esoteric metaphysical speculation, the younger New England men were departing from the Evangelical emphases which Fuller held dear. Philosophy could never be set up as an 'oracle', as he had earlier written to Ryland. 'Philosophy' he stated, 'is out of its place, when seated upon the *bench* by the side of God's word: the *bar* is the highest station to which it ought to be admitted'.[80]

In all these extracts Fuller's independence of judgment, practical 'down to earth' agenda and commitment to a 'spirit of free enquiry' (one of his favourite phrases), are all clear. His Evangelicalism is highlighted by his commitment to the simple core truths of the gospel, truths that had to be lived as well as believed. Chief among these was his frequently stated commitment to the scriptures as the word of God. Though various human authorities, including Edwards and the very best of contemporary philosophy could come to the 'bar' of the court, it was God's word, and God's word alone, that should sit in judgment.[81] This is

---

78   Morris, *Andrew Fuller*, 1st edn, p. 384-85. 'Mr Scott' is, once again, the Evangelical Anglican Thomas Scott. Fuller may well have had Edwards Jr and Stephen West themselves in mind when he made these comments, particularly in relation to their attempts to modify and 'improve' Edwards Sr's theory of the will. See Foster, *New England Theology*, p. 224-69.

79   Robison, 'Particular Baptists in England', p. 36.

80   Ryland, *Andrew Fuller*, pp. 229-30. Also worth noting is Ryland's footnote to this quotation: 'Philosophy is human opinion, formed without the Bible. Is that more an oracle than human opinion formed from it? I grant that right reason never errs; but what is, at all times, called philosophy, may: and, to say, that we make right reason or true philosophy our oracle, is taking it for granted, that we have found out what right reason and true philosophy is, in all cases, which is more than can be justly pretended.'

81   Cf. Fuller's letter to Timothy Dwight, 1 June 1805, cited in A.G. Fuller, *Andrew*

important because, for Fuller, a spirit of free enquiry did not mean abandoning the Bible as his supreme standard. David Bebbington has written that some liberal Evangelicals of the nineteenth century drifted from their biblical roots in favour of a completely unfettered, supposedly 'presuppositionless' pursuit of a spirit of free enquiry:

> It was held that a condition of progress in scientific knowledge is a total lack of presuppositions... The belief that it is possible to operate without any presuppositions was the result of exaggerating one aspect of enlightenment teaching. An emphasis on free enquiry was exalted above one of the four evangelical characteristics, biblicism.[82]

My contention is that this was one of the traits which Fuller, in 1795, recognized in some of the New England men. It was a trait that he was determined to resist. This chapter has clearly shown the influence of progressive American thinking on Fuller. But as some of the 'human authorities' from the school he held most dear drifted from one of the defining Evangelical characteristics, Fuller remained tenaciously wedded to the Bible as God's authoritative word.

Fuller as a Theologian

This final chapter on Fuller's thought concludes with a brief assessment of his importance as a theologian. His significance was clearly recognized by contemporaries outside the Particular Baptist denomination on both sides of the Atlantic. Especially noteworthy were the honorary doctorates he was urged to accept from two prestigious New England colleges. Fuller declined them both. Writing to Samuel Hopkins in 1798, he expressed his gratitude at the honour he had heard the New Jersey College had conferred on him earlier that year. It was, he said, 'such a token of respect'. He continued: 'I esteem it as coming from that quarter which, beyond any other in the world, I most approve.' But he did not, he believed, have the 'qualifications which are expected to accompany such titles', and in addition thought all such 'titles in religion' to be contrary to Jesus' words in Matthew 23.8: 'Do not be called Rabbi...for you are all brothers.'[83]

Fuller, in *Fuller's Works*, I, p. 85, where Fuller stated that Edwards Sr's 'sermons on justification have afforded me more satisfaction on that important doctrine than any human performance which I have read'. The qualification that Edwards' work was a 'human' performance was a typical Fuller touch.

82   Bebbington, *Evangelicalism*, p. 76.

83   Fuller to S. Hopkins, 17 March 1798, Fuller Letters (4/5/1). Fuller had earlier

If Timothy Dwight (1752-1817),[84] the President of Yale from 1795 to his death, had heard of Fuller's views about titles it did not stop him writing to the Kettering pastor in 1805, informing him that 'The corporation of Yale College at the last public commencement conveyed on you the degree of Doctor of Divinity'. Dwight, a maternal grandson of Edwards Sr, stated that: 'As this act is the result of the knowledge of your personal character and your published works only, and as such degrees are not inconsiderately given by this body, I flatter myself that it will be regarded by you in the light of a sincere testimony of respect to you.'[85] The letter and testimony were handed to him personally by the Professor of Chemistry at Yale, Benjamin Silliman, who was in England, presumably on College business.[86] Once again, in his written reply to Dwight, Fuller was courteous in declining the honour. After doing so he stated that:

> The writings of your grandfather, President Edwards, and of your uncle, the late Dr Edwards, have been food to me and many others...some pieces I have met with of yours have also afforded me much pleasure... I have requested Mr Silliman to procure of my bookseller all that he can furnish of what I have published, which I hope you will accept and furnish with a place in the college library, as a token of my grateful esteem.[87]

Fuller's importance and power was recognized by English and Scottish contemporaries. Thomas Chalmers (1780-1847),[88] the father of Scottish 'Common Sense' philosophy, was one such who paid tribute to him. Fuller actually stayed with the young Chalmers in Kilmany in 1813, on the last of his missionary tours of Scotland on behalf of the Baptist Missionary Society. Kirkby cites a comment of Chalmers'

---

expressed his views on doctorates forcefully to Ryland, as 'John Ryland Jr Letter to Andrew Fuller', Bristol Baptist College library (G 97 B Box A [n.d but internal evidence shows late 1793]), shows. The letter is Ryland's reply to Fuller's strictures on Ryland's own honorary doctorate. Ryland regretted having received this, but he regarded being called 'Dr' as a 'nickname', and thought using it preferable to having to constantly explain that he had rejected it, leaving him open to the accusation of 'false pride'. He received the doctorate earlier in 1793 from Brown University, Rhode Island. See Haykin (ed.), *Armies of the Lamb*, p. 153 n.

84   For Dwight see *DEB*, I, pp. 336-37.

85   T. Dwight to Fuller, 18 March 1805, in A.G. Fuller, *Andrew Fuller*, in *Fuller's Works*, I, p. 85.

86   For a note on Silliman see Haykin (ed.), *Armies of the Lamb*, p. 200 n.

87   Fuller to T. Dwight, 1 June 1805, in A.G. Fuller, *Andrew Fuller*, in *Fuller's Works*, I, p. 85.

88   See *DEB*, I, pp. 210-212.

biographer, William Hanna: 'This visit of Mr Fuller was one of the incidents in his Kilmany life to which Mr Chalmers always looked back on with pride and pleasure. He could not refrain from referring to it when introducing a remark of Fuller's into one of his theological lectures.' Once again it appears that Fuller had not been overawed by meeting an acknowledged 'great man', urging Chalmers to abandon his habit of reading his sermons from a manuscript and instead preach extempore.[89]

Fuller's ability as a theologian is shown too in comparison with other leading Evangelicals of his age. Bruce Hindmarsh in one of his studies on John Newton states:

> [Newton's] most vigorous intellectual period was from 1758 to 1764. After that he grew increasingly satisfied with a 'pass the buck' approach to theology, typically referring inquirers to Jonathan Edwards, for example, on the knotty problem of moral and natural inability, or to John Owen on the propriety of the free offer of the gospel, rather than working out these arguments afresh for himself. While it is no disgrace that Newton was more a pastor than a theologian, it is one of the most serious indictments of the English Evangelical Revival that it produced so few theologians of stature.[90]

Fuller was influenced by and appealed to both Owen and Edwards. He too emphasized the distinction between natural and moral inability, and pleaded that the gospel should be offered, freely and indiscriminately, to all. He too was a pastor. But he never engaged in 'pass the buck theology', and he could never be accused of not 'working out arguments fresh for himself'. Given all this, it is easy to forget that Fuller had no formal theological training, indeed little formal education at all, receiving only 'the barest rudiments of English instruction'.[91] He was from simple farming stock, the 'very picture of a blacksmith', as William Wilberforce memorably put it.[92] But Wilberforce too was an admirer.[93] If it is true that Evangelical Revival produced few theological thinkers of real 'stature' then there is surely enough evidence in this

---

89   Although when Fuller met him Chalmers was only 33 and his reputation was yet to be firmly established. See Kirkby, 'Theology of Andrew Fuller', p. 20. Note too the quotation from Chalmers cited by Haykin, *One Heart and Soul*, p. 7, warmly appreciative of the Fullerite Particular Baptists in general.

90   Hindmarsh, 'The Politically Correct Evangelicalism of John Newton', in Rawlyk and Noll (eds), *Amazing Grace*, p. 53.

91   A.G. Fuller, *Andrew Fuller*, in *Fuller's Works*, I, p. 1.

92   F.K. Brown, *Fathers of the Victorians* (Cambridge: Cambridge University Press, 1961), p. 505.

93   Ryland, *Andrew Fuller*, 2nd edn, pp. ix, 138.

study of his thought to show that Fuller was one of those theologians.

As far as his own denomination was concerned, by the end of the eighteenth century Fuller was acknowledged (at least by Evangelical Calvinists), to be their premier theologian. Ryland, a significant thinker in his own right, considered Fuller 'the most judicious and able theological writer that ever belonged to the Baptist denomination'.[94] Ivimey writing soon after Fuller's death, believed that the Kettering pastor enjoyed a high and, in many ways, 'unrivalled station' as the denomination's theologian.[95] These are just two of many comments that could have been cited. Certainly *The Gospel Worthy* was the most influential text in weaning the majority of Particular Baptists away from High Calvinism. Ryland cites the example of an older minister, Joshua Thomas, who initially opposed *The Gospel Worthy*, but 'came over to Mr Fuller's views at last'.[96] He would have been one of many. In 1797 a group of Deacons in a Baptist Church in Hull wrote to the Evangelical Baptist Pastor Joseph Kinghorn. The Hull church wanted Kinghorn to help them to find a minister, and specified the sort of man they were looking for. Amongst other things they were clear that he was to be a 'lively, zealous and affectionate preacher' and 'orthodox'. The letter has a marginal note explaining the meaning of 'orthodox'. It says 'of Mr Fuller's sentiments'.[97] The numerical and spiritual growth that will be considered in the following chapters was certainly driven and shaped by the Edwardsean Evangelical Calvinism that became known as Fullerism. Fuller's achievement in writing *The Gospel Worthy*, and subsequently defending and modifying his thinking, was considerable.

Nevertheless (as much of the material in this and the previous chapter makes abundantly clear), Fuller's triumph was not complete. Older High Calvinists would continue to reject 'duty faith', and their criticisms would be taken up by a new generation. Key leaders of the nineteenth-century Strict Baptist movement such as William Gadsby and J. C. Philpot were scathing in their condemnation of Fuller. For Gadsby, Fuller was 'the greatest enemy the church of God ever had, as his sentiments were so much cloaked in the sheep's clothing'. Fuller was blamed for the erosion of true Calvinistic principles amongst the

---

94   Cited by Clipsham, 'Development of a Doctrine', p. 99.

95   *HEB*, IV, p. 532

96   Ryland, *Andrew Fuller*, p. 131. For Thomas, who was a minister at Leominster, see *HEB*, I, pp. 65, 73.

97   Cited by Kirkby, 'Theology of Andrew Fuller', p. 11. The letter is dated 23 March 1797, from three Deacons at George Street Baptist Church in Hull, to Kinghorn who was pastor of St Mary's Baptist Church, Norwich. The original is held in the archives at St Mary's. Cf. Watts, *Dissenters*, I, p. 460, who states that 'Fullerism became the new orthodoxy of the [Particular Baptist] denomination'.

Particular Baptists, for opening the door to mixed communion and, along with it, Arminianism.[98] This view has some supporters today,[99] but Kenneth Dix's verdict is fair, and deserves to be quoted in full:

> The Strict Baptists did not treat Fuller with the respect he deserved as the leading Baptist theologian of his day. There was a failure to accept Fuller's testimony of his commitment to 'strict Calvinism', or of the very gracious way he wrote of his opposition to mixed communion principles. There were certainly times when Fuller made statements which might have been construed as a departure from the particularist position, but this was not the case. His belief in an atonement that was sufficient for all men but efficacious only for the elect, offended high-Calvinists, but he never gave up the seventeenth-century confessions. Andrew Fuller was no more responsible for any shift from orthodox Calvinism in the nineteenth century than the men who framed the 1677 Confession could be held responsible for the path taken by some of their opponents into the chilling winds of high-Calvinism.[100]

This is an assessment with which I heartily concur. Certainly nineteenth-century Strict Baptists regarded Fuller as their *bête noire*, and so an analysis of his theology is important in any description of the emergence of the Strict and Particular Baptist Community.[101] But the nineteenth-century shift away from what Fuller termed 'strict Calvinism' was far more attributable, as Ian Sellers states, to 'the tide of nineteenth-century opinion [which] was running against religious particularism of any form'.[102] Those who laid the 'blame' for the erosion of Calvinistic distinctives amongst the Particular Baptists at Fuller's door were wrong.[103] Rather than abandoning Calvinism and opening the door to Arminianism, Fullerism actually opened the door to expansive gospel ministry by allowing increasing numbers within the Particular Baptist denomination to hold together strict Calvinism and invitational

---

98   K. Dix, *Strict and Particular: English Strict and Particular Baptists in the Nineteenth Century* (Didcot: Baptist Historical Society, 2001), pp. 37 n., 103; Haykin, 'Particular Redemption in the Writings of Andrew Fuller', p. 108.

99   See especially G.M. Ella, *Law and Gospel in the Theology of Andrew Fuller* (Eggleston, Co. Durham: Go Publications, 1996), *passim*.

100   Dix, *Strict and Particular*, pp. 269-70.

101   Oliver, 'Emergence of a Strict and Particular Baptist Community', p. 119.

102   I. Sellers, 'John Howard Hinton, Theologian', *BQ* 33.3 (July, 1989), p. 123. For more detail see also Dix, *Strict and Particular*, p. 70. Evangelical Calvinism would enjoy a significant resurgence at the end of the nineteenth century in the person of C.H. Spurgeon.

103   Rinaldi, 'The Tribe of Dan', pp. 36-40, details this 'erosion of distinctives' amongst erstwhile Particular Baptists in the nineteenth century.

gospel preaching. That he was able to do this so successfully was a large part of his genius as a theologian.

Conclusion

In the first section of this work I have sought to show how Fuller developed a vibrant Evangelical theology. The basis was biblical, the focus was the atonement and the aim was to encourage activism in the pursuit of conversions. If Ernest Payne was guilty of overstatement when he spoke of the 'revolution' effected by Fuller's work, he was not wrong to use such a dramatic term, for undoubtedly it *was* revolutionary for many. Through *The Gospel Worthy* and the subsequent works in which its author defended its key tenets and further modified his views on the atonement, a vitally important contribution to the revitalization of denominational life was made. This is the conclusion to the first half of this book. In the following three chapters the focus shifts from Fuller's theology to the practical outworking of that theology in his own life and the life of the Particular Baptist denomination. The second half of this study will attempt to show that this practical outworking was no less revolutionary than the theology itself.

CHAPTER FIVE

Fuller's Pastoral Ministry

Being now devoted to the ministry

By now it should be clear that, although Fuller was a theologian of real stature, his context for 'doing theology' was local and trans-local pastoral ministry. This context was an important influence on his changing views, but it was also the setting in which he worked out his theology in practice. In this, the first of three chapters on his life and ministry, the focus is on how his new theology fed through into a pastoral ministry which became thoroughly Evangelical. In particular Fuller developed a thoroughly *evangelistic* ministry, with a clear conversionist agenda driving much of what he did. This is seen in this chapter through an examination of his work as a pastor, with his congregations at Soham and Kettering and also within his own family, in his wider preaching ministry, and finally through his involvement in the life of the Northamptonshire Association.

The Development of Fuller's Evangelistic Local Church Ministry

The young Fuller first began occasionally taking church services at Soham in 1771, and in 1775 was ordained as their pastor. As noted in chapter two, 1775 was an important year in the development of Fuller's thought, when, as a result of reading Abraham Taylor's tract on the 'Modern Question', his commitment to High Calvinism began to weaken considerably. But this did not immediately affect his preaching, as his continuing uncertainty concerning 'indiscriminate offers of the gospel', together with his innate caution and a certain degree of apprehension, all combined to hold him back. In his own words: 'I…durst not, for some years, address an invitation to the unconverted to come to Jesus.'[1]

By the late 1770s however, his thought had developed to the extent that there was now an unsustainable tension between theology and practice. Fuller, doubtless with the same fear and trepidation which would later accompany his decision to publish *The Gospel Worthy*, introduced the new evangelistic note of direct appeal into his public ministry. The result was consternation and dissatisfaction at Soham, although the exact extent of the opposition is unclear.[2] A degree of antagonism was almost inevitable, considering the views of the previous pastor, John Eve, and the disputes through which the church had only recently passed. Ryland wrote that: 'A tinge of false Calvinism infected some of the people, who were inclined to find fault with his ministry, as it became more searching and practical, and as he freely enforced the indefinite calls of the gospel.' Ryland, working with free access to all Fuller's private papers, was able to date the beginning of this opposition precisely – to December 1779.[3] Fuller's renewed theology was now leading to a parallel change in his preaching.

In the years immediately following 1779 Fuller was worried that his sermons were still not 'searching and practical' enough. 'Surely I do not sufficiently study the cases of the people in my preaching!', he wrote in his diary on 29 July 1780. 'I find, by conversation today, with one seemingly in dying circumstances, that but little of my preaching has been suited to her case.' Fuller's conclusion was that an increased amount of time spent in pastoral visiting would make his sermons more 'experimental', by which he meant more suited to his people's experience.[4] But still he struggled to break decisively from his past as far as his practical ministry was concerned.

This continuing struggle is further indicated by his behaviour towards his father, who by the close of January 1781 was dying. Fuller's mother was a member at Soham and was, according to Gunton Fuller, 'a woman of excellent Christian character'.[5] His father, however, although a

---

1   Ryland, *Andrew Fuller*, p. 32. Fuller's comment is made with respect to where he stood at the end of 1774, although the position would remain unchanged for a further five years.

2   Morris, *Andrew Fuller*, 2nd edn, p. 34, was more negative than Ryland, *Andrew Fuller*, p. 44, who only spoke of 'the unkindness of a few'. Fuller himself, 'Narrative', 9 September 1781, p. 47, referred to the 'reproach of some and the indifference of others'. Ryland experienced similar opposition to his own preaching at Northampton, as did Sutcliff at Olney. See G. Gordon, 'The Call of Dr John Ryland Jr', *BQ* 34.5 (January 1992), p. 216; Haykin, *One Heart and Soul*, p. 151-52.

3   Ryland, *Andrew Fuller*, p. 44.

4   Ryland, *Andrew Fuller*, p. 77.

5   A.G. Fuller, *Men Worth Remembering*, p. 12.

'hearer' or regular attender, had not joined the church and appears to have been unconverted. Certainly this was Fuller's view, and the son agonized over Robert Fuller's 'eternal state'. Despite his now developing pulpit ministry he was hesitant to speak to his father, although his heart was 'being much drawn out' in prayer to God for him. By 26 January, with his father's health clearly failing, the son plucked up some courage and the following conversation is recorded in Fuller's diary:

> Son: Have you any outgoings of soul, father, to the Lord?
> Father: Yes my dear, I have.
> Son: Well, father, the Lord is rich in mercy to all that call upon him. This is great encouragement.
> Father: Yes, my child, so it is; and I know, if I be saved, it must be by him alone. I have nothing to recommend me to his favour...but my hopes are very small.

Robert Fuller's words show he had imbibed the language and attitudes of High Calvinism through his attendance at Soham. But his son too, despite his comment that 'the Lord is rich in mercy to all that call upon him', continued to show its influence (assuming, as the diary entry indicates, that this was where the conversation ended).[6] It is one of a number of pointers indicating that his evangelistic ministry may have developed quite slowly, even after his 1779 breakthrough. In fact there is really nothing at all in this exchange that could not have been said by a High Calvinist. Probably Fuller found it easier to put his new principles into practice in the pulpit than one-to-one, and doubtless his hesitation here was due in some degree to a natural reticence in speaking with his father. But this still falls rather short of what we might have expected from him at this stage of his career, and contrasts sharply with later examples of his evangelistic ministry, including where elderly and much respected relatives were concerned.[7] Fuller did not find the break from High Calvinism easy. And yet certainly in the pulpit his approach was changing. One indication of this was that by the early 1780s his preaching was beginning to see moderate success, with some conversions and an increased number wanting to hear him. But opposition to him was hardening too and Fuller found himself increasingly unhappy at Soham, not just, it has to be said, because of his growing Evangelicalism.

One of the central problems was that the church was poor and struggled to support their pastor. Fuller's stipend of £13 a year, despite

---

6   Ryland, *Andrew Fuller*, pp. 87-88.
7   See Ryland, *Andrew Fuller*, p. 317, for a letter to an elderly relative.

an additional £5 from the Particular Baptist Fund in London, was woefully inadequate. Attempts to supplement this, first by running a small shop and then a school, failed. Fuller, with his growing family, found he was simply unable to manage. Even the success of his preaching was a source of frustration, as the meeting house was not large enough to accommodate those who wanted to come and the people were unwilling to look for a more suitable place of worship, even when their landlord raised the rent.[8] Fuller's unhappiness regularly surfaced in his diary, and against this background some of the ministers of the Northamptonshire Association who had become his friends, particularly at this stage Robert Hall Sr, began to suggest that he moved to a new church.

The protracted negotiations which surrounded Fuller's eventual acceptance of the call to the pastorate of the 'Little Meeting' at Kettering in 1782, a call that had originally come over a year earlier, occupy considerable space in all the early biographies.[9] The events which surrounded Fuller's move are dealt with in more detail in chapter seven of this book. Suffice to say here that whatever other struggles he was going through, Fuller would not compromise his newly found evangelistic principles. Indeed, these were principles to which he was becoming increasingly committed. Fuller's induction at Kettering took place on 7 October 1783 (following the usual trial period of a year's ministry). The personal statement of faith Fuller offered to the church at this time contained an article that was both a statement of his theology and a declaration of intent for his future ministry. It is worth quoting in full:

> I believe it is the duty of every minister of Christ plainly and faithfully to preach the gospel to all who will hear it; and, as I believe the inability of men to spiritual things to be wholly of the moral, and therefore of the criminal kind – and that it is their duty to love the Lord Jesus Christ, and trust in him for salvation, though they do not; I therefore believe free and solemn addresses, invitations, calls, and warnings to them, to be not only consistent, but directly adapted as means, in the hand of the Spirit of God, to bring them to Christ. I consider it as part of my duty that I could not omit without being guilty of the blood of souls.[10]

This part of Fuller's personal confession indicates that a sea change had taken place in both theology *and* practice. In fact, with its

---

8   A.G. Fuller, *Andrew Fuller*, in *Fuller's Works*, I, pp. 18-19; Ryland, *Andrew Fuller*, p. 44.

9   See e.g. A.G. Fuller, *Andrew Fuller*, in *Fuller's Works*, I, pp. 19, 24-34.

10   Ryland, *Andrew Fuller*, p. 68. There were twenty articles in all, many affirming Fuller's Calvinist orthodoxy.

Edwardsean distinction between natural and moral inability and its warm practical tone, this particular part of his statement reads like a summary of the main arguments of *The Gospel Worthy*, still two years away from publication, although by now basically ready in manuscript form. The gap between faith and practice had closed. Indeed, throughout his life Fuller was to feel keenly the inadequacies of his previous approach to preaching. The development of his Evangelical theology had led to the development of an Evangelical ministry, with a conversionist agenda that was clear for all to see. Some examples of Fuller's evangelistic efforts in the context of his local church work at Kettering, spanning the thirty two years of his ministry there, serve to emphasize and illustrate this development.

Examples of Fuller's Evangelistic Ministry

By the time Fuller began his ministry at Kettering he had effectively thrown off his inhibitions in evangelism both in his preaching and his work with individuals. One example of his personal work is contained in a letter to the son of a friend, written from Kettering in 1799. The boy was extremely ill, and in contrast to his earlier conversation with his father, Fuller did not on this occasion spend time enquiring whether he had 'any outgoings of soul to the Lord'. Rather, his appeal was direct. 'The invitations of the gospel are universal', he wrote, continuing: 'Repent of your sin and you shall find mercy; believe his gospel with all your heart, and you shall live... Every one that thus asketh receiveth; and he that seeketh findeth; and to him that knocketh, the door of mercy will be opened.' Fuller concluded the letter: 'If the Lamb of God, that taketh away the sin of the world, be not a comfort to you, you are comfortless. Look to him, my dear young friend, and live.'[11] Although this was written sixteen years after his move to Kettering, the letter is illustrative of his approach from a much earlier date. Also, although these words were written rather than spoken face to face, Fuller's biographies and diaries show that he was more than prepared to challenge someone in person.[12] Fuller's commitment to personal evangelism, with his willingness to openly offer the gospel 'indiscriminately' (significantly, the friend's son was a young man he hardly knew), is clear.

An example of evangelistic preaching comes from a sermon given at a ministers' meeting held at Clipstone, on 27 April 1791[13] (although

---

11   Ryland, *Andrew Fuller*, p. 325. See also the letter on p. 326, which is in the same vein.

12   A.G. Fuller, *Andrew Fuller*, in *Fuller's Works*, I, pp. 78-80.

13   The original sermon was entitled the 'Instances, Evil and Tendency of Delay in

almost certainly its content had already been preached already at Kettering, and perhaps elsewhere).[14] This sermon had a significant part to play in the formation of the BMS, and it will be considered again in chapter six. But it is worth quoting here because a large number of Fuller's other sermons survive only in note form, and sometimes those notes are brief.[15] This particular message was later published by Fuller himself and, because it survives in a more complete form, is likely to give a better impression of his style and approach. The context in which the sermon was given is also worth noting. Admittedly this was an open meeting, with many people other than pastors present. Nevertheless, if Fuller preached in this way at what was essentially a *ministers'* meeting, it is surely reasonable to conclude that the approach he adopted with his own church was at least as evangelistic and applied as that shown here.

The particular section of the sermon that concerns us is the final one. As Fuller dealt with the 'evil nature and dangerous tendency' of delay, he declared that 'sinners' only have an opportunity to escape God's wrath 'as long as life lasts'. A fountain is flowing that one day will be sealed off; a door is open which one day will be shut. Fuller briefly answered the charge, that to urge people to come to Christ clashed 'with the Scripture doctrine of decrees', with what by now was his stock argument – men had the natural ability to come and so they had no excuse. He then proceeded to his appeal:

> Thoughtless sinner! trifle no longer with the murder of time, so short and uncertain in its duration; the morning of your existence; the mould in which you receive an impression for eternity; the only period in which the Son of Man has

---

the Concerns of Religion'. It was later published as *The Pernicious Consequences of Delay in Religious Concerns* (Clipstone: J.W. Morris, 1791). For the text see *Fuller's Works*, I, pp. 145-51. All subsequent quotations from it are taken from these pages.

14   Fuller's first published work was his sermon on 'Walking by Faith' as preached at the Northamptonshire Association meeting of 2 June 1784. But entries in his 'Diary and Spiritual Thoughts [1784-1799]', Bristol Baptist College Library (G 95 b), for 25 April and 23 May 1784, show that he had already preached this message at least twice, at Kettering and on a return visit to Soham. His entries for the 1790s are much less detailed and by then Fuller was no longer including this sort of information, but the likelihood must be that he had already preached his 1791 association address at Kettering. For the published version of his 1784 message, see the discussion on the 1784 'Prayer Call' below.

15   Although many of the 'Sermons and Sketches' included in *Fuller's Works*, I, still contain passages which indicate that a strong evangelistic appeal had been made. See e.g. the sermon 'The Prayer of Faith, Exemplified in the Woman of Canaan', n.d., p. 241: 'O my hearers! let us agonize to enter in at the straight gate... Incline your ear and come to him; hear and your souls will live.'

power to forgive sins! Should the remaining part of your life pass away in the same careless manner as that which has already elapsed, what bitter reflection must needs follow! How cutting it must be to look back on all the means of salvation as gone for ever; the harvest past the summer ended, and you not saved!

Fuller concluded his message in the following way:

> My dear hearers! consider your condition without delay. God says to you, today, if ye will hear his voice, harden not your hearts. Today may be the only day you have to live. Go home, enter the closet, and shut the door; confess your sins; implore mercy through our Lord Jesus Christ; 'Kiss the Son, lest he be angry, and ye perish from the way, when his wrath is kindled but a little. Blessed are all they that put their trust in him.'

As to style, some of Fuller's evident power in the pulpit survived the transfer of his sermon to the printed page. Ryland commented on Fuller as a preacher, saying that he 'loved men' and had 'an evident unction from the Holy One'. Although there were some who excelled him for 'fluency' and popular appeal (Ryland was thinking particularly of Samuel Pearce), Fuller was an effective, extempore preacher.[16] Some critical remarks concerning Fuller's preaching do appear in the other biographies, and it does seem that this was not his greatest gift. Hayden summarizes some of these comments. Fuller lacked 'easy elocution', and his voice although 'strong' could also be 'heavy'.[17] In addition, he seems to have spent little time in preparation for some of his weekly local church preaching, with Gunton Fuller stating that 'it was not often that Mr Fuller's preparations for the pulpit were elaborate'. As we shall see, time would increasingly be at a premium for Fuller as his ministry progressed. Nevertheless he could certainly rise to the occasion for something like the Clipstone meeting, and he was clearly a popular speaker. Certainly, there is little difficulty in believing his son's comment: 'Sleepy hearers were not often found in Mr Fuller's congregation.'[18]

As to the content of this part of the Clipstone message, a number of points are worth highlighting. Fuller's use of scripture, couching his appeal in biblical terms, is striking. His use of Psalm 2 (the words, 'kiss the son, lest he be angry'), echoes the use he made of it in *The Gospel Worthy*. In fact Fuller proceeded from scriptural argument and theology, with the judicious use of Jonathan Edwards once again, to his appeal.

---

16   Ryland, *Andrew Fuller*, p. 144.

17   Hayden, 'The Life and Influence of Andrew Fuller', p. 5; Morris, *Andrew Fuller*, 1st edn, pp. 66-67.

18   A.G. Fuller, *Men Worth Remembering*, pp. 61, 80.

The themes and approach of his theological writings were also the themes and approach of his preaching. All this drives home the point made earlier, that the gap between theology pastoral practice had closed. The days when he 'durst not address an invitation to the unconverted', despite all his doubts concerning High Calvinism as a system, had gone. Both his preaching and what we might term his 'personal work' had indeed become 'experimental'; that is searching, practical and thoroughly evangelistic.

The Growth of the Church at Kettering

Throughout his pastorate at Kettering, the work of the 'Little Meeting' grew steadily. According to the church book, there had been 88 members when Fuller became pastor, and by the time of his death in 1815 this had increased to 174. Certainly this was not spectacular, although account needs to be taken of 146 who died, moved away or were excluded during this period. In total 232 people were received into membership during Fuller's pastorate.[19] In addition there were an increasingly large number of non-members regularly attending who, together with the children of members, could swell the congregation to over a 1000 strong. A number of those who came each Sunday walked in from surrounding villages.[20] The meeting house had to be enlarged twice to accommodate those who were now attending, steps the Kettering church were more willing to take than their counterparts at Soham had been.[21] Moreover, throughout the period of Fuller's ministry, Kettering remained a small and relatively poor market town with a population of no more than 3300.[22] In addition the Congregational church, whose minister, Thomas Toller, Ryland described as 'justifiably popular', was strong. The town also boasted a

---

19   'Church Book, Kettering Baptist Church, 1773-1815'. Entry for 23 February 1815. Of the 174 members at Fuller's death, 100 were women. Members were suspended or excluded for a variety of reasons, most commonly sexual misconduct and 'drinking to excess', e.g. pp. 107, 136.

20   Ryland, *Andrew Fuller*, pp. 246, 383.

21   In 1786 and 1805. Ryland, *Andrew Fuller*, p. 374.

22   R.L. Greenall, 'After Fuller: Baptists in 19th Century Kettering', in Greenall (ed.), *The Kettering Connection*, pp. 33-46. By the time of Fuller's death in 1815, Kettering was actually in severe economic decline. The collapse of the eighteenth-century staple trades of wool combing and worsted weaving had badly affected the town. Fuller himself, Fuller to J. Deakin, 25 October 1812, in E.A. Payne, 'Letters to James Deakin' *BQ* 7 (1934-35), p. 368, described Kettering as 'a place of but little wealth and of only 3000 inhabitants'.

congregation of Wesleyan Methodists and, towards the end of Fuller's time, Evangelical preaching in the Church of England.[23] Toller, reflecting back on this period in his farewell sermon, commented that in the early years of the nineteenth century Kettering was known as 'the Holy Land', because almost everyone seemed to attend some place of worship.[24] The evidence strongly suggests that in this comparatively small and declining market town, with significant competition from other churches, Fuller was an effective pastor.

Nevertheless there were problems. The failure to translate the large number of hearers to a more significant increase in the membership was not uncommon in the context of the period,[25] but the likelihood is that Fuller had less time for personal 'follow up' or in-depth pastoral work than most ministers. This was certainly true from 1792 onwards when he was away from his church for up to three months of the year, travelling round the country on behalf of the BMS. Ryland noted that Fuller admitted that these journeys were 'some impediment to his Pastoral duties'. Morris was stronger, and surely more honest, when he said that 'in discharging the duties of the Pastoral Office, Mr Fuller was not [entirely] successful...his numerous and, perhaps still more important engagements did not afford him sufficient opportunity.'[26] Fuller admitted as much himself. In October 1794 he wrote to Ryland lamenting the extent to which his role with the mission was 'interfering' with his work at Kettering. 'I long to visit my congregation', he said, 'that I may know of their spiritual concerns and preach to their cases'.[27] There is little doubt that, as Stanley notes, his work for the BMS was both to the 'detriment' and 'regret' of the church, although they were generally supportive of the mission work and of Fuller's role in it.[28] It was only from 1811 that Fuller had an assistant at Kettering, John Keen Hall, the nephew of his old friend Robert Hall Sr.[29] The pace at which Fuller worked for the BMS will be considered at length in chapter six. Suffice to say that given the pressures he was under, it is remarkable that Fuller saw the growth in his congregation that he did, and was as loved a pastor as he seemed to be.[30]

---

23 Ryland, *Andrew Fuller*, p. 383.

24 Greenall, 'Baptists in Kettering', p. 35.

25 See Bebbington, *Evangelicalism*, p. 21.

26 Ryland, *Andrew Fuller*, p. 155; Morris, *Andrew Fuller*, 1st edn, p. 74.

27 Ryland, *Andrew Fuller*, p. 155. Cf. comments of Ryland's own, p. 381.

28 Stanley, *History of the BMS*, p. 20.

29 G. Laws, *Andrew Fuller: Pastor, Theologian, Ropeholder* (London: Kingsgate Press, 1942), p. 8.

30 On April 23 1815, two weeks before Fuller's death and after his condition had been pronounced as 'hopeless', George Wallis, a young deacon at Kettering, wrote in

Evangelistic Work amongst Young People

One further aspect of Fuller's ministry at Kettering worth highlighting is the work he did with young people. His concern for his own children is exemplified in a letter to Robert, one of his sons from his first marriage. Robert Fuller (1782-1809) had 'acquired a habit of roving', as Ryland put it.[31] Following two failed apprenticeships and spells in the army and in the marines (both of which ended with his father buying him out, at Robert's request), his father got a place for him as a crew member on a merchant ship. But while he was waiting to board he was press-ganged into the navy, later receiving 350 lashes, a punishment he was fortunate to survive, before being discharged in 1804. Father and son were reunited in London, where Robert was nursed back to health by a doctor who had formerly been in Kettering who was known to Fuller. But in 1805 Robert disappeared once more, joining the Marines for a second time. He was never seen by his family again, dying off the coast of Lisbon, Portugal, in March 1809. Just four months prior to Robert's death Fuller had written to him, a warm-hearted letter showing much practical concern as well as urging him, as he had done many times previously, to turn to Christ:

> Do not despair. Far as you have gone, and low as you are sunk in sin, yet if from hence you return to God by Jesus Christ, you will find mercy. Jesus Christ came into the world to save sinners, even the chief of sinners. If you had been ever so sober and steady in your behaviour towards men, yet without repentance towards God and faith in Christ, you could not have been saved. And if you return to God by him, though your sins be great and aggravated, yet you will find mercy.[32]

---

his diary: 'What a loss as individuals and as a church we are going to sustain. Him that has so long fed us with the bread of life, that has so affectionately, so faithfully, and so fervently counsell'd, exhorted, reprov'd, and animated; by doctrine, by precept, and by example the people of his charge; him who has <u>liv'd</u> so much for <u>others</u>! Shall we no more hear his voice?' 'Diary of George Wallis', Fuller Baptist Church, Kettering. Wallis was the son of Samuel Wallis and the nephew of George and Beeby Wallis. He was 61 years a member at Kettering, becoming a deacon in 1813 and then serving for 50 years. He died in April 1863 aged 88.

31   This account of Robert Fuller is based on Fuller, 'Diary and Spiritual Thoughts', entry for 21 July 1800; Ryland, *Andrew Fuller*, pp. 297-304; A.G. Fuller, *Men Worth Remembering*, pp. 68-73. Kirkby, 'Theology of Andrew Fuller', pp. 24-27, and especially Haykin (ed.), *Armies of the Lamb*, pp. 221-22; 283-88, deal with Robert Fuller in some detail.

32   The text of the letter is in A.G. Fuller, *Men Worth Remembering*, pp. 71-72,

Fuller's behaviour towards his errant son appears to have been exemplary,[33] and contrasts favourably with what John Ryland Jr's attitude to one of his children appears to have been.[34] The Sunday after he had received news of his son's death Fuller wept in the pulpit at Kettering. An article in the *East Midland Baptist Magazine* for 1895, by a Rev D. P. McPherson, gives an account of a talk the writer had with an old lady in Kettering who had been eight years of age at the time of Fuller's death. 'She remembered Fuller's greatest grief; a prodigal son had gone abroad and sorrowful tidings came back respecting him.'[35] Yet unknown to Fuller it appears that Robert may have professed a Christian commitment on his final voyage. Certainly this was what Gunton Fuller believed and he cited the testimony of a Mr Waldy, a deacon in the Baptist church at Falkirk, whom Gunton Fuller met in 1845. According to Waldy, he had served with Robert on this last voyage and reported that Robert 'was a very pleasing, nice youth, and became a true Christian man'. This ending is not as implausible as it first appears, as letters written by Robert to his father and half-sister Sarah (which are now lost), together with a report from the ship's captain, gave Fuller himself some hope that his son had come to repentance and faith at the end of his life. If Gunton Fuller's account is to be believed then Haykin's words are fitting: 'Andrew Fuller's many prayers for his wayward son were answered and that verse from Psalm 126 powerfully illustrated: "They that sow in tears shall reap in joy."'[36]

Fuller's experiences with Robert form the background to his concern for young people within the congregation at Kettering. Every year, from at least the early 1790s, he would preach a new year's sermon particularly aimed at children and 'youth'. On these occasions, according to Ryland, Fuller would 'pour forth all his heart...exhorting and charging every one, as a Father [sic] doth his children'.[37] One of these sermons, entitled 'Advantages of Early Piety', gives an example of

---

and is reproduced by Haykin (ed.), *Armies of the Lamb*, pp. 221-22.

33   In his 'Diary and Spiritual Thoughts', entry for 21 July 1800, Fuller wrote: 'My ? (sic) has been tried and continually wrung with anguish about my unhappy son.'

34   This was John Tyler Ryland, a child born to Ryland Jr's first wife Elizabeth (née Tyler) in 1786. See S. Read, 'Further Information on the Ryland Family', *BQ* 36.4 (October, 1995), pp. 202-203. Read speculates that Ryland's attitude towards his son may have been because he was blamed for the death of his mother, seven weeks after the birth. Fuller's own letters show a warm mix of spiritual and practical concern for Robert.

35   Cited by Kirkby, 'Theology of Andrew Fuller', p. 24.

36   Haykin (ed.), *Armies of the Lamb*, p. 286.

37   Ryland, *Andrew Fuller*, p. 383.

what was said on those occasions.[38]

Fuller took as his text Psalm 90.14: 'O satisfy us early with thy mercy, that we may rejoice and be glad all our days', which he preceded to interpret as a prayer on behalf of the youth of Israel. He began by declaring: 'I hope I need not say that this prayer…is expressive of the desires of your minister and your parents; you know it is so. Oh that it might express your own!' Fuller preceded to make two points, firstly concerning the need for an 'early participation in Divine mercy', and secondly that this was the way to lasting happiness in the future. Part of the message included reminding those present that during the past year there had been five funerals of young people from the congregation, 'some of them under twenty years of age, and others of them but little past that period'. For Fuller, the lesson was clear: 'None of them seem to have thought much of dying, yet they are gone from the land of the living! Hark! From their tombs I hear the language of solemn warning and counsel!' He closed by pleading with his hearers to come to Christ:

> What shall I say more? Will you, my dear young people, will you drink and be satisfied at the fountain of mercy; a fountain that is wide open and flows freely through our Lord Jesus Christ? You cannot plead the want of sufficient inducements. Ministers, parents, Christians, angels, the faltering voice at death, the solemn assurance of a judgement to come, and, above all, the sounding of the bowels of Jesus Christ, all say, Come.

Ryland recorded that 'many young people' who later believed 'traced their first serious impressions' to these occasions.[39] Fuller wrote to Ryland in March 1810 that he had begun a weekly meeting in his vestry at Kettering for 'earnest' young people, and there were now four waiting for baptism. At one stage he appears to have been meeting with them on both Monday and Friday nights, times that he said were 'much thronged'.[40]

Fuller's evangelistic impulses also drove him to reach out to younger people who were beyond the immediate orbit of his family and the church. Gunton Fuller recorded that, some time in the 1800s (a period when Fuller had very little time for pastoral work amongst his members), his father was devising a scheme to evangelize amongst young lacemakers who worked in Kettering. This involved getting hold of some of the white wrapping paper the girls used and printing some 'little hymns' on them, some of which he planned to compose himself. In a letter to a friend Fuller enthused about the plan: 'Every child who

---

38   *Fuller's Works*, II, pp. 421-26, esp. 425-26. The sermon is n.d..

39   Ryland, *Andrew Fuller*, p. 383.

40   Ryland, *Andrew Fuller*, pp. 251-52.

comes for a small quantity of thread will find it wrapped up in a paper containing a short impressive hymn addressed to its heart.'[41] Not the most plausible of Fuller's schemes, it is unlikely this was ever implemented. But the Kettering pastor's evangelistic concerns are, once again, clear.

Fuller's Expository Preaching

Of course Fuller engaged in a range of pastoral work which was not directly evangelistic, and he covered a variety of topics in his preaching. At one stage Fuller kept a notebook entitled 'Families that attend at the Meeting', in which details of members – their names, families and 'particular cases' – were recorded. Fuller added that a 'review of these may help me in my preaching'. Significantly this book dates from the period before he began work as secretary of the BMS.[42] His sermons included expository preaching which was specifically designed to build up more mature believers, in addition to textual preaching that might be described as more 'inspirational' and more suited to occasional 'hearers'. Ryland listed the biblical books he systematically covered, from the time when he began his habit of regular expository preaching on a Sunday morning in April 1790.[43] His published *Expository Discourses on the Book of Genesis* stand as an example of this type of preaching, as do his *Expository Discourses on the Apocalypse.*[44]

Particularly when expounding Revelation, Fuller took more time in preparation than was his normal practice.[45] Fuller dedicated the published edition of the sermons to his church (as he had done with the volume on Genesis), and he clearly loved his people. And yet even here, as he expounded the scriptures to believers, a concern for the spread of the gospel was never far from the surface. In particular, his New England influenced post-millennialism, with its concomitant belief that great success would 'attend the preaching of the gospel' even before the

---

41   A.G. Fuller, *Men Worth Remembering*, p. 88.

42   August 1788. Ryland, *Andrew Fuller*, p. 381.

43   Ryland, *Andrew Fuller* p. 382. The full list is: Psalms, Isaiah, Joel, Amos, Hosea, Micah, Nahum, Habakkuk, Zephaniah, Jeremiah, Lamentations, Daniel, Haggai, Zechariah, Malachi, Genesis, Matthew, Luke, John, Revelation, Acts, Romans and 1 Corinthians as far as 4.5.

44   *Fuller's Works*, III, pp. 1-198; pp. 201-306. These appeared in 1806 and 1815 respectively, the former originally as a two volume work.

45   A.G. Fuller, *Men Worth Remembering*, p. 61. Cf. Fuller's own comments, *Discourses on the Apocalypse*, in *Fuller's Works*, III, pp. 201-202.

millennium dawned, underpinned these messages.[46] Fuller believed that
he and his hearers were living at the time of the 'pouring out of the
seven vials' described in Revelation 16, and that this period was
immediately prior to the commencement of the millennium.[47] The
pouring out of the vials would be a time 'full of wars and struggles' and
yet also of great victories.[48] As he preached through Revelation Sunday
by Sunday between 1809 and 1810, he was ready to believe that a time
of 'great success' was at hand. He wrote in his opening dedication 'that
we have seen enough, amidst all the troubles of our times, to gladden
our hearts; and trust that our children will see greater things than
these'.[49] Some of what Fuller preached was highly speculative and
makes strange reading today, as does much written on Revelation by
past generations (the Puritans are a prime example).[50] But what is
beyond doubt from these messages is that Fuller delighted in and looked
forward to the spread of the gospel. There is a powerful case for saying
that evangelism always remained to the fore throughout his pastorate.
This was true too, of the wider ministry he exercised.

Fuller's Wider Preaching Ministry

In addition to his work at Kettering Fuller also travelled regularly,
preaching at other churches, both near to home and further afield. A
significant proportion of this, even after 1792, was separate from his
work as secretary of the BMS. Fuller preached at the opening of new
church buildings, to theological students at Bristol and Stepney and on
behalf of various societies, for example The British and Foreign Bible
Society, which was formed in 1804.[51] In particular he was increasingly

---

46   See *Discourses on the Apocalypse*, in *Fuller's Works*, III, e.g., pp. 293-94.

47   Fuller, *Discourses on the Apocalypse*, in *Fuller's Works*, III, p. 391. Cf. the
comments of E.A. Payne, *The Baptist Union: A Short History* (London: Carey Kingsgate
Press, 1959), p. 17.

48   Fuller to J. Saffery, 14 October 1811, 'Andrew Fuller Letters to John Saffery',
Angus Library, Oxford, (II/273).

49   Fuller, *Discourses on the Apocalypse*, in *Fuller's Works*, III, p. 202. The
dedication was not written until 1815, the year of Fuller's death.

50   Cf. the comment by D.A. Carson, *New Testament Commentary Survey*
(Leicester: IVP, 5th edn, 2001), p. 127: 'It is a little known fact that the
Puritans...produced far more commentaries on Revelation than on any other book, most
of them eminently forgettable and mercifully forgotten.' Fuller clearly used some of
these commentaries in his own preparation. There is a strong case for saying that the
present generation is no more discerning!

51   See *Fuller's Works*, I, e.g. pp. 413, 515-21, 391, 417.

invited to give addresses at the ordinations and inductions of new ministers, and Fuller's *Works* contain at least twenty four examples of this type of preaching.[52] On these occasions Fuller often took the opportunity to encourage pastors to preach evangelistically. To quote just one instance, in a message entitled 'The Nature of the Gospel, and the Manner in Which it Ought to be Preached', he urged the unnamed minister to be 'faithful', 'fearless' and full of love or 'great affection' as he declared the gospel. The apostles and Christ himself were the examples as to both the manner and method in preaching. He was to study hard and think deeply, but preach 'plainly' and simply so his hearers could understand. 'Preaching the gospel' was absolutely fundamental to a minister's work.[53] Another sermon, entitled 'Churches should exhibit the Light of the Gospel', shows that he also sought to challenge churches as to their evangelistic responsibilities.[54] 'The end of your existence', Fuller stated, 'is to hold forth the word of life'. This they were to do by supporting their pastor and commending the gospel themselves, particularly by living 'blameless' lives. The latter was, Fuller believed, a 'powerful way of preaching the gospel. It speaks louder than words – louder than thunder.' Whether by word or example, Christ was to be commended.

His major role in promoting evangelism in the churches was doubtless through the impact of his theological works, in particular *The Gospel Worthy* itself. But he could also play a more direct personal role in helping to promote his brand of Evangelical Calvinism in a local church setting. An example of this was when he travelled to give the charge at the induction of Francis Franklin, at what was to become Queens Road Baptist Church in Coventry. The church had had some struggles with issues relative to High Calvinism, but Fuller's involvement in this service was, according to the official history of the church, 'conclusive proof' of where they now stood in 'the evangelistic spectrum'. In 1803 Fuller would return to preach a 'charity sermon' in support of the Sunday School, an event at which £44 was raised.[55] His evangelistic efforts could not be confined to a local church pastorate. In engaging in this sort of work, Fuller was making yet another

---

52   See e.g. *Fuller's Works*, I, pp. 478-509.

53   'The Nature of the Gospel, and the Manner in Which it Ought to be Preached', in *Fuller's Works*, I, pp. 494-96. The sermon is n.d. but internal evidence suggests post 1800.

54   'Churches Should Exhibit the Light of the Gospel' (n.d.), in *Fuller's Works*, I, pp. 531-34. The quotations which follow in this paragraph are from these pages.

55   C. Binfield, *Pastors and People: The Biography of a Baptist Church, Queen's Road, Coventry* (Coventry: Alan Sutton, 1984), pp. 27, 33. Franklin became the church's assistant minister.

contribution to the revitalization of his denomination.

Fuller and the Revival of Particular Baptist Life

That Fuller's ministerial career coincided with a time of significant growth within his denomination is attested by a number of sources. In 1793 Fuller wrote a letter detailing 'the state of religion in Northamptonshire'.[56] This firstly indicated the triumph of Fuller's own brand of Evangelical Calvinism amongst Particular Baptists in the county. Out of 21 churches, there were 4 or 5 who embraced 'what is called the High Calvinist scheme'. These included the Rushden church pastored by William Knowles, the church that we saw opposed Fuller after *The Gospel Worthy* was first published. But the rest, according to Fuller, made 'no scruple' about openly 'exhorting' people to believe the gospel. The county with which both Gill and Brine had been associated was now coming down decisively on the 'affirmative side' of the 'Modern Question'. Ministers could and should offer the gospel indiscriminately to all.[57]

But the letter also indicated something else. The churches which embraced what Fuller here termed 'Moderate Calvinism' were growing. Fuller spoke of a 'readiness discovered in many parts of the county for hearing the gospel', and of a 'considerable increase' among the churches. Indeed he could be more specific, stating that: 'Seven or eight new churches have been raised amongst [us] within the last 20 years.' There is no reason to doubt the figures Fuller gave, particularly as he expected his correspondent, possibly a General Baptist layman, to publish them. When we put this together with the number of people regularly coming to hear Fuller in Kettering, the figures indicate that something highly significant was occurring.

Nor was this growth confined to Northamptonshire. The 1790s saw the publication of several volumes of John Rippon's *Baptist Annual Register*, which provides what Nuttall describes as a 'fine contemporary record of [English Particular Baptist] churches'.[58] The formation of such a comprehensive survey was in itself an indicator of the health and

---

56   G.F. Nuttall, 'The State of Religion in Northamptonshire (1793) by Andrew Fuller', *BQ* 29.4 (October, 1981), pp. 177-79. All quotations and information in this paragraph and the next are from Fuller's letter and Nuttall's introductory remarks. Fuller was writing here of the churches within the county of Northamptonshire, not the Northamptonshire Association as a whole.

57   Nuttall, 'Northamptonshire and the Modern Question, *passim.*

58   G.F. Nuttall, 'The Baptist Churches and Their Ministers: Rippon's Baptist Annual Register', *BQ* 30.8 (October, 1984), pp. 383-87.

confidence of the denomination.[59] In Volume One of the *Register* (covering the period from 1790 to the first part of 1793), there were 326 churches listed; in Volume Three (which covered 1798-1801), 361 churches were recorded by Rippon.[60] These figures can be compared with those quoted in chapter one, which suggested that in the 1750s there were only 150 Calvinistic Baptist churches in England and Wales (in Rippon's surveys the Welsh churches were counted separately and do not appear in the figures quoted above).[61] If these statistics are even approximately right (the complete accuracy of the 1750s figure is open to some question), then something of great significance was happening.[62] The late-eighteenth century was, of course, a time of rapid population growth, but this was certainly outstripped by the growth of the Particular Baptist churches.[63] In addition to his figures Rippon also provided extensive notes, in Volume Three of the *Baptist Annual Register*, on many of the congregations listed. Page after page reveals that many churches were experiencing 'considerable additions', facing 'the pleasing necessity' of enlarging their meeting houses and were increasingly involved in village preaching.[64] It is surely correct to say that a revitalization of Particular Baptist life in England was taking place.

Fuller, as the denomination's leading theologian and one of its leading figures overall, has a significant place in this story. He

---

59   As was the launching of the *Baptist Magazine* in 1809 and the formation of a 'General Union' of (Particular) Baptist churches in 1812. See Payne, *Baptist Union*, pp. 17-19; 20-25.

60   John Rippon, *The Baptist Annual Register*, I (London: Dilly, Button and Thomas, 1793), pp. 8-13; III (London: Button, Conder, Brown et al., 1801), pp. 3-40. Rippon edited the *Baptist Annual Register* from 1790 to 1801. For Rippon, who is also significant because of his contribution to Baptist hymnody, see K.R. Manley, 'John Rippon D.D. (1751-1836) and the Particular Baptists' (DPhil thesis, University of Oxford, 1967), forthcoming as, *'Redeeming Love Proclaim': John Rippon and the Particular Baptists* (Studies in Baptist History and Thought, 12; Carlisle: Paternoster, 2003).

61   Dix, *Strict and Particular*, makes a (rare) mistake when he says that: 'During the eighteenth century the number of Particular Baptist churches grew steadily', although he is correct to speak of a 'marked acceleration in the closing decades of the century', p. 1.

62   Cf. the comments of Payne, *Baptist Union*, p. 19.

63   Bebbington, *Evangelicalism*, p. 21.

64   See Rippon, *Baptist Annual Register*, III, e.g. pp. 5-9 for numerous examples. One of those involved in reaching out in village preaching was Sutcliff in the regions surrounding Olney, another William Steadman from his base at Bradford in the north of England. See James, 'William Steadman', pp. 265-66.

undoubtedly made an important contribution to the revitalization of the denomination. But this renewal of Particular Baptist life was not confined to growth at home; it also, as Nuttall states, involved 'vigorous mission and interest across the oceans'.[65] This too would be part of Fuller's evangelistic ministry. Part of the seed-bed for formation of the BMS was certainly the renewal of theology in which Fuller played such a key role. But important too was the so-called 1784 'Call to Prayer' issued by the Northamptonshire Association.

Fuller was a central figure in association life. As noted in chapter two, his involvement in the Northamptonshire Association had a bearing, both directly and indirectly, on the development of his thought. Clearly, through events like the yearly assembly usually held in the week after Whitsun, it had an impact on his practice too. But Fuller was a net contributor to association life. He preached regularly at association events, as well as being the moderator of the yearly assembly five times.[66] He wrote the annual newsletter to the churches on no less than ten occasions, the first as early as 1782 on 'The Excellence and Utility of the Grace of Hope'; the last in the year of his death, 'On The Situation of The Widows and Orphans of Christian Ministers', clearly with his own family in mind.[67] But it was his involvement in the 'Call to Prayer' that was particularly strategic, and which I will consider here in some detail.

Fuller and the Prayer Call of 1784

The so-called 'Prayer Call of 1784' was a hugely significant event, not only in the life of the Northamptonshire Association, but also in the wider Particular Baptist denomination and beyond. It directly resulted in the establishment of monthly prayer meetings in many churches, specifically to pray for Revival throughout the known world. The 'Call' certainly paved the way for the founding of the BMS,[68] and has been the subject of a number of studies, the most important of which remains that

---

65   Nuttall, 'Baptist Churches and their Ministers', p. 383.

66   Elwyn, *Northamptonshire Baptist Association*, pp. 100-101. The years were 1782, 1795, 1804, 1808 and 1813 respectively.

67   See *Fuller's Works*, III, pp. 308-63, for the texts of these letters. Note also T.S.H. Elwyn, 'Particular Baptists of the Northamptonshire Association as Reflected in the Circular Letters, 1765-1820', Part 1, *BQ* 36.8 (October, 1996), pp. 368-81 / Part 2, 37.1 (January, 1997), pp. 3-19.

68   Stanley, *History of the BMS*, pp. 4-6. See Morris, *Andrew Fuller*, 2nd edn, pp. 95-98, for the view of one of Fuller's contemporaries.

of Ernest Payne.[69] John Sutcliff was clearly the key figure in issuing the 'Prayer Call' to the Northamptonshire Association, but Fuller had an important role too, and the following account seeks to bring this out.

In looking at the background to the 'Call to Prayer', Jonathan Edwards is once again a central figure. In April 1784 John Ryland received, from John Erskine in Edinburgh, a parcel of books which included a treatise written by Edwards entitled *An Humble Attempt to Promote Explicit Agreement and Visible Union of God's People in Extraordinary Prayer*, which had originally been published in 1748.[70] Edwards' *Humble Attempt* was rooted in the movement to establish regular prayer meetings for Revival which had begun in the 1740s and subsequently criss-crossed the atlantic.[71] The so called 'Concert of Prayer' actually began in Scotland, where a number of ministers who were part of the growing trans-atlantic Evangelical network with Edwards, such as John McLaurin of Glasgow and William McCullough of Cambuslang, had committed themselves and their churches to pray for Revival.[72] Edwards sought to set up something similar in New England, and a sermon he preached on the subject in 1747 was later revised, expanded and published as the *Humble Attempt*. Ryland was deeply impressed with what he read and lost no time sending the work to Sutcliff and Fuller.[73]

In his treatise Edwards urged that regular prayer meetings be established, specifically so that 'fervent and constant' prayer to God could be made for the 'effusions of the blessed Spirit' which would lead to the rapid growth of God's Kingdom.[74] His appeal was based solidly

---

69   E.A. Payne, *The Prayer Call of 1784* (London: Kingsgate Press, 1941). See also Haykin, *One Heart and Soul*, pp. 153-71.

70   For the text see *Edwards Works*, Hickman (ed.), II, pp. 280-312.

71   For details see M.J. Crawford, *Seasons of Grace, Colonial New England's Revival Tradition in its British Context* (Oxford: Oxford University Press, 1991), pp. 229-31.

72   See Susan O'Brien, 'Eighteenth Century Publishing in Transatlantic Evangelicalism', in M.A. Noll, D.W. Bebbington and G.A. Rawlyk (eds), *Evangelicalism: Comparative Studies in Popular Protestantism in North America, The British Isles and Beyond, 1700-1990* (Oxford: Oxford University Press, 1994), pp. 41, 45, for the transatlantic Evangelical network. Cf. W.R. Ward, 'Baptists and the Transformation of the Church, 1780-1830', *BQ* 25.4 (October 1973), pp. 170-71, who refers to what he terms 'the literary freemasonry' of the Revival.

73   Ryland, *Andrew Fuller*, p. 98 n. The *Memoir* of Edwards by Sereno Dwight, written in 1830, contains a letter from Edwards to Erskine where he promises to send him a copy of the *Humble Attempt*. See, *Edwards' Works*, Hickman (ed.), II, p. xcv.

74   *Edwards' Works*, Hickman (ed.), II, p. 312. All the following quotations from the *Humble Attempt* are from pp. 280-312 of this edition.

on scripture, but he also referred in detail to the times in which he and his readers were living. Edwards viewed his age both as 'one of great apostasy' and as a 'day of the wonderful works of God'. Examples of 'spiritual calamities' included the persecution of the Huguenots in France and what he saw as a general 'deluge of vice and immorality'. Examples of God's works of 'power and mercy' included the British defeat of French forces in North America and especially the spiritual Revivals which had recently occurred in both Europe and the New World. Edwards believed that these 'late remarkable religious awakenings...[should] justly encourage us in prayer for the promised glorious and universal outpourings of the Spirit of God.' The balance between divine sovereignty (God sending his Spirit) and human responsibility (the need to appropriate God's blessing through prayer), was typical of Edwards. But it is important to underscore the fact that his argument was tied not only to biblical theology but also to his reading of the 'signs of the times'. The *Humble Attempt* was rooted in the cultural, political and ecclesiastical context of the eighteenth century.

A phrase like 'the promised glorious and universal outpourings of the Spirit of God' hints at Edwards' optimistic post-millennial eschatology, with his accompanying belief in the imminence of 'the latter day glory'. This was allied with some speculative interpretations of biblical prophecy. These included projections that the purity of the Protestant church would be restored between 1750 and 1800, that Roman Catholics would come to embrace the gospel between 1800 and 1850, and that Christ's millennial reign could possibly begin round about the year 2000.[75] The Northamptonshire men wanted to distance themselves from some of these more questionable aspects of Edwards' thinking. Later, when Sutcliff brought out an English edition of the *Humble Attempt* in 1789, he took the opportunity to make this explicit. 'As to the author's ingenious observations on the prophecies', he stated, 'we entirely leave them to the reader's judgement'.[76] This is another indication of the independence and, most would say, discernment of Fuller, Ryland and Sutcliff. But they nevertheless broadly shared Edwards' eschatology, a point that will already be clear in Fuller's case from the discussion of his preaching on Revelation.[77] These views, particularly the belief that

---

75   *Humble Attempt*, in *Edwards' Works*, Hickman (ed.), II, e.g. p. 306. For a detailed discussion of Edwards' millennial views see J.A. De Jong, *As The Waters Cover the Sea, Millennial Expectations in the Rise of Anglo-American Missions, 1640-1810* (Kampen: J.H. Kok NV, 1970), pp. 124-37.

76   Sutcliff's Preface to the English edition in *Edwards' Works*, Hickman (ed.), II, pp. 278-79.

77   Fuller's expositions on Revelation were certainly influenced by the *Humble*

the sovereign God was about to work in an unprecedented way, proved a great motivation to prayer and action.[78]

Whatever reservations they may have had as to some of the details, the Northamptonshire pastors were clearly struck by the central appeal of the *Humble Attempt* and the basis on which it was made. There had already been concerns expressed in the association, for example in 1782, about the need for prayer given the state of the churches and the nation. Its leading figures were clearly fertile ground for the challenge of Edwards' words. Yet Payne is surely right that it was the *Humble Attempt* itself that was primarily instrumental in 'stirring individuals and churches' to prayer.[79] A number of the association's key men were determined to respond to what they had read. They met together on 11 May, a meeting that Fuller recorded in his diary: 'Devoted this day to fasting and prayer, in conjunction with several other ministers, who have agreed thus to spend the second Tuesday of every other month, to seek the revival of real religion, and the extension of Christ's kingdom in the world.' This was an important preliminary meeting and Fuller appears to have kept this personal commitment to bi-monthly prayer and fasting.[80] The real breakthrough, however, came at the annual association meeting which took place at Nottingham on the 2 and 3 June.

Fuller preached one of the sermons on the opening day of this significant meeting, taking as his text 2 Corinthians 5.7, 'We walk by faith not by sight'. This was later published as *The Nature and Importance of Walking by Faith*.[81] The message was wide ranging, but contained two elements that are particularly worth noting. The first was a strong challenge to those present to be concerned for 'the interest of Christ' in the whole world. The prophecies of the Bible teach the church to look forward to a time 'when the earth shall be full of the knowledge of the Lord, as the waters cover the sea'. The situation in the world was currently very different from this, but there was no place for despair.

Attempt, see *Fuller's Works*, III, p. 251, for an explicit reference. The fact that the French revolution occurred in 1789, the year that the *Humble Attempt* was being reprinted, would only have reinforced the view that God was shaking the world at large.

78   For the connection between post-millennialism and the modern missionary movement see De Jong, *As the Waters Cover the Sea*, *passim*. On a more popular level, I.H. Murray, *The Puritan Hope, Revival and The Interpretation of Prophecy* (Edinburgh: Banner of Truth, 1971), pp. 131-55, deals with the BMS in some detail.

79   Payne, *Prayer Call of 1784*, pp. 4-5.

80   Ryland, *Andrew Fuller*, pp. 96-98.

81   *The Nature and Importance of walking by Faith* (Northampton: T. Dicey, 1784), in *Fuller's Works*, I, pp. 117-34. The following quotations are taken from pp. 131 and 134.

'God forbid!' declared Fuller, 'The vision is yet for an appointed time... Let us take encouragement, in the present day of small things, by looking forward.' The similarities between Fuller's preaching and the general argument in the *Humble Attempt* are striking.[82]

The second element of Fuller's address to highlight is his call to 'earnest and united prayer'. He appealed to his hearers: 'Let us pray much for an outpouring of God's Spirit upon our ministers and churches, and not upon those only of our own connexion and denomination, but upon all that in every place call upon the name of Jesus Christ our Lord, both theirs and ours!' Fuller's world vision was once again clearly evident, as was an element of Evangelical 'catholicity' as Fuller urged prayer for those who were not Particular Baptists.[83] Fuller was echoing Edwards' 'Call to Prayer' and re-applying it strongly to his own context. The conclusion to his message contained one of his most passionate appeals:

> Christians, Ministers, Brethren, all of us! Let us realize the subject. Let us pray, preach and hear, and do everything we do with eternity in view! Let us deal much with Christ and with invisible realities. Let us, whenever called, freely deny ourselves for his sake, and trust him to make up the loss. Let us not faint under the present difficulties, but consider them as opportunities afforded us to glorify God... In one word let us fight the good fight of faith, and lay hold of eternal life!

When Fuller's association sermon was published later that year, he appended to it some notes which he entitled, 'Persuasives to General Union in Extraordinary Prayer for the Revival and Extent of Real Religion'. Fuller set out seven specific points:

> I. Consider Christ's readiness to hear and answer prayer, especially on these subjects.
>
> II. Consider what the Lord has done in times past, and that in answer to prayer.
>
> III. Let the present religious state of the world be considered to this end.
>
> IV. Consider what the Lord has promised to do for the church in times to come.

---

82   Cf. Haykin, *One Heart and Soul*, p. 163. Clearly the *Humble Attempt* made a big impression on Fuller.

83   Although, as I shall have cause to note again in chapter six, Fuller was not as ecumenically minded as some of his colleagues. This was particularly marked as far as Fuller's attitude to Wesleyan Methodists was concerned. See e.g. Fuller to W. Ward, 16 July 1809, Fuller Letters (4/5/2), where Wesley is described as a 'dishonest man' and a 'crafty Jesuit'. By contrast Fuller's friend Samuel Pearce was prepared to preach in Methodist chapels. See Payne, 'Some Samuel Pearce Documents', p. 30.

V. If we have any regard to the welfare of our countrymen, connection and friends, let this stimulate us in our work.

VI. Consider what is suggested is so very small.

And lastly. It will not be in vain, whatever be the immediate and apparent issue of it.[84]

As Thornton Elwyn states, these 'make abundantly clear what was in the mind of the people [i.e. the leading ministers] at Nottingham'.[85] Fuller was an important figure in the issuing of the 'Call to Prayer'. He was also prepared to make his own personal response to the challenge that he himself had been involved in throwing down.

The following day, after having referred directly to Fuller's sermon, Sutcliff launched the association's own 'Prayer Concert'. Member churches were urged to establish meetings, on the first Monday of each month, the 'grand object' of which would be prayer for Revival. Less than two months had passed between Ryland receiving the *Humble Attempt* to the 'Call' being issued. Both the world vision and the commitment to pray for denominations other than their own, which had been important in Fuller's sermon, were present in the circular letter that Sutcliff wrote. Churches should not focus their prayers too narrowly. Rather, 'let the whole interest of the redeemer be affectionately remembered'. The strong and unambiguous missionary thrust was also plainly stated: 'Let...the spread of the gospel to the most distant parts of the habitable globe be the object of your most fervent requests', the 'Call' declared.[86] This breadth of vision, particularly the rejection of a narrow denominational emphasis, was a hallmark of Evangelicalism. The missionary emphasis, which was absolutely central, was highly significant in the light of later developments.

On his return to Kettering Fuller quickly set up a monthly meeting along the lines suggested. For the first few of these Fuller sought to stir up those who had come by reading passages from the *Humble Attempt*. This was followed by opportunities for singing and for extempore prayer, focused on the over-arching theme of Revival. There are a number of references to these meetings in his diary, and it appears that Fuller found these times to be both a challenge and an encouragement. On 6 December 1784 he recorded that they had had an 'affecting meeting of prayer' for the 'revival of real religion'. On this occasion he

---

84 See Elwyn, *Northamptonshire Baptist Association*, p. 17; Payne, *Prayer Call of 1784*, p. 2. These seven points are not appended to *Walking by Faith* in the American edition of *Fuller's Works*.

85 Elwyn, *Northamptonshire Baptist Association*, p. 17.

86 Haykin, *One Heart and Soul*, pp. 164-65; Elwyn, *Northamptonshire Baptist Association*, p. 17.

found 'much pleasure in singing', and also 'freedom to God in prayer'. On 7 March 1785 he wrote that he 'enjoyed Divine assistance at the monthly prayer meeting, in speaking on continuing in prayer, and in going to prayer, though I felt wretchedly cold before I began'.[87]

Within a few years the 'Call to Prayer' had spread beyond the boundaries of the Northamptonshire Association. For example, in 1786 it was taken up by Particular Baptist churches in Warwickshire and in 1790 by the Western Association. The re-igniting of the 'Concert of Prayer' had led to a significant movement. It was yet another sign of the life and vigour that was to increasingly characterize the English Particular Baptists, not just in the Northamptonshire Association but in many other places too.[88] But for Fuller perhaps the most significant development was the broadening of his horizons. In the light of future events a diary entry for 3 September can be seen as significant. Again the year was 1784: 'Employed nearly all day in searching out Paul's journeys into Asia, Macedonia and Greece. O that I might enter into the spirit of that great man of God! Felt much pleasure in this day's work.'[89] Fuller, having developed an evangelistic ministry in his local church context, was now developing a similar concern for world-wide mission and Revival.

Conclusion

This chapter has shown that, particularly after he moved to Kettering in 1782, Fuller developed a pastoral ministry the hallmark of which was an evangelistic concern. Moreover, as his ministry progressed, his evangelistic horizons were to widen, particularly as a result of the Northamptonshire Association's 1784 'Call to Prayer'. Through involvement in this Fuller developed a new breadth of vision as to what could be achieved, both at home and abroad. Once again the work of Edwards, mediated to Fuller and the other Northamptonshire men in his circle through the trans-atlantic Evangelical network, was important as Fuller and his friends responded to the unique challenges and opportunities of the late-eighteenth century. The Revival of Particular Baptist life was part and parcel of the wider Evangelical Revival. That such a Revival was taking place among the English Particular Baptists is certain. Decline had been arrested and remarkable growth had taken its place. In the early 1790s, this growth was about to enter a new phase

---

87   Ryland, *Andrew Fuller*, pp. 103-105; cf. T. George, *Faithful Witness: The Life and Mission of William Carey* (Leicester: IVP, 1991), pp. 48-49.

88   Ryland, *Andrew Fuller*, p. 98; Payne, *Prayer Call of 1784*, p. 11.

89   Ryland, *Andrew Fuller*, p. 100.

with the formation of the BMS. Through the work of the mission, Fuller's new world focus would be given practical expression.

CHAPTER SIX

Fuller and the Baptist Missionary Society

I feel that willingness to exert myself

Late in 1792, Fuller called at the London home of the Evangelical Clergyman Thomas Scott. Fuller spoke of the impression made by his fellow Particular Baptist William Carey, when he had preached at the Northamptonshire Association meeting on 30 May earlier that year. Carey had taken as his text Isaiah 54.2-3: 'Enlarge the place of thy tent, and let them stretch forth the curtains of thine habitations: spare not, lengthen thy cords, and strengthen thy stakes.' Carey's two points, as Fuller related them, were that they should '*expect* great things' and then '*attempt* great things'. This was presented to Scott by Fuller as being one of the key events leading to the formation of the Baptist Missionary Society.[1]

The 'Particular Baptist Society for Propagating the Gospel Among the Heathen' (henceforth the BMS), was founded on 2 October 1792. William Carey was not only the central figure in its formation but also its first missionary, eventually arriving in India with his companion John Thomas (1757-1800) on 10 November 1793.[2] Fuller had called on

---

[1]   John Scott, *The Life of Thomas Scott* (London: Seeley, 1836), p. 115. This meeting between Scott and Fuller is also mentioned in Murray, *The Puritan Hope*, p. 130.

[2]   For Carey see especially E. Carey, *Memoir of William Carey, DD* (London: Jackson and Walford, 1836); S.P. Carey, *Memoir of William Carey, DD* (London: Hodder and Stoughton, 1923); George, *Faithful Witness*. It could be argued that technically Thomas was the first missionary, as it was Thomas who was the first to be accepted by the home committee when it met at Kettering on 9 January 1793, with Carey then volunteering to go as his companion. But this would be to ignore a number of factors, not least that the BMS had been formed largely to put into effect what Carey had proposed. See Stanley, *History of the BMS*, pp. 16-17. For Thomas see C.B. Lewis, *The Life of John Thomas* (London: Macmillan, 1873).

Scott in his capacity as secretary of the new society, not just to share information but also to seek a donation, and his 'collecting book' shows that Scott did indeed become a contributor.[3] In his account of Fuller's visit, Scott's son and biographer hinted at the huge significance of what was happening. Where the BMS was leading, other societies, like the London Missionary Society and the Church Missionary Society, would soon follow.[4] Doubtless Baptist historians have sometimes claimed too much for the BMS, and to talk of Carey as the 'father of modern missions' is in many ways misleading.[5] Thomas and Carey were not the first Protestant missionaries to be sent out by European churches, and Carey and Fuller were themselves influenced by the efforts of American missionaries such as David Brainerd, as we have already seen. Roman Catholicism had been active in overseas mission for many years.

Yet despite all this, there is no doubt that something of huge importance *was* happening. As Stanley states: '[The] early missionaries of the BMS were among the first impressions of a renewed endeavour by Western Christians to refashion the rest of the globe in a Christian image – a movement which was to have profound implications for the history of the non-European world over the next two centuries.'[6] There were precedents, but nevertheless the founding of the BMS marks a turning point. By 1792 the Particular Baptists were, as noted in chapter five, growing strongly and no longer in danger of becoming the

---

3   J. Wilson, *Memoir of Thomas Wilson, Esq.* (London: John Snow, 2nd edn, 1849), pp. 126-27 n., cited by Stanley, *History of the BMS*, p. 21. Many other Evangelical Anglicans were supportive. See e.g. B. Wood to Fuller, 15 December 1812, Fuller Chapel Letters, II, 65, where Wood stated: 'I believe I have been a subscriber to your mission ever since 1792.' Following the fire at the missionaries' base of operations at Serampore in India, in March 1812, Wood collected £130 from his congregation for the continuing work of the BMS.

4   Scott, *Thomas Scott*, p. 115. The Congregational LMS was formed in 1795, the Anglican CMS in 1799. Thomas Scott was to be the first secretary of the CMS, which was known as 'The Society for Missions in Africa and the East' until 1812. Carey had met Scott several times when the latter was Curate at Olney between 1781-85.

5   Some misleading historiography on this subject, from Baptists and others, is summarized by W.H. Brackney, 'The Baptist Missionary Society in Proper Context: Some Reflections on the Larger Voluntary Religious Tradition', *BQ* 34.8 (October, 1992), p. 364. Young, 'Fuller and the Developing Modern Missions Movement', is one who falls into this trap. See e.g. pp. 2-3 of his Abstract where he states: 'it is a commonplace that the modern missions movement had its real beginning with the formation of the Baptist Missionary Society.'

6   Stanley, *History of the BMS*, p. 1. Stanley summarizes European Protestant missionary activity up to 1792, pp. 1-2. Cf. M.R. Watts, *The Dissenters. 2: The Expansion of Evangelical Nonconformity* (Oxford: Clarendon Press, 1995), pp. 13-14.

'dunghill' that Fuller had once feared. From this position of renewed strength and vigour they were about to be involved in something of global significance.

The formation and early years of the BMS constitutes a vast area of research, and there is a wealth of primary and secondary material to help in this task.[7] Fuller's own role was multi-faceted and wide ranging, and therefore a comprehensive account of his involvement is beyond the scope of this study. What this chapter shows, by focusing on certain key areas, is that Fuller's contribution was highly significant. It was a contribution that greatly extended his evangelistic ministry; indeed at times he was pushed almost to breaking point as he gave himself in unceasing activity to the work of the mission.

Fuller and the Founding of the BMS

The key figure in the formation of the BMS was certainly William Carey, as Ryland[8] and also Fuller himself acknowledged. 'The origins of the society', Fuller said, 'will be found in the workings of our brother Carey's mind'.[9] Carey and Fuller first met at the 1782 Northamptonshire Association meeting at Olney, when Carey was only twenty one years old, and 'still feeling his way to the Baptist position'.[10] But evidence that Fuller had a particularly important role in the theological formation of the younger man is lacking. It was Robert Hall Sr's *Help to Zion's Travellers*, published in 1781 four years before *The Gospel Worthy*, that was probably the most important extra-biblical work that Carey read. 'I do not remember ever to have read a book with such raptures' he said, and years later he was to inform Fuller that 'its doctrines are the choice of my heart to this day'.[11] By the time *The Gospel Worthy* was published, Carey had already imbibed the warm Evangelical Calvinism

---

7   See the list of MS sources in E.D. Potts, *British Baptist Missionaries in India, 1793-1837* (Cambridge: Cambridge University Press, 1967), pp. 249-67. See also E.A. Payne, 'Carey and his Biographers', *BQ* 19.1 (January, 1961), pp. 4-12. The authoritative history of the society is by Stanley, *History of the BMS*.

8   Ryland, *Andrew Fuller*, pp. 147-48.

9   *Periodical Accounts Relative to the Baptist Missionary Society*, 1, (Clipstone: J.W. Morris, 1800 [1794]), p. 1. See also E.F. Clipsham, 'Andrew Fuller and the Baptist Mission', *Foundations*, 10.1 (January, 1967), p. 4. Clipsham attempts what he terms a 'tentative appraisal' of Fuller's role in this brief, but suggestive study.

10   Payne, *Prayer Call of 1784* , p. 4.

11   E. Carey, *William Carey*, pp. 15-16. Cf. Brown, *English Baptists*, p. 116; Haykin, 'The Elder Robert Hall', 1', p. 20. Carey probably read *Help to Zion's Travellers* in 1782-3.

by then prevalent amongst the leading figures of the Northamptonshire Association. Doyle Young's argument, that 'Fuller, no less than Carey, should carry the title "Father of Modern Missions"', is clearly misleading.[12]

This is not to say that Fuller did not have a significant role in the genesis of the BMS. Once again one of Fuller's sermons was important. This was the address he gave at the Clipstone ministers' meeting held on 27 April 1791, and referred to in the previous chapter. As noted already, the original title of this message was 'The Instances, Evil, And Tendency of Delay, in the Concerns of Religion', and before giving his stirring evangelistic appeal, Fuller had some points to make to those who said that 'the time has not yet come' for world mission.[13] He suggested that it was because of the prevailing 'procrastinating spirit' that 'so few and so feeble efforts had been made for the propagation of the gospel in the world'. The argument which followed was powerful and obviously had a profound effect on many of those who heard him and many others who later read the message in its printed form. Referring to the 'great commission' of Matthew 28.19-20, Fuller stated:

> When the Lord Jesus commissioned his apostles, he commanded them to go and teach 'all nations' and preach the gospel to 'every creature'; and that notwithstanding the difficulties and oppositions that would lie in their way. The apostles executed their commission with assiduity and fidelity; but, since their days, we seem to sit down half contented that the greater part of the world should remain in ignorance and idolatry. Some noble efforts have indeed been made; but they are small in number, when compared with the magnitude of the object.

Fuller had just stopped short of saying that Matthew 28.19-20 was binding on all believers in every age, although it could be argued that this was implicit in the point he was making. The apostles had taken the gospel to 'all nations'; Fuller was increasingly convinced of the need for similar action in his own day. He continued:

> Are the souls of men of less value than heretofore? No. Is Christianity less true or less important than in former ages? This will not be pretended. Are there no opportunities for societies, or individuals, in Christian nations, to convey the gospel to the heathen? This cannot be pleaded as long as opportunities are found

---

12   Young, 'Fuller and the Developing Modern Missions Movement', p. 246. The title 'Father of Modern Missions' should not strictly be applied to Carey either, as has already been noted. Although guilty of overstatement, Doyle is, however, quite correct in pointing out that Fuller's role in the early years of the BMS was crucial.

13   Fuller, *Pernicious Consequences of Delay*, in *Fuller's Works*, I, pp. 145-51. All subsequent quotations from this sermon are from these pages.

to trade with them, yea, and (what is a disgrace to the name of Christians) to buy
them, and sell them, and treat them with worse than savage barbarity? We have
opportunities in abundance; the improvement of navigation, the maritime and
commercial turn of this country, furnish us with these; and it deserves to be
considered whether this is not a circumstance that renders it a duty peculiarly
binding on us.

Fuller's appeal was predicated on the eternal truth, relevance and
power of the gospel. But it was also tied to the circumstances of the age
in which he and his hearers lived. Rather than being 'impracticable',
real opportunities had opened up for taking the gospel to unreached
peoples, opportunities which Christians in late-eighteenth century
Britain were particularly well placed to exploit.[14] Also worth noting at
this point are Carey's words, that it was the accounts of Captain Cook's
voyages to Australia and the South Seas that were 'the first thing that
engaged my mind to think of missions'.[15] Thus the founding of the BMS
can only be understood in its late-eighteenth century context. With an
allusion to the 1784 Prayer Call, Fuller further drove home his appeal
for action:

> We *pray* for the conversion and salvation of the world, and yet neglect the
> ordinary *means* by which those ends have been used to be accomplished. It
> pleased God, heretofore, by the foolishness of preaching, to save them that
> believed; and there is reason to think it will still please God to work by that
> distinguished means. Ought we not then at least to try by some means to convey
> more of the good news of salvation to the world around us than has hitherto been
> conveyed? The encouragement to the heathen is still in force, *"Whoever shall call
> upon the name of the Lord shall be saved:* but how shall they call on him in whom
> they have not believed? and how shall they believe in him whom they have not
> heard? and how shall they hear without a preacher? and how shall they preach
> except they be sent?"

---

14   Fuller would later extend this argument to include believers in North America.
Writing in 1806 to a Philadelphia ship owner, Robert Ralston, he stated: 'Of all the
nations upon earth, I think it is the duty of Britain and North America to disseminate the
gospel. We have more commerce with mankind, more gospel knowledge, more liberty
and more wealth, than perhaps any other nation', *The Last Remains of Andrew Fuller:
Sermons, Essays, Letters, and Other Miscellaneous Papers, not included in his
Published Works* (Philadelphia: American Baptist Publication Society, 1856), pp. 287-
88, cited by Haykin (ed.), *Armies of the Lamb*, p. 211-12, who records that Ralston was
a staunch supporter of the BMS.

15   E. Carey, *William Carey*, p. 18; Stanley, *History of the BMS*, p. 8. Probably
these were the accounts of Cook's second and third voyages, published in 1784.

The twin emphases, on divine sovereignty and human responsibility, were by now absolutely typical of Fuller. Prayer was vital, but it had to be accompanied by action, for although it was God who did the work he worked through 'ordinary means', in particular the 'foolishness of preaching'. As he was later to say, 'The Hindoos [sic] can never be converted by mere *human means*, though we are equally persuaded they will never be converted without them'.[16] Fuller was applying the thoroughgoing Evangelical Calvinism of *The Gospel Worthy* to the subject of overseas mission. His central message to his Particular Baptist audience was clear. The time to make a real effort to convey 'more of the good news of salvation to the world around us had come'. As he was later to write to John Fawcett of Hebden Bridge, 'we now think we ought to do something more than pray'.[17] As he bluntly put it at Clipstone, 'we wait for we know not what'.

The importance of Fuller's Clipstone message for the founding of the BMS is brought out in all the major accounts,[18] as is that of a sermon by John Sutcliff, *Jealousy for the Lord of Hosts Illustrated*, that was preached on the same day.[19] After dinner that evening Carey proposed that something should be done, immediately, to set up a mission society. The fact that this did not happen there and then has been portrayed by some of Carey's biographers as showing that the leading Northamptonshire ministers, including Fuller, were dragging their feet. Indeed, 'they would not rise and build the Lord's house', according to S. Pearce Carey.[20] But, as Stanley points out, this is inherently unlikely in view of what had just been preached. The delay was almost certainly due more to practical considerations, although Carey was doubtless frustrated by it.[21] After the Clipstone meeting another key moment came in May 1792 when, following the active encouragement of Fuller, Ryland and Sutcliff, Carey was ready to publish himself on the subject of world mission.

Carey's famous pamphlet was entitled *An Enquiry into the Obligations of Christians to use Means for the Conversion of the*

---

16   *Fuller's Works*, II, p. 821.

17   Fuller to J. Fawcett, 28 January 1793, in Fawcett Jr, *John Fawcett*, p. 294. Fuller wrote at least fifteen almost identical letters to Baptist ministers all over the country in the latter half of January 1793. See Stanley, *History of the BMS*, p. 17.

18   See e.g. Morris, *Andrew Fuller*, 2nd edn, p. 103.

19   This appears to be Sutcliff's only extant sermon, published later in 1791. See Haykin, *One Heart and Soul*, pp. 206-10, where the full text of the message is included in an appendix, pp. 355-65.

20   S.P. Carey, *William Carey*, p. 69.

21   See the discussion in Stanley, *History of the BMS*, pp. 10-11.

Heathens.[22] Stanley states that some of Carey's language 'corresponded closely to a passage in Fuller's April 1791 sermon on the dangerous tendency of delay'.[23] The particular example of this that Stanley notes is on page eight of the *Enquiry*. Carey stated that 'the work (of world mission) has not been taken up or prosecuted of late years, except by a few individuals, with the zeal and perseverance with which the primitive Christians went about it'. He continued:

> It seems as if many thought the commission [i.e. the 'great commission', Matthew 28.19] was sufficiently put in execution by what the apostles and others have done; that we have enough to do to attend to the salvation of our own countrymen; and that, if God intends the salvation of the heathen, he will some way or other bring them to the gospel, or the gospel to them. It is thus that multitudes sit at ease, and give themselves no concern about the greater part of their fellow sinners, who, to this day, are lost in ignorance and idolatry.[24]

Fuller in the *Instances, Evil, And Tendency of Delay* had spoken of 'the few and feeble efforts [that] have been made for the propagation of the gospel in the world', referred to the work of the apostles and the 'great commission', and spoke scathingly of those who put things off to 'another time'.[25] There are a number of other similarities too, all within the space of a few pages. Was Carey copying Fuller? That Carey was drawing from Fuller's Clipstone sermon is, in fact, by no means certain. It is possible that Fuller had borrowed from Carey rather than vice versa, given that Fuller had seen and critiqued an early MS of the *Enquiry* before he had preached at Clipstone.[26] Moreover, Carey daringly argued that the 'great commission' was still 'binding' on present day disciples, and did so at length.[27] This was a theme that Fuller had not developed in his Clipstone sermon. The *Enquiry* was very much Carey's own work. Nevertheless, on balance it is probable that Carey drew on Fuller's sermon at least to some extent (note especially Carey's comment: 'It has been said that some learned divines have proved from Scripture that the time is not yet come that the heathen

22   W. Carey, *An Enquiry into the Obligations for Christians to use Means for the Conversion of the Heathens* (London: Kingsgate Press, 1961 [1792]). The text is also reproduced in George, *Faithful Witness*, pp. E.1-57. Subsequent references are from the London edn.

23   Stanley, *History of the BMS*, p. 12.

24   Carey, *Enquiry*, p. 8.

25   *Fuller's Works*, pp. 147-48. For more parallels see Carey's *Enquiry*, pp. 12-13.

26   As Stanley notes, *History of the BMS*, p. 12.

27   Carey, *Enquiry*, especially pp. 6-13.

should be converted...').[28] Once again, Fuller's influence is highlighted.

Carey went on to preach his celebrated sermon on Isaiah 54.2-3 at the annual association meeting held at Friar Lane, Nottingham, on Wednesday 30 May 1792. His motto has passed into Baptist folklore as 'Expect Great things from God; Attempt great things for God,' but probably the shorter title that Fuller reported to Scott, and referred to subsequently,[29] was accurate.[30] At the business meeting the following morning it seemed once again that no firm proposal to form a society would be made. But, with Carey's prompting, it was Fuller who submitted the following resolution: 'that a plan be prepared against the next ministers' meeting at Kettering, for forming a Baptist society for propagating the Gospel among the Heathen.'[31]

Consequently when the BMS was finally formed, on 2 October 1792, the founding meeting took place in Fuller's own town.[32] At least fourteen men crammed themselves (the dimensions of the room were twelve feet by ten), into the back parlour of the home of Martha Wallis, widow of the deacon Beeby Wallis who had been influential in Fuller first coming to Kettering. In addition to Fuller one of his current deacons, Joseph Timms, was also present, probably acting as the nominal 'host'.[33] Fuller was the 'natural choice' to act as the society's secretary and was duly appointed at this meeting.[34] His part in the formation of the BMS had been a significant one. His role in the following years was to be greater still.

---

28   Carey, *Enquiry*, p. 12.

29   Cf. Fuller to J. Fawcett, 30 August 1793, Fuller Letters (4/5/1), where Fuller recorded Carey's headings as: '1. Let us *expect* great things; II. Let us *attempt* great things.' Fuller continued: 'I feel the use of his sermon to this day. Let us pray much, hope much, expect much, labour much; an eternal weight of glory awaits us!'

30   See E.A. Payne, 'John Dyer's Memoir of Carey', *BQ* 22.6 (April, 1968), pp. 326-27; A.C. Smith, 'The Spirit and Letter of Carey's Catalytic Watchword: A Study in the Transmission of Baptist Tradition', *BQ* 33 (1989-90), pp. 226-37, although Ryland, *Andrew Fuller*, p. 150, has the longer title. The full text of Carey's sermon has not been preserved.

31   Rippon (ed.), *Baptist Annual Register*, I, pp. 375, 419. See also Stanley, *History of the BMS*, p. 14.

32   See *Periodical Accounts*, 1, pp. 3-4, for details of this meeting and the text of the resolutions passed.

33   S.P. Carey, *William Carey*, pp. 88-93; *Periodical Accounts*, 1, pp. 3-4. There were only thirteen subscribers, but Carey does not appear on this list and he was certainly present. Probably he was too poor to afford a subscription.

34   Clipsham, 'Andrew Fuller and the Baptist Mission', p. 5.

Fuller's Role as Secretary of the BMS

As the secretary of the BMS, from its inception to his death in 1815, Fuller was to make a massive contribution to the Society. His self-understanding of his task is revealed in an image that would be picked up by most biographers, both of Fuller and Carey. Ryland recorded that Fuller, whilst on a journey with a 'confidential friend', had remarked:

> Our undertaking to India really appeared to me, on its commencement, to be somewhat like a few men, who were deliberating about the importance of penetrating into a deep mine, which had never before been explored. We had no one to guide us; and while we were thus deliberating, Carey, as it were, said, 'Well, I will go down, if you will hold the rope'. But before he went down...he as it seemed to me, took an oath from each of us, at the mouth of the pit, to this effect – that 'while we lived, we should never let go of the rope'.[35]

The phrases 'as it were' and 'as it seemed to me' probably indicate that the rope holding image originated with Fuller rather than Carey. Certainly it was Fuller, out of the original founders, who took his role in supporting Carey, Thomas and subsequent missionaries most seriously, and no one in Britain made a contribution which even approached his in terms of its significance. As Brackney puts it, Fuller was the key 'executive', who became the 'voluntary superintendent in the operation of the society'.[36]

As secretary Fuller issued the regular *Periodical Accounts* of the Society[37] and supplied missionary news to Rippon's *Baptist Annual Register*, as well as to the *Evangelical Magazine* and *Baptist Magazine*.[38] He also took the lead role in the selection of missionaries, and wrote regularly to those in the field.[39] All this was in addition to his work promoting the BMS through voluminous letter writing and regular speaking engagements. These included short visits to individuals and churches, together with longer tours which would see him covering vast

---

35   Ryland, *Andrew Fuller*, p. 157. Cf. Laws, *Andrew Fuller*, whose work was subtitled *Pastor, Theologian, Ropeholder*. The 'confidential friend' was almost certainly Ryland himself.

36   Brackney, 'BMS in Proper Context', p. 370.

37   Although this was originally done by Samuel Pearce until his death in 1799, Ryland *Andrew Fuller*, p. 147.

38   See the (incomplete) list of articles in Ryland, *Andrew Fuller*, 1st edn, pp. 230-35. Ryland omitted this list from the second edition.

39   The bound volume containing the transcriptions of Fuller's Letters to Serampore is 600 pages long.

distances as he traversed the British Isles. He also 'championed' the cause of Christian missions, during a time where the right to engage in missionary work overseas was regularly under serious threat. There are many areas here that could be followed up in detail. In attempting to assess Fuller's role I will focus in particular on his theological contribution, his work as a political apologist and his journeys to promote the cause in the churches. Once again the treatment will be thematic rather than chronological, and I will work through each of these three areas in turn.

Fuller's Theological Contribution

E.F. Clipsham, in his article 'Andrew Fuller and the Baptist Mission', argues that Fuller played a vital theological role for the BMS. He quotes B. Grey Griffith: '[Fuller] was pre-eminently the thinker, and no movement can go far without a thinker.'[40] Fuller was indeed in a unique position to influence the theological direction of the young society. This was something he did in a number of ways, particularly through regular correspondence with those who had been sent overseas. Clipsham highlights four areas where Fuller made a particular contribution.

Firstly, Clipsham states that Fuller emphasized that 'God has uniquely and finally revealed himself in Jesus Christ'. Secondly, Fuller was clear that 'In the gospel, God is freely offering Christ to the world' (with the corollary that the missionaries too must offer Christ). If the first point was hardly a matter of debate amongst Particular Baptists, the second certainly had been, and continued to be an issue for a significant minority. Fuller carried his emphasis on the free, indiscriminate offer of the gospel over into his work as a missionary theologian. He wrote to John Rowe, the first representative of the BMS in Jamaica, telling him that he carried a gospel 'which addresses itself alike to the civilized and the uncivilized; a gospel that commends itself to every man's conscience in the sight of God.'[41]

---

40   Clipsham, 'Andrew Fuller and the Baptist Mission', p. 8. The quotation from Griffith is from his Presidential address to the Baptist Union Assembly, 27 April 1942. The text of this address is reprinted in H.L. Hemmens, E.A. Payne, B.G. Griffith et al, *Baptist Missionary Society Ter-Jubilee Celebrations, 1942-4: Programmes of Meetings and Services...With some of the Sermons and Speeches And a Statement of Contributions to the Celebrations Fund* (London: Baptist Missionary Society, 1945), pp. 31-47. The quotation is on p. 36. I am grateful to John Barclay for this reference.

41   Written on Rowe's departure, 8 Dec 1813. *Periodical Accounts*, 5, pp. 290-93. Rowe arrived at Montego Bay on 23 Feb 1814, see Stanley, *History of the BMS*, pp. 70-71.

A third stress was that 'only those means...consistent with the nature of the gospel [were] worthy of a Christian Missionary'. In other words the character and conduct of the missionaries was important. 'Beware that you do not misrepresent your blessed Lord and his glorious gospel', he advised Carey and Thomas before they set out.[42] Clipsham could have developed this point further by highlighting the way that Fuller habitually urged missionaries and their families to nurture a deep spirituality. For example, in a letter of 1806 to two missionary couples about to set sail he wrote: 'there is the greatest necessity for us all to keep near to God... Beware of drawing a veil between him and you... Be very conversant with your Bibles.'[43] The fourth emphasis was eschatological, namely that 'the final triumph of Christ and his cause is assured'. A passage from one of Fuller's earliest letters to Carey, not cited by Clipsham, illustrates this, the final one of Fuller's central theological concerns:

> For my part, I believe in God, and have little doubt that a matter, begun as this was, will meet His approbation... I confess I feel sanguine, but my hopes are fixed in God. Instead of failing in the E. Indian enterprise, I look to see not only that but many others accomplished.[44]

Fuller, to quote Carey's dictum again, was *attempting* great things precisely because he *expected* great things. Fuller's Evangelical Calvinism, with its optimistic eschatology and strong practical concern, is evident throughout these extracts.

Clipsham's instinct for what was important is sound, although his analysis is open to question in one respect. He at least infers that some of these points were Fuller's particular contribution.[45] But the extent to which Fuller was, for example, responsible for the belief that 'The final triumph of Christ and his cause is assured' is doubtful. Certainly such a belief was all pervasive in the early days of the BMS. But this was because it was held by all the leading figures of the Northamptonshire

---

42   Fuller to W. Carey and J. Thomas, 20 March 1793, in *Periodical Accounts*, 1, pp. 36-40.

43   Fuller to 'Mr and Mrs Chater and Mr and Mrs Robinson', 5 April 1806, in Ryland, *Andrew Fuller*, p. 161. For these missionaries see Stanley, *History of the BMS*, pp. 54-55, 140, 168. Cf. Fuller to Jabez Carey, 18 Aug 1815 in the *Baptist Magazine*, 66 (1874), pp. 467-68, cited by Haykin, *Armies of the Lamb*, p. 264.

44   Fuller to W. Carey, in S.P. Carey, *William Carey*, p. 112. The letter is n.d. by S.P. Carey, but it was probably written early in 1793.

45   Although Clipsham, 'Andrew Fuller and the Baptist Mission', p. 6, certainly acknowledges the obvious point, that the belief that 'God has uniquely and finally revealed himself in Jesus Christ' was not 'peculiar to Fuller or his associates'.

Association, and had been shot through much of English Particular Baptist life by the 1784 'Concert of Prayer'.[46] The second point, that 'In the gospel, God is freely offering Christ to the world' has, of course, more claim to be seen as a distinctive contribution of Fuller. But even here, this chapter has shown that Carey himself came to believe this through another route. The early BMS was in fact of theological 'thinkers', both at home and abroad.

Yet there is no doubt that Fuller made a real contribution to the theological shaping of the mission. The fact that he played a vital role in helping to create and sustain the Evangelical Calvinism that was characteristic of the BMS during his period as secretary is certain. One should add that *The Gospel Worthy* was *the* key text in creating the ecclesiastical climate (amongst the Particular Baptists), where a venture such as the BMS could be accepted and supported, and would prosper. It is surely significant that the regions that were most resistant to Fuller's work, namely London and East Anglia, were the least fertile in terms of support for the new society.[47] Where Fuller's theology was accepted support was forthcoming. There is much evidence then to support Timothy George's comment, that Fuller was indeed the 'leading theologian of the missionary movement'.[48]

Fuller's Political and Apologetic Contribution

What I have described as Fuller's 'political and apologetic' contribution to the BMS is what Clipsham describes as his work as the 'champion of Christian Missions'.[49] Fuller was sensitive to the fact that, from the time Carey and his party had slipped into Calcutta without an official permit from the British East India Company, the mission to India hung by the 'slenderest of political threads'.[50] Fuller was extremely careful not to do

---

46   See e.g. James, 'William Steadman', pp. 274-75, for the example of how Edwards' eschatological expectations were broadly shared by Steadman.

47   For the lack of support for the BMS in these areas see Stanley, *History of the BMS*, pp. 17-18. W. Carey to Fuller, 11 Feb 1793, 'Letters to and from Andrew Fuller and Others in the Fuller Family', 3, wrote, 'I expected the London people would do as they have done'. This, and other MS Fuller letters in this collection, are held at Bristol Baptist College (G 95 B). For opposition to *The Gospel Worthy* see e.g. Fuller to Thomas Steevens of Colchester, 18 May 1793, 'I know the opposition made to "Andrew Fuller" in S_____ and N_____', Fuller Letters (4/5/1). S. and N. are almost certainly Suffolk and Norfolk.

48   George, *Faithful Witness*, p. viii.

49   Clipsham, 'Andrew Fuller and the Baptist Mission', p. 11.

50   Stanley, *History of the BMS*, p. 24; George, *Faithful Witness*, p. 91.

anything that would jeopardize the future of the work. In this he was helped by some of the Anglican Evangelicals who made up the 'Clapham Sect', such as William Wilberforce and particularly Charles Grant, who was described by Fuller as a 'faithful friend'. It was Grant, once the East India Company's senior merchant in India and from 1805 the deputy chair of its Court of Directors, who advised him to be careful when sending goods which could be turned into money, a move which could have laid the missionaries open to an accusation that they were acting as traders.[51] Fuller was grateful for this sort of inside information, but needed no encouragement to be scrupulously thorough in his efforts to avoid offending the authorities.

The BMS had made significant advances in India in the years following 1793. For example, in 1799 Joshua Marshman (1768-1837), William Ward (1764-1823), Daniel Brunsdon and William Grant came to India to augment the work of the mission.[52] Of these Marshman and Ward were by far the most significant (Grant died from cholera and dysentery less than a month after their arrival in India). Together with Carey, Marshman and Ward became known as 'the Serampore trio', deriving their name from the missionaries base of operations form 1800 onwards. Carey engaged in extensive bible translation work and Ward, a printer, was instrumental in establishing a press at Serampore so that the scriptures and other literature could be printed and distributed. The first Hindu convert was Krishna Pal (d. 1822), a carpenter converted and baptized in 1800. Despite this success (indeed, in part because of it), the mission was regularly under threat from those who wanted the missionaries recalled. This was particularly true in 1807-8 and again in 1813. The situation that arose in 1807 can be taken as an example.

A mutiny amongst the East India Company's sepoy[53] troops stationed at Vellore in 1806 was attributed by some to interference with the religious views of Indians,[54] and for a time the missionaries had to operate under severe restrictions. Carey wrote to Fuller, urging the home committee to 'try to engage men such as Mr Grant, Mr Wilberforce and others to use their influence to procure for us the liberty we want, viz. liberty to preach the gospel throughout India.' 'Do your utmost', Carey

---

51   Clipsham, 'Andrew Fuller and the Baptist Mission', pp. 12, 17 n.

52   For information in this paragraph see S. Neill, *A History of Christian Missions* (The Pelican History of the Church, 6; Harmondsworth, Middlesex: Penguin, 1964), pp. 262-4; Potts, *British Baptist Missionaries in India*, p. 172; George, *Faithful Witness*, pp. 122; 129-132.

53   That is an India soldier in European service.

54   See J.C. Marshman, *The Story of Carey, Marshman and Ward, The Serampore Missionaries* (London: Alexander Strahan, 1864), pp. 117-18. The European garrison at Vellore, in the Madras presidency, was attacked with considerable loss of life.

urged, 'to clear our way'.[55] At home the missionaries were attacked in various periodicals, and plans were made to introduce a motion in the Company's Court of Proprietors which would lead to the expulsion of Carey and his colleagues.[56]

Fuller's response was both restrained and thorough. He worked privately, together with his Clapham friends visiting a number of the directors, whilst at the same time preparing a statement defending the Indian mission. This was to be distributed at a meeting on 7 June 1807 where the possible recall of the missionaries was to be discussed. Grant persuaded Fuller, however, that it would be better to leave the matter in the hands of himself and some others on the committee who were sympathetic. This low key approach paid off and (with Fuller watching anxiously from the gallery of India House), the motion was defeated.[57] According to Gunton Fuller, some involved with the LMS had been critical of Fuller's careful approach whilst he had been in London, describing Grant as 'timid and irresolute' and urging Fuller to disregard the advice of his friend and 'act on the offensive'.[58] But Fuller's tactics were almost certainly correct, showing him to be a safe pair of hands as far as looking after the Society's interests was concerned.

By the end of the year however, the attacks against the missionaries had intensified. A tract was printed by the press at Serampore which became known as 'The Persian Pamphlet'. This was unwisely negative about Islam, using intemperate language to accuse Muslims of perverting God's commands, thereby incurring the 'wrath of God'. Carey knew nothing of this tract, and was alarmed when parts of it were read to him. It was actually written by a Muslim convert to Christianity, and it appears that Ward, who by now was supervising the press day- to-day, had not properly read the pamphlet before running it off. Its circulation was immediately stopped, but the damage had been done, and it appeared for a while that the missionaries' presses might be closed. In Britain, a series of pamphlets were produced attacking Carey and his colleagues. The first of these being Thomas Twining's *A Letter to the Chairman of the East India Company, on the danger of Interfering in the Religious Observances of the Natives of India*, which

---

55   W. Carey and others to BMS, Serampore, 2 September 1806, BMS MSS, Angus Library, Oxford, quoted in Potts, *Baptist Missionaries in India*, p. 178. 'Mr Wilberforce' is William Wilberforce, the Evangelical social reformer and parliamentarian, another member of the 'Clapham Sect'.

56   Young, 'Fuller and the Developing Modern Missions Movement', p. 223.

57   Morris, *Andrew Fuller*, 2nd edn, p. 142-43; Ryland, *Andrew Fuller*, pp. 156-57; Stanley, *History of the BMS*, pp. 24-26.

58   A.G. Fuller, *Men Worth Remembering*, p. 119; Marshman, *Carey, Marshman and Ward*, p. 124.

had appeared earlier in 1807.[59] Twining, a member of the famous tea trading family, believed that the activities of the missionaries could result in no less than the expulsion of the British from India, and sought to spread the accusation they were responsible for the Vellore massacre. Other writers criticized the missionaries in much the same vein. Perhaps most significantly, a pamphlet was published by an anonymous 'Bengal Officer' (a Major Charles Stewart),[60] which contrasted the breadth and tolerance of Hinduism with the narrowness and bigotry of Christianity, and in the *Edinburgh Review* Carey and his co-workers were famously attacked by Sydney Smith as a 'nest of consecrated cobblers'.[61] But these were only a few of a large number of attacks. This time Fuller believed he had to write a public defence and produced his *Apology for the Late Christian Missions to India* in 1808.[62]

Fuller's *Apology* was divided into three parts, and the edition in his *Works* also contains an appendix, which was originally published separately. Clipsham's assessment of the work as a whole is that it was 'not a polished literary production', in some respects 'tedious' and 'repetitive'. Fuller, now working under intense pressure, had to produce the work in a short space of time, and was answering specific and detailed allegations.[63] But it was a more or less effective rebuttal, defending both the character of the missionaries and the basis on which they worked, and Clipsham's judgment is a little harsh.[64] Nevertheless, Fuller does return repeatedly to the same issues as he answers the charges against the missionaries. Consequently the best way to approach the *Apology* is to consider some of the main themes which occur, rather than working systematically through the text.[65]

---

59   The tract is wrongly attributed to Richard Twining, a director of the East India Company, by Clipsham, 'Andrew Fuller and the Baptist Mission', p. 13. Thomas Twining, who actually wrote four 'Letters' on the 'danger of interfering in the religious opinions of the natives in India', the last in 1808, was one of Richard Twining's sons. See *DNB*, XIX, pp. 1314-316.

60   Stewart had served as an officer in the East India Company's Bengal Army from 1781 to 1808. *DNB*, XVIII, pp. 1163-164; J.C. Marshman, *Carey, Marshman and Ward*, p. 153.

61   See *Edinburgh Review*, 12 (1808), 'Publications Respecting Indian Missions'. Cf. Morris, *Andrew Fuller*, 2nd edn, pp. 279-80.

62   Fuller, *Apology*, in *Fuller's Works*, II, pp. 763-836.

63   As Clipsham also points out, 'Andrew Fuller and the Baptist Mission', p. 13.

64   Although J.C. Marshman was certainly guilty of serious overstatement when he wrote: 'On no occasion did [Fuller's] controversial acumen appear to greater advantage,' J.C. Marshman, *Carey, Marshman and Ward*, p. 155.

65   A more detailed treatment of Fuller's *Apology* can be found in my chapter 'Fuller as a Missionary Apologist', in Haykin (ed.), *Fuller as an Apologist*.

Fuller's *Apology for the Late Christian Missions to India*

Fuller rejected the charge that Baptists were at all to blame for Vellore, pointing out that no evidence had been produced to substantiate what had become a repeated accusation.[66] Dealing with the 'Persian Pamphlet' was more difficult. Fuller privately agreed that its publication had been an error, and pointed out in the *Apology* that it had not been written by one of the missionaries. But he was also able to show that an anonymous English 'translation' of the pamphlet that was circulating, which at one point described the Hindus as 'barbarians', was inaccurate. Fuller believed that this translation was done expressly 'to inflame the minds of the directors and the government against the missionaries'. He obtained a second translation from a student at the Baptist Academy in Bristol, where Ryland was now Principal, which he printed alongside extracts of the first. It was about the best Fuller could have done in the circumstances, but by 1808 Carey's prompt reaction in withdrawing the pamphlet had already mollified the authorities – on the ground in India at least.[67]

Elsewhere in the *Apology* Fuller defended the missionaries themselves, chiefly by reproducing some written testimonies as to their character.[68] He also sought to show that accounts of contemporary Hindu practices from Twining and particularly Stewart were highly selective. Some of Fuller's strictures on the majority religion in India, based on information received from the missionaries, can seem harsh when read today. But the 'Serampore Trio' could write sympathetically on aspects of the culture, and a book by Ward on the manners and customs of Hindus is described by Stephen Neill as 'as one of the best and most sympathetic delineations of Hindu thought ever produced by a foreigner'.[69] What they could not accept were some of the practices such as ritual infanticide, *ghat* murders, where the sick and dying were exposed on the banks of the Ganges, and *sati*, where widows threw themselves on the funeral pyres of their dead husbands.[70] These and other such practices were rigorously opposed. The social concern that Fuller had earlier shown in his Clipstone sermon, where he attacked

---

66   Fuller, *Apology*, in Fuller's *Works*, II, e.g. pp. 768-69.

67   Morris, *Andrew Fuller*, 2nd edn, p. 145

68   In the Appendix. *Fuller's Works*, II, pp. 829-31.

69   Neill, *History of Christian Missions*, pp. 264-65. Ward's book was originally published in 1811.

70   See George, *Faithful Witness*, pp. 149-52. *Ghats* were the steps leading down to the river. Fuller, *Apology*, in *Fuller's Works*, II, describes some of these customs and rituals, e.g. pp. 765-66; 796-800.

slavery, was also evident here. In addition, Fuller and the missionaries were not prepared to compromise on their belief in the uniqueness of Christ and their responsibility to proclaim him. In fact Fuller was now ready to say that the great commission was not 'confined to the apostles', and that the contemporary church was 'obliged to do its utmost' in the 'use of those means Christ has appointed for the discipling of all nations'. This was non-negotiable and the *raison d'être* of their missionary activity.[71]

But the most important theme to emerge from the *Apology* was Fuller's plea for toleration for the Serampore missionaries. Twining had argued that the activities of Carey and his colleagues were actually against 'the mild and tolerant spirit of Christianity'[72]. He clearly believed that Carey and his colleagues should not be allowed to make converts, arguing that 'our religious subjects in India' should be 'permitted quietly to follow their own religious opinions.' Fuller's answer to these points was carefully nuanced. Any attempt to coerce Indian Hindus or Muslims to follow Christ would be quite wrong, and indeed impossible. If any so-called 'missionary' tried to do this, or deliberately sought to disturb the 'peace of society', they could have no complaints if they were dealt with severely by the government. Overthrowing another religion by force was anathema to Fuller, as were any 'measures subversive of free choice'. As an English Nonconformist, grateful for the 1689 Act of Toleration, but still experiencing significant social and legal discrimination at home, Fuller was committed to freedom of conscience in religion.[73]

But when Fuller came to define toleration positively, it was clear that his views were very different from Twining's. In a statement crucial to his argument, Fuller wrote that 'toleration was a legal permission not only to enjoy your own principles unmolested, but to make use of all the fair means of persuasion to recommend them to others'. In other words, people should be free not only to hold to certain principles, but also to *propagate those principles* through all reasonable means. Only this view of toleration squared with the scriptures. In fact Twining's views were actually corrosive of religious freedom. Turning the tables on his opponent, Fuller argued that Twining was himself being 'intolerant' by saying that Christians in India 'must not be allowed to make proselytes', or indeed circulate the scriptures in the Indian languages. This was not 'toleration' but 'persecution'. Later on in the tract he appealed directly

---

71   See Fuller, *Apology*, in *Fuller's Works*, II, pp. 817-18.

72   For these and other quotations in this paragraph, unless otherwise stated, see Fuller, *Apology*, in *Fuller's Works*, II, pp. 763-64; 768.

73   For a discussion of Fuller's views on 'civil and religious liberty', see A.G. Fuller, *Men Worth Remembering*, pp. 197-203.

to Edward Parry, Chair of the East India Company:

> May I not take it for granted, sir, that a British government cannot refuse to tolerate protestant missionaries; that a protestant government cannot forbid the free circulation of the Scriptures; that a Christian government cannot exclude Christianity from any part of its territories?... I trust I may.

Fuller had argued for a distinctively Christian view of toleration, with a commitment to a free and truly tolerant society which was not incompatible with evangelistic activity or indeed claims to absolute truth.

At this stage there was a real possibility the missionaries would be recalled. But Fuller's trust was not, after all, misplaced. Although the influence of Grant and others on board of the East India Company was crucial in safeguarding the interests of the mission, what Stanley describes as Fuller's 'political discretion' was important as well.[74] A more impetuous or less thorough secretary would almost certainly have endangered the work. Fuller's 'political contribution' allowed the work of conversions to continue and flourish, not just in India, but, as the society grew, in other parts of the world too.[75]

It is against this background that Fuller's treatment of any missionary who showed a taste for radical politics needs to be viewed. Those reproved in no uncertain terms included Jacob Grigg (1769-1835), sent to begin a mission in Sierra Leone in 1795, and John Fountain (1767-1800), who arrived in India in 1797.[76] Fountain especially alarmed and indeed angered Fuller by openly making his republican views known. As early as September 1797, just a few months after Fountain's arrival in India, Fuller warned him concerning his 'too great edge for politicks'.[77] Later, in 1800, he would write to William Ward deploring Fountain's 'rage for politics', lamenting that he 'seemed incapable of refraining from talking about them in any company'.[78] Fountain died in

---

74   Stanley, *History of the BMS*, p. 25.

75   The Society sent missionaries to the West Indies from 1813, see Stanley, *History of the BMS*, p. 70. Grigg's abortive work in Sierra Leone is referred to below.

76   For these men see B. Amey, 'Baptist Missionary Society Radicals', *BQ* 26.8 (October, 1976), pp. 363-76; Young, 'Fuller and the Developing Modern Missions Movement', pp. 208-11.

77   Fuller to J. Fountain, 7 September 1797 in A.G. Fuller, *Men Worth Remembering*, p. 143; cf. Stanley, *History of the BMS*, p. 24. As early as 25 March 1796, before Fountain had even sailed from London, Fuller had warned him that 'all political concerns are only affairs of this life', Fuller to J. Fountain, bound volume of Fuller Letters, (III/170), p. 23.

78   Fuller to W. Ward, 21 September 1800, bound volume of Fuller Letters

India in 1801, but not before he had almost been recalled by the home committee. Grigg had in fact been expelled from Sierra Leone in 1797, an action by the governor, Zachary Macaulay (another member of the Evangelical 'Clapham Sect'), that had Fuller's full support.[79]

Fuller believed, quite correctly, that this sort of behaviour endangered the whole mission. His strong treatment of these men, with the full backing of the BMS committee, is unsurprising in the circumstances. But his view that missionaries should 'stand aloof' from any radical political involvement was not only based on concerns for the continuance of the work. It also sprang from a deeper biblical conviction that 'Jesus spent His [time] in accomplishing a moral revolution in the hearts of men'. Missionaries, indeed 'good men in general', should do likewise.[80] Consequently his advice to Fountain contained the following: 'Well does the apostle charge us who have engaged to be soldiers of Christ, not to entangle ourselves in the affairs of this life.'[81] Fuller's social concern has already been noted, but his attitude to the activities of men such as Grigg and Fountain reflected his overriding focus on evangelism, or 'accomplishing a moral revolution in the hearts of men'. For Fuller, it was this that was the major work of Christian mission. Nothing was more important, and nothing could stand in its way.

Fuller's Contribution to Promoting the Work of the BMS and Raising Funds at Home

One of Fuller's first duties when he became secretary at the society's inaugural meeting in 1792 was to attempt to raise some funds. Given that the subscriptions and promises of money, collected in Fuller's snuffbox, amounted to £13 2s 6d, this was his most pressing task.[82] One of a number of letters he wrote in January 1793 to promote the work was to John Fawcett of Hebden Bridge, a letter from which we have already cited. Fuller had never met Fawcett, but this did not stop him making a strong appeal for support: 'Any sums of money conveyed...will be thankfully received. The sooner the better, as the time is short.' Carey, of course, was still in the country at this stage and Fuller wrote that the prospective missionary would in fact be in

(III/170), p. 136.

79   Stanley, *History of the BMS*, p. 24.

80   Fuller to W. Carey, 18 January 1797, Fuller Letters (4/5/1). See also E.A. Payne, 'Andrew Fuller as Letter Writer', *BQ* 15.7 (July, 1954), p. 295.

81   Fuller to J. Fountain, 7 September 1797, in A.G. Fuller, *Men Worth Remembering*, p. 144.

82   Ryland, *Andrew Fuller*, p. 150; Laws, *Andrew Fuller*, pp. 61-62.

Yorkshire within the next few weeks to 'visit a relation'. If Fawcett were to 'hear him preach', Fuller assured him, he would certainly 'give him a collection'. Most significantly, in the light of future developments, he concluded his letter by offering to come to Yorkshire to preach himself. 'I feel that willingness to exert myself' he said, so that if an 'excursion of two to three weeks' would promote the cause of the mission, 'I would cheerfully engage in it'.[83]

Fawcett became an enthusiastic supporter of the BMS and wasted no time in collecting £200 from churches in his region, which he sent to Fuller in March 1793, adding: 'my heart is much affected...to see so much regard for the gospel, and for precious souls.'[84] Fuller would continue to write letters to promote the society, often spending upwards of ten hours a day at his desk, mostly giving himself to the work of the BMS. He would also visit individuals to solicit support, and pay one off visits to churches for the same purpose. But it was his longer tours, not only to places such as Yorkshire but also further afield, that probably did most to raise awareness and support for the mission. It was through this unstinting work that Fuller's commitment to the BMS was supremely shown.

As noted in chapter five, Fuller was regularly away from Kettering for up to three months of each year, travelling huge distances on behalf of the society. As late as 1814, by which time his health was deteriorating rapidly, he was working at an extraordinary pace. Morris recorded Fuller's itinerary, for May to July of that year. In May and June he was due to go to Olney, Bedford, Leicester, Essex and London, although Fuller noted he had to be in Kettering on 26 June, 'which is our Lord's Supper day'. In July he was in the north of England, on successive Sundays in Liverpool, Manchester, Leeds, Newcastle and Hull. As Fuller surveyed this forthcoming programme, it is little surprise that he wrote: 'May the Lord strengthen me for these labours.'[85] During this year, Fuller travelled 600 miles in one month alone, collecting, by his own reckoning, about a pound a mile.[86] In all he travelled many times to London, and at one time or other visited most of the counties in England, including one journey into the High Calvinist bastion of

---

83   Fuller to J. Fawcett, n.d. but between February and April 1793, in Fawcett Jr, *John Fawcett*, p. 296.

84   J. Fawcett to Fuller, n.d. but received 22 Mar 1793, Fuller Chapel Letters, I, 4.

85   Morris, *Andrew Fuller*, 1st edn, p. 156.

86   Fuller to W. Ward, 5 September 1814, Fuller Letters (4/5/2). Cf. Fuller to J. Deakin, 14 August 1812, in 'Letters to James Deakin', p. 365. Fuller estimated that the journey to Wales was also 'about a 600 miles excursion'. Still he raised what he usually aimed for – 'my old price, a pound a mile'. See also Stanley, *History of the BMS*, p. 20

Norfolk.[87]

But even more remarkable were journeys to Ireland (in 1804), Wales (in 1812) and Scotland (at regular intervals between 1799 and 1813).[88] The extensive Scottish journeys are the best documented of all his tours on behalf of the mission. Fuller kept a journal of his first journey, which included details of travel arrangements, preaching engagements and people met, together with various observations on the life of the Scottish churches. Information concerning the other trips can be extracted from different letters recorded by Ryland.[89] In all he visited Scotland five times – in 1799, 1802, 1805, 1808 and 1813 – producing what was described as a 'hallowed excitement' and enjoying great personal popularity.[90] As Stanley notes, 'by his later years Fuller was probably better known, and certainly better loved, in Scotland and the North of England than in London'.[91] After 1799 Fuller aimed to make his Scottish visits 'triennial', but at the very end of his life this would be something that even he would fail to manage.

A number of points can be made from a study of the material relating to his Scottish visits. The first is that Fuller canvassed support from a range of denominations, bringing him into contact with a much wider network of ministers and other friends than he had previously experienced. He was positive about many non-Baptist Evangelicals in Scotland, and they in turn welcomed him. In Edinburgh in 1799 he had his first face to face meeting with his own and Ryland's correspondent, the Church of Scotland minister John Erskine, whom he described as 'an excellent old man', full of 'kindness and goodness'.[92] Fuller was also impressed with a number of other ministers 'in the Kirk', as he also was by the Independents, Robert Haldane (1764-1842) and his brother James (1768-1851).[93] Descended from the prestigious Haldane family of Gleneagles, the brothers, particularly Robert, were men of considerable

---

87   Fuller to J. Deakin, 14 August 1812, in 'Letters to James Deakin', p. 365.

88   Doyle, 'Fuller and the Developing Modern Missions Movement', pp. 243-54, includes much material from Fuller's tours and ⌐horter journeys, giving a flavour of the pace at which Fuller worked.

89   Ryland, *Andrew Fuller*, pp. 164-83 reproduced the bulk of the journal, and also included much primary evidence from the other Scottish tours, pp. 184-212.

90   Ryland, *Andrew Fuller*, p. 156; F.A. Cox, *History of the Baptist Missionary Society of England from 1792 to 1842* (London: T. Ward, 1842), p. 21. On his first journey to Scotland he was accompanied by Sutcliff, on the last, for part of the tour, by William Steadman.

91   Stanley, *History of the BMS*, p. 20.

92   Ryland, *Andrew Fuller*, pp. 168-69.

93   *DEB*, I, pp. 500-503; *Dictionary of Scottish Church History and Theology*, pp. 385-86.

means, and following Evangelical conversions used their wealth to employ itinerant preachers and build sizeable 'tabernacles' in major Scottish centres at the beginning of the nineteenth century. These were free of pew rents and designed to reach the underprivileged classes. From 1799 James Haldane was himself pastor of the congregation which met which met at the former circus building in Edinburgh until a large purpose built tabernacle was opened in 1801. Together the brothers stood for a lively Evangelicalism with a strong commitment to mission both at home and abroad (In 1796 Robert had actually attempted to undertake a self-financed evangelistic tour to Bengal). It was at their instigation that Fuller had come to Scotland, and they and their churches were to prove fertile soil for the message of the BMS.

Fuller was welcomed into the pulpits of the Haldanes' growing connexion, and preached at the circus on his first visit. He recorded his initial impressions in his journal: 'Certainly these appear to be excellent men, free from the extravagance and nonsense which infect some of the Calvinistic Methodists in England; and yet trying to imbibe and communicate their zeal and affection.'[94] One of those who heard him was Christopher Anderson (1782-1852), a member of the circus church who was 'much impressed by Fuller's powerful public appeals on behalf of the Baptist mission'.[95] Anderson 'had been deeply influenced by the aims and ministry of the Haldanes', but lost his membership of their connexion in 1801 when he became a Baptist (although not a Scotch Baptist).[96] A year later he offered for missionary service with the BMS at a personal interview with Fuller, which took place during the Kettering pastor's second Scottish tour. Anderson subsequently studied with Sutcliff in Olney and Ryland in Bristol, although it was judged that, because of health problems, it would be unwise for him to go overseas. Instead he founded a Baptist church in Edinburgh on the English single pastor model. Anderson was a convinced Evangelical

---

94   Ryland, *Andrew Fuller*, p. 169.

95   A.C. Smith, 'Christopher Anderson and the Serampore Fraternity' in D.E. Meek (ed.), *A Mind for Mission; Essays in Appreciation of the Rev. Christopher Anderson 1782-1852* (Edinburgh: The Scottish Baptist History Project, 1992), p. 25. For information in this paragraph, in addition to Smith, see *Dictionary of Scottish Church History and Theology*, p. 11.

96   J.M. Gordon, 'The Early Nineteenth Century' in D.W. Bebbington (ed.), *The Baptists in Scotland: A History* (Glasgow: The Baptist Union of Scotland, 1988), p. 34. See D.B. Murray, 'An Eighteenth Century Baptismal Controversy in Scotland' in S.E. Porter and A.R. Cross (eds), *Baptism, the New Testament and the Church: Historical and Contemporary Essays in Honour of R.E.O White* (JSNTSupp Series, 171; Sheffield: Sheffield Academic Press, 1999), pp. 428-29, for a guide to Scottish church life during this period for the 'unwary'.

Calvinist, principles he had imbibed, at least in part, through his friendship with Fuller, Sutcliff and Ryland.[97]

In contrast to his generally appreciative view of the Haldanes' connexion, Fuller was often far less positive about the Scotch Baptists (whose churches were led by a plurality of elders). The Scotch Baptists were, in turn, often wary of him, especially so on his first visit. A question put by Sutcliff, Fuller's travelling companion on this first journey, captures what the Northamptonshire men were most concerned for. Fuller approvingly recorded in his journal that 'Brother S' had asked a Scotch Baptist elder whether his religion 'allowed a proper and scriptural place for the exercise of the affections?' Clearly neither Fuller or Sutcliff thought it did.[98] The Scotch Baptists owed much to Alexander MacLean, whose Sandemanian views were noted briefly in chapter four.[99] Their intellectualized view of faith probably accounted for what Fuller and Sutcliff saw as the arid nature of many of their churches. But Fuller had further strictures to offer. Scotch Baptist life exhibited little tolerance and was prone to frequent schisms over matters of minor importance.[100] Most centrally, they were not sufficiently committed to the spread of the gospel. One might summarize by saying that for Fuller, the Scotch Baptists were not Evangelical enough. For their part, on more than one occasion the Baptists refused to have Fuller preach for them. The relationship improved on journeys subsequent to 1799, with MacLean supporting the work of the BMS, but it remained uneasy right to the end.[101]

---

97   As early as 1807 Anderson had been Fuller's chosen successor as secretary of the BMS on the event of his death. But Anderson was not acceptable to some on the BMS committee, and was not appointed in 1815. He became the Serampore missionaries 'trusted advocate' during their struggles with the home committee in the late 1820s. See Stanley, *History of the BMS*, pp. 3-4; A.C. Smith, 'Christopher Anderson and the Serampore Fraternity', in Meek (ed.), *A Mind for Mission*, pp. 25-37.

98   See Ryland, *Andrew Fuller*, pp. 168-70.

99   See *Dictionary of Scottish Church History and Theology*, pp. 364 and 744 for John Glas and Robert Sandeman respectively. By the time of Fuller's first visit to Scotland MacLean had come to repudiate the name 'Glasite' quite vehemently, considering that the Glasites had become 'wordly'. But his theological debt to Glas and Sandeman remained considerable.

100   Cf. Fuller to J. Deakin, 25 Feb 1804, in Payne, 'Andrew Fuller and James Deakin, 1803', p. 328: 'I do not know how it is, but there is something about the Baptists in your country that seems to *divide* and *scatter*, on almost every difference that occurs'.

101   Ryland, *Andrew Fuller*, pp. 183. For MacLean's support for the BMS see his sermon, 'The Duty of Using Means for the Universal Spread of the Glorious Gospel of Christ', in Rippon (ed.), *Baptist Annual Register*, 3, p. 377. This was originally preached

Fuller's contacts with the Haldanes and ministers in the Church of Scotland were significant, although, as Stanley notes, pan-evangelicalism had its limits for Fuller.[102] He remained implacably opposed to infant baptism and, at a time when the attitudes of other Particular Baptists were softening, was a strong supporter of closed communion. Consequently, the introduction of open communion at Serampore in 1805 was repeatedly lamented by Fuller[103] and, largely because of his strictures, the trio reverted to a policy of strict communion in 1811.[104] Nevertheless his Scottish tours do show him actively practicing a form of Evangelical ecumenism. Fuller's concern was not that people became Baptists (although he would have welcomed Anderson's 'conversion', as well as that of the Haldanes in 1808). Rather the need was to make people (including Baptists!), Christians.[105] As he explained to a group of Scotch Baptists in 1802, 'free preaching to the unconverted' was the priority.[106] Issues of Baptist church polity, however significant they might be, were of secondary importance.

A second point to note is that he achieved the aim for which he had initially set out, namely raising funds for the mission. In fact the Scottish visits made a vital contribution to the continuing work of the BMS. Wherever Fuller preached he took collections, and he also solicited money by visiting ministers and prominent Christian laypeople house to house. He often preached to thousands, for example to over four thousand at the Haldanes' tabernacles in Edinburgh and Glasgow on his second tour in 1802 (these estimates are of course, Fuller's own). These were extraordinary experiences for Fuller, but the verdict of his hearers on these occasions appears to have been extremely positive. As far as collecting money was concerned, Ryland commented that 'he always disliked violent pressing for contributions...he chose, rather, to tell a plain unvarnished tale; and he generally told it with good effect'. Nevertheless he was never coy about fund raising.[107] To help the Bible

---

in Edinburgh in 1795. I am indebted to Dr Derek Murray for this reference.

102 Stanley, *History of the BMS*, p. 22-23.

103 See e.g. Fuller to W. Carey, 1 Nov 1806, Fuller Letters (4/5/2).

104 See T. George, 'Controversy and Communion: The Limits of Baptist Fellowship from Bunyan to Spurgeon', in Bebbington (ed.), *Gospel in the World*, pp. 52-53, and especially, E.D. Potts, '"I throw away the guns to preserve the ship": A Note on the Serampore Trio', *BQ* 20.3 (July, 1963), pp. 115-117, for an account of what both Carey and Ward referred to as the 'mixt [sic] business'.

105 M.A.G. Haykin, 'Hazarding all for God at a Clap: The Spirituality of Baptism Among British Calvinistic Baptists', *BQ* 38.4 (October, 1999), p. 193.

106 Ryland, *Andrew Fuller*, p. 190.

107 From the very beginning. See e.g. 'John Davis, Minister at Waltham Abbey 1764-1795', *BQ* 39.8 (October, 2002), p. 410, and Davis' comment of 5 November

translation at work at Serampore, and as an inducement for Fuller to consider visiting Scotland, Robert Haldane had arranged for £100 to be transferred to BMS funds. Suitably encouraged, Fuller agreed to embark on his first tour. Ryland recorded that one evening during that first journey, in October 1799, a lady commented: "'O sir, why did you not come here before?" Fuller (with his tongue perhaps only slightly in his cheek), responded: "Why madam, every man, as Sir Robert Walpole said, has his price; and till that gentleman there [Robert Haldane] sent me a hundred pounds, I did not know it would be worthwhile to visit you.""[108]

The sums Fuller collected (carefully recorded in his journal or diary), could vary from £20 from a small congregation to upwards of £200 at somewhere like the Edinburgh circus. It greatly aided the work going on in India, with collections often specifically ear marked for the Bible translation work.[109] Thanks in large part to the Haldane brothers, Fuller may well have been able to exceed his stated pound a mile target on his Scottish tours. It is almost impossible to imagine this sort of fund raising for foreign missions taking place in, say, the sixteenth century. These events, once again, mark out Fuller as an eighteenth-century Evangelical, who played a significant part in the continuing spread of Evangelical life.

A third and central point regarding his missionary tours through Scotland is the way they highlight his activism. As already noted, this was a central tenet of Evangelicalism, and one which his journal and letters illustrate perhaps more strongly than any of the material considered so far in this study. In 1805, by then on his third journey, Fuller kept up his usual exhausting pace. An extract from a letter to his wife (written from Lancaster, in the north of England), gives a flavour of what was happening:

> The last letter I wrote to you, was from Glasgow, Tuesday, July 23. (This letter is wanting.) Since then, I have preached at Paisley, Greenock, Saltcoats, Kilmarnock, Kilwinning, Air [sic], and Dumfries. I am now on my way to Liverpool, I have not been in bed till tonight, since Lord's Day night, at Irvine, in Scotland. I have felt my strength and spirits much exhausted; yet hitherto the Lord

---

1794, preserved in his private papers: 'Mr Andrew Fuller from Kettering here begging for mission giving to India.' Davis' papers are now held in the Essex Record Office, Chelmsford (A10720).

108   Ryland, *Andrew Fuller*, p. 164. This anecdote is also recorded in A. Haldane, *The Lives of Robert and James Haldane* (London: Hamilton and Adams, 3rd edn, 1853), pp. 298-99.

109   Ryland, *Andrew Fuller*, pp. 185, 212.

hath helped and my health is good.[110]

This sort of punishing schedule was not at all unusual for Fuller in Scotland. A typical day would see him travel upwards of forty miles, visit, preach and collect (on a Sunday usually three times) and then stay up into the evening talking with ministers. Nor was he always able to report to his wife that his health was bearing up. As early as 1793, within four months of the founding of the BMS, Fuller had suffered what he termed a 'paralytic stroke'.[111] One side of his face was left temporarily paralyzed, and though he recovered, from this point on he was to suffer severe headaches for the rest of his life. In 1801 he was seriously ill again, and unable to preach for three months. He wrote to Carey: I have for the past fortnight been very ill, having nearly lost my taste, smell, voice and hearing. Yesterday I was worked violently by an emetic – last night a blister was laid on my stomach – today I can but just move about… The pain in my stomach has been as a acute, I think, as gout.[112] Unsurprisingly many of his friends, he later told Joshua Marshman, had apprehended his 'going after dear brother Pearce'.[113]

Fuller's letters relating to his BMS tours give ample evidence that his work for the society continued sap to his strength.[114] The open air preaching that he was sometimes asked to do can hardly have helped, particularly when the weather was poor. For all his illnesses, the remedies of the day, such as hot tiles wrapped in a flannel and applied to the stomach when he was in pain, could only give temporary relief.[115] All this needs to be set alongside the other demands of his ministry. Fuller had many other duties as secretary of the BMS. He also continued to write and (when he was there), pastor the church at Kettering. One of his letters, from as early as 1801, captures the dilemma he was increasingly facing:

> Pearce's memoirs are now loudly called for. I sit down almost in despair… My wife looks at me with a tear ready to drop, and says, 'My dear, you have hardly time to speak to me'. My friends at home are kind, but they also say, 'You have no time to see us or know us, and you will soon be worn out'. Amidst all this there

---

110   Fuller to Ann Fuller, 1 August 1805, in Ryland, *Andrew Fuller*, pp. 197.

111   Payne, 'Andrew Fuller as a Letter Writer', p. 292.

112   Fuller to Carey, 19-20 August 1801, Fuller Letters (4/5/2), also cited by Payne, 'Andrew Fuller as a Letter Writer', p. 293.

113   Fuller to J. Marshman, 19 November 1801, Fuller Letters (4/5/2), also cited by Payne, 'Andrew Fuller as a Letter Writer', p. 293.

114   Ryland, *Andrew Fuller*, pp. 196-97, 202, 207, gives ample evidence that these frequent tours were affecting his health.

115   Payne 'Andrew Fuller as a Letter Writer', p. 293.

is 'Come again to Scotland – come to Portsmouth – come to Plymouth – come to Bristol'.[116]

In 1801 Robert Hall Jr, having heard that Fuller had indeed recently visited Plymouth and Bristol, expressed his fears for Fuller's health in a letter to Ryland: 'If he is not more careful he will be in danger of wearing himself out before his time. His journeys, his studies, his correspondencies [sic] must be too much for any man.'[117] In fact from 1800 onwards Fuller was rarely well.

Despite Fuller's failing health it never seems to have occurred to him to slacken his pace. A member of the Kettering congregation wrote to Ryland: 'Mr F.'s exertions are too much for his health... Dear sir, pray for us, that so valuable a life may yet be continued.'[118] When advice to slow down was given, Fuller felt unable to heed it. Against this background, perhaps the remarkable thing was not that 'his exertions proved greater than nature was able to sustain, and [that] he sunk under them into a premature grave", but rather that he managed to survive until 1815.[119] As late as 1813, on what would be his final tour of Scotland, Fuller was often preaching in the open air in bad weather.[120] But following his return he became ill once more, and in the last eighteen months of his life grew steadily weaker. In March 1815 Fuller's 'ghastly, cadaverous appearance' as he preached at the ordination of J. Mack at Clipstone startled his friends. On descending from the pulpit Fuller said: 'I am very ill – a dying man.'[121] He was right, preaching and

---

116   A.G. Fuller, *Men Worth Remembering*, pp. 91-92. The letter is from 'March 1800'.

117   R. Hall Jr to J. Ryland Jr, 25 May 1801, G.F. Nuttall, 'Letters from Robert Hall to John Ryland, 1791-1824', *BQ* 34.3 (July, 1991), p. 127. The original is held in the library of the Selly Oak Colleges, Birmingham. Cf. Hall's comments recorded by A.G. Fuller, *Andrew Fuller*, in *Fuller's Works*, I, p. 108, where following Fuller's death Hall spoke of 'the series of unceasing labours and exertions, in superintending the mission to India, to which he most probably fell a victim'.

118   Ryland, *Andrew Fuller*, p. 344. Cf. Fuller to Ann Fuller, 25 July 1813, 'Letters to and from Andrew Fuller and Others of the Fuller Family', Bristol Baptist College Library (G 95 B), 13, which shows that as late as 1813, on what would be his final tour of Scotland, Fuller was often preaching in the open air in bad weather.

119   Ryland, *Andrew Fuller*, p. 381. This was the background too for the terseness and irritability that could occasionally creep into some of Fuller's letters. See e.g. Fuller to I. Mann and R. Aked, 2 September 1806, Fuller Letters (4/5/2). This letter is also cited by Haykin, *Armies of the Lamb*, pp. 215-19.

120   Fuller to Ann Fuller, 25 July 1815, 'Letters to and from Fuller', Bristol Baptist College,

121   A.G. Fuller, *Men Worth Remembering*, pp. 187-88.

leading communion only once more at Kettering, before, in his son's words, 'he came into the house to die'. When the congregation at Kettering learned of his death during a service on 8 May 1815, an 'audible wail went up' and John Keen Hall, who was preaching, immediately closed the meeting.[122] When news of Fuller's death reached India, William Ward, one of the original 'Serampore trio', spoke of Fuller having had 'as large a share as any man on earth' in the establishment and promotion of the mission, and of having 'left no living person who can fill his place'.[123] It is no exaggeration to say that Fuller had given his life for the BMS. Ward's words were a fitting epitaph, as was the comment of J.W. Morris: 'He lived and died a martyr to the Mission.'[124]

Conclusion

In all the areas surveyed in this chapter, Fuller added a new dimension to his evangelistic ministry and in doing so made a hugely significant contribution to the BMS. Indeed, no one 'at home' did more during his own lifetime to further its work. His unstinting work on behalf of the BMS captures particularly well one aspect of Bebbington's 'quadrilateral' of Evangelical distinctives, namely 'activism'. Indeed, Fuller could stand as a supreme example of eighteenth- and nineteenth-century Evangelical activism, giving himself to the work of the society until his health was quite broken. Jonathan Edwards wrote, in his *Narrative of Surprising Conversions*, that:

> Persons after their own conversion, have commonly expressed an exceeding great desire for the conversion of others. Some have thought that they should be willing to die for the conversion of any soul...and many have, indeed, been in great distress with desires and longing for it.[125]

This description of Evangelical activism in the pursuit of conversions

---

122   A.G. Fuller, *Men Worth Remembering*, p. 188-91

123   W.R. Ward, *A Sketch of the Character of the Late Rev Andrew Fuller* (Bristol: J.G. Fuller, 1817), p. 16. The sermon was originally preached at the Lal Bazaar Chapel, Calcutta, 1 October 1815. Ward and the other Serampore missionaries were deeply concerned about the direction the BMS might take following Fuller's death, as it turned out, with good reason.

124   Morris, *Andrew Fuller*, 2nd edn, p. 49.

125   J. Edwards, *A Narrative of Surprising Conversions* (London, 1737), p. 47, in *Edwards Works* (ed.), Hickman, I, p. 357.

fits Fuller perfectly,[126] as do the words of the Evangelical authoress and contemporary of Fuller, Hannah More. 'Action is the life of virtue', she wrote at the beginning of the nineteenth century, 'and the world is the theatre of action'.[127] Although Fuller never went further afield than Britain and Ireland, in a very real sense, the 'world' *had* become 'his theatre of action', as he developed a ministry that was integral to the fostering of world-wide mission.

---

126   In a sermon preached at Bedford, 6 May 1801, cited by Morris, *Andrew Fuller*, 2nd edn, p. 149, Fuller stated: 'And what if…we should a few of us lose our lives? We must die some way; and can we desire to die in a better cause. In carrying the glad tidings of eternal life to jews and gentiles [sic], Stephen and James, with many others, fell sacrifices at an early period: yet no one was discouraged on this account, but rather stimulated to follow the example.'

127   H. More, *An Estimate of the Religion of the Fashionable World* (London, 1808), p. 146, cited by Bebbington, *Evangelicalism*, p. 12.

CHAPTER SEVEN

Fuller and the Spiritual Life

I wanted more spirituality

In his diary Fuller recorded that on 6 June 1786 he rode from Kettering to Northampton to take part in the annual meetings of the association. Whilst there he was generally encouraged by reports from the churches, and 'had a very affecting time in communicating experiences with friends'. He was also, together with Sutcliff, one of the preachers that year. Fuller clearly enjoyed the association. But his experience of preaching produced the following comment: 'I wanted more spirituality.'[1] This desire for 'spirituality' was clearly important to Fuller throughout his life. This final main chapter sets out to examine Fuller's spiritual life. The first half of the chapter charts his movement away from an introspective piety and a preoccupation with indwelling sin. This movement was long and protracted, but as in his theology and ministry, his spirituality would eventually become thoroughly Evangelical. The chapter concludes by seeking to identify and draw together the threads of the mature Fuller's Evangelical spirituality.

Attempts to define 'spirituality' are legion. This is partly because the term has both a secular and general religious use, as well as a specifically Christian one. But there are also many different ways of understanding Christian spirituality, and some of these definitions are so broad as to include almost all of human experience.[2] Whilst this is unhelpful, an alternative meaning which focuses only on prayer or what have traditionally been termed 'the spiritual exercises' is too narrow for the purposes of this study. More useful is the definition of John

---

1   Ryland, *Andrew Fuller*, pp. 118-19.

2   For a brief and useful discussion see A.E. McGrath, *Christian Spirituality* (Oxford: Blackwell, 1999), pp. 1-7. McGrath includes a representative sampling of the different ways writers have sought to define specifically Christian spirituality. See also I.M. Randall, *Evangelical Experiences: A Study in the Spirituality of English Evangelicalism 1918-1939* (Carlisle: Paternoster, 1999), pp. 1-2.

Cockerton, who treats spirituality as 'that way of regarding Christian living which highlights and articulates the believer's personal relationship to God'.[3] Following this I will understand Fuller's spirituality as 'his way of relating to God', a definition which has many loose ends, but which allows for analysis of a broad range of 'lived experience'.[4] When Fuller himself used the term, as he often did, it was with the sense of 'practical godliness'. Indeed 'spirituality' and 'godliness' were virtually synonyms in his writing. The definition given above therefore reflects Fuller's own.

Introspection and the Struggle for Assurance

Fuller's spirituality, from his conversion in 1769 to at least 1790, was characterized by introspection, and throughout this period he was often unhappy. The agonies he went through as he considered the possibility of moving from Soham to the pastorate at Kettering serve as an illustration of this. The first contact from the Kettering church came in 1779, but Fuller's induction there did not take place until 1783. His diary entries for the intervening period make for grim reading, as through them he revealed the deep distress he felt as he weighed his options.[5] As noted in chapter five, the Soham church could not adequately support him and his family financially, and some were opposed to his preaching following his introduction of direct evangelistic appeals at the end of 1779. The Kettering church would provide the stipend he needed, was committed to an Evangelical Calvinism, and would be generally supportive. But Fuller hesitated as some at Soham pleaded with him to stay, and he subjected himself to rigorous self-examination regarding his motives for wanting to leave.

On 12 July 1781 he wrote the following in his diary: 'Have been trying, today, to examine my heart, by putting to myself such questions as these: "Would it be most agreeable to my conscience to continue after all, with my people? Is it likely, in so doing, I should please God, and contribute to the welfare of his cause...?"' Fuller could not, at this stage, see how he could answer 'yes' to these questions. He continued: 'I am now going to the church meeting. O for wisdom, and a quick

---

3   J. Cockerton, *Essentials of Evangelical Spirituality* (Grove Spirituality Series, 49; Nottingham: Grove Books, 1994), p. 3.

4   Randall, *Evangelical Experiences*, p 2. Cf. P. Sheldrake, *Christianity and History* (London: SPCK, 1991), p. 52, who argues that Christian spirituality is concerned with the conjunction of theology, communion with God and practical Christianity.

5   See Ryland, *Andrew Fuller*, pp. 44-63.

understanding in the fear of the Lord!' Fuller broke off his entry to attend the meeting at which his position was discussed. But when he returned home later that night to record the result his state of mind had not improved: 'The meeting house has been a Bochim today – a place of weeping! I have told the church to expect my removal, in a quarter of a year. Oh my soul! I seem unable to endure such attacks on my feelings!'[6]

In despair, Fuller next consulted a number of different ministers as to what to do. These included Robert Hall Sr and other Northamptonshire Association ministers, who all advised Fuller to move, and Robert Robinson of Cambridge who, much to Hall Sr's annoyance, suggested Fuller stayed, at least for the time being. The 'quick understanding' for which Fuller had prayed had not been given, and the expected 'removal' within three months did not take place. Following further struggles Fuller finally concluded that his 'continuance' at Soham 'would not be to my or their profit', and he was finally inducted to the pastorate at Kettering, following a year's trial, in October 1783.[7] It was the end of what his early biographers knew many readers would regard as an excessive, tortuous and even 'ridiculous' process, although they tried to present it positively.[8] Ryland was not exaggerating when he commented: 'Men who fear not God would risk the welfare of a nation with fewer searchings of heart than it cost him to determine whether he should leave a little dissenting church, scarcely containing forty members besides himself and his wife.'[9]

But Fuller's tendency towards introspective self-examination is revealed even more clearly by his painful lack of assurance of salvation. One diary entry in particular stands out, although a number of others in the same vein could also have been cited. On 12 September 1780 he wrote:

> Very much in doubt respecting my being in a state of grace... The Lord have mercy on me, for I know not how it is with me. One thing I know, that if I be a Christian at all, real Christianity in me is inexpressibly small in degree. O what a vast distance is there between what I ought to be, and what I am! If I am a saint at

---

6   Ryland, *Andrew Fuller*, p. 50-53 for information in this and the next paragraph. 'Bochim' was the place where the Israelites wept in Judges 2.5.

7   Fuller, 'Narrative', 26 May 1782, p. 50.

8   Ryland, *Andrew Fuller*, pp. 43-44; A.G. Fuller, *Men Worth Remembering*, p. 46.

9   Ryland, *Andrew Fuller*, p. 44. Ryland's own call from College Lane in Northampton to the Bristol Academy and Broadmead Baptist Church was also long and protracted. See Gordon, 'The Call of Ryland Jr', *passim*. Ryland's 'call' was issued in 1792 and not accepted until 1794.

all, I know I am one of the least of all saints. I mean, that the workings of real
grace in my soul are so feeble, that I hardly think they can be feebler in any true
Christian... I think of late, I cannot in prayer consider myself as a Christian, but as
a sinner casting myself at Christ's feet for mercy.[10]

Gilbert Laws comments on this extract, saying of Fuller, 'even yet he
is inclined to look within himself instead of looking off to Jesus'.[11]
Certainly introspective soul searching is clearly seen in this extract, as is
the complete lack of assurance of salvation. And Fuller's remedy for
this lack of certainty regarding whether he was really a Christian was
yet more self-examination – a constant searching inside himself, looking
for evidence of the 'working of real grace' in his soul. On 25 November
he wrote that he had been under 'heavy affliction' for a week and
'incapable of writing'. He continued:

I only observe, that some days I seemed to find no material workings of sin, nor
exercises of grace; sometimes I felt worse. One day I dreamed that I was dead:
waking and finding it but a dream, I trembled at the thought of what would
become of such a sinful creature, were this dream realized! Here I stopped,
painfully stopped: at length I answered, 'Lord I *have* hoped in thy salvation'. Here
I wept, and thought I would hope still. O that it may not be in vain.[12]

The final sentences were about as optimistic as Fuller's diary entries get
during this period.[13] The impression given is that, a full eleven years
after his initial conversion experience, he was close to despair.

It is important to be aware that his diary does not necessarily give a
totally rounded picture of his spiritual life at this time. Bruce
Hindmarsh, in his study of John Newton, comments that because his
subject's diary was used as a means of 'disciplined self examination' in
the Puritan tradition, its confessional and sometimes 'self recriminatory'
tone were not necessarily reflective of his spirituality as a whole. In
other words, taken on its own, the diary is likely to be a distortion of
Newton's spiritual life, a distortion created by the medium itself.[14] The
same is likely to be true for Fuller, and Hindmarsh's words of caution
need to born in mind, particularly as Fuller's diary is one of the primary
sources for understanding his spirituality. Probably his state of mind

---

10   Ryland, *Andrew Fuller*, p. 78. Cf. p. 119: 'I have a fountain of poison in my
nature...and am far from a spiritual frame of mind.'

11   Laws, *Andrew Fuller*, p. 38.

12   Ryland, *Andrew Fuller*, p. 87.

13   An impression gained from Ryland, *Andrew Fuller*, which is supported by an
examination of Fuller's 'Diary and Spiritual Thoughts'.

14   Hindmarsh, *John Newton*, p. 222.

was often brighter than the extracts above, and others like them, would lead one to believe. Nevertheless there is every reason to think that his struggle for assurance and lack of joy were very real. This anxiety continued long after he had finally moved to Kettering. Although it gradually did begin to ease, this only happened painfully slowly.

The Reasons for Fuller's Struggle

Why did Fuller struggle with doubt and introspection in this way, and for so long? Temperament is likely to have been a factor, and this will be touched on later in this chapter. But clearly Fuller was influenced by his background in High Calvinism, as the constant agonizing and desperate searching for 'some outgoings of soul to God' indicate. He had rejected the High Calvinist teaching that a subjective 'warrant' was necessary before someone could come to God for salvation, and yet he continued to struggle with what in many ways was an extension of this approach, as he looked inside himself for the evidence that would confirm that he really was one of the elect. But we need to probe a little deeper, and see that for Puritanism too, assurance was a struggle.[15] To receive assurance demanded much personal effort and rigorous self-examination. Journals were often kept, and Fuller's diary, although less systematic than Newton's journal, fits this pattern. Most importantly, for many of the Puritans assurance was, in the words of the seventeenth-century divine Thomas Brooks, 'a pearl that most want, a crown that few wear'.[16] Put another way, rather than being part of normal Christian experience, it was the possession of only a few. 'Assurance', as Bebbington states, 'was by no means the norm'.[17]

This Puritan view had been influential in shaping the High Calvinist view of assurance. But it is perhaps significant that some of the classic expressions of it are found in the writings of John Bunyan, in *Pilgrim's Progress* and particularly in *Grace Abounding to the Chief of Sinners*, both of which we know Fuller had read directly. *Grace Abounding* was Bunyan's 'spiritual autobiography'. In it he stated:

> How can you tell you are elected? And what if you should not [be elected]? How then? O Lord, thought I, what if I should not indeed? It may be you are not, said

---

15 See Bebbington, *Evangelicalism*, pp. 43-45; D. Gillett, *Trust and Obey: Explorations in Evangelical Spirituality* (London: Darton, Longman and Todd, 1993), pp. 42-46.

16 T. Brooks, *Heaven on Earth* (Edinburgh: Banner of Truth, 1961[1645]), p. 15. See also Gillett, *Trust and Obey*, p. 43.

17 Bebbington, *Evangelicalism*, p. 45.

the tempter: it may be so indeed thought I. Why then, said Satan, you had better leave off and strive no further, for if indeed you should not be elected and chosen by God, there is no talk of you being saved... By these things I was driven to my wits end, not knowing what to say, or how to answer these temptations.

Bunyan struggled long and hard with these thoughts. Later in *Grace Abounding* he stated: 'I could not believe that Christ had love for me; alas, I could neither hear him, nor see him, nor feel him, nor savour any of his things; I was driven as with a tempest.'[18] Some similarities, in content and tone, between these extracts and those from Fuller's diaries will be obvious. There is no evidence which directly links Bunyan with Fuller's struggle for assurance. But it is certainly possible that reading him and other Puritans reinforced the tendency towards doubt, introspection and self-examination which was part of his inherited High Calvinist milieu. This was in contrast to his reading of the Puritans elsewhere, which had confirmed him in his move away from High Calvinism. As Fuller took his leave of High Calvinism, it was this mutation of the Puritan emphasis on self-examination that he found hardest to break free from.

Further Struggles

By 1785, the year after the association's 'call to prayer' had been issued, there were some signs that Fuller was beginning to feel a little less unhappy. For example, diary references to 'tender feelings' and 'affections' slowly begin to mount up. This was so, particularly in connection with his preaching, the now regular monthly prayer meetings for Revival and the periodic meetings he had with other ministers.[19] It seems that Fuller was at his happiest and least introspective when he was engaging in some spiritual work with others. In the light of future developments, a decision he made on 25 September 1785, that from that point on he would not write in his diary unless there was something substantial or 'material' to note, is probably significant.[20] Certainly this prefigures the more factual diary, journal and commonplace book entries of the 1790s and beyond. But in the mid- to late- 1780s it was a

18   J. Bunyan, *Grace Abounding to the Chief of Sinners* (Harmondsworth, Middlesex: Penguin, 1987 [1666]), paragraphs 59-61, p. 19; paragraph 78, p. 23. The first of these extracts is also cited by Gillett, *Trust and Obey*, pp. 44-45, in his exposition of the Puritan view of assurance.

19   See Ryland, *Andrew Fuller*, p. 107; cf. pp. 110, 113, 118.

20   Ryland, *Andrew Fuller*, p. 111: 'It can answer no end to write, when there is nothing to write about.'

resolution he found it hard to keep, and the self-recriminatory tone often resurfaces. And yet even here it is possible to discern a shift, as Fuller more regularly bemoans a lack of activity and usefulness in God's service, rather than the possibility of 'his not being in a state of grace'. For example in January 1786, reviewing his spiritual progress during the preceding year, he wrote: 'Some painful reflections, in thinking on my vast deficiencies. Another year is gone; and what have I done for God? O that my life were more devoted to God! I feel as if I could wish to set out afresh for heaven; but, alas! my desires seem but too much like those of the sluggard.'[21] The accusatory tone remains, but its focus was subtly changing.

1786 to 1789 were, however, extremely painful years for Fuller. This was partly due to the death of his daughter at the age of six,[22] and partly due to a period of severe spiritual depression. Undoubtedly these were linked, although Fuller tended to treat them as separate 'trials'. His final surviving diary entry for 1786 was made on Sunday 11 June. Fuller had recently heard Robert Hall Sr preach, taking as his text Proverbs 30.2: 'Surely I am more brutish than any man'. Fuller was convinced these words were far more applicable to him than to his friend and mentor, so he proceeded to preach on them himself that Sunday.

The next diary entry that Ryland could discover was dated 3 October 1789, over three years later. Ryland recorded that between 16 to 18 leaves had been torn out (presumably by Fuller himself), but in his 3 October entry the Kettering pastor also confessed to have written nothing for 'about a year and a half', for, he said, 'it seemed to me that my life was not worth writing'.[23] Fuller described it as a time of 'lukewarmness', 'backsliding', and much 'hardness of heart'. Looking back on this period eight years later, in a letter to John Thomas in India, he wrote of 'a deep dejection' that had gripped him, which although he 'strove to throw it off in company' returned as soon as he was in private.[24] For a period of over three years Fuller was, by his own reckoning, both struggling as a Christian and struggling with depression.

The recommencement of his diary at the end of 1789 did not signal any great change, although reading Jonathan Edwards seemed to bring some relief. On 20 January 1790 he wrote: 'During the last quarter of a year I seemed to have gained some ground in spiritual things. I have read some of Jonathan Edwards' sermons, which have left a deep impression on my heart.' Fuller was reading from Edwards' *Practical*

---

21   Ryland, *Andrew Fuller*, p. 117.

22   In April 1786. A.G. Fuller, *Men Worth Remembering*, pp. 63-65. At this stage Fuller had already lost three children in infancy.

23   Ryland, *Andrew Fuller*, p. 119.

24   Fuller to J. Thomas, 16 May 1796, in Ryland, *Andrew Fuller*, pp. 119; 159.

Sermons, published posthumously in 1788 by John Erskine in Edinburgh. The fact that Fuller was clearly in possession of this at least by 1789 is an indication that the Northamptonshire ministers were by this time fully linked up with the wider Evangelical network.[25] Particular messages he noted include 'God the Christian's Portion' from Psalm 73.25 and 'The Importance of a Thorough Knowledge of Divine Truth' from Hebrews 5.12.[26] Both, as the titles suggest, were strongly God centred. In the sermon entitled, 'The Importance and Advantage of a Thorough Knowledge of Divine Truth', Edwards urged that this pursuit of divine truth should not be 'speculative', but warmly 'spiritual' and 'practical'. To acquire this knowledge a person should be 'assiduous' in reading the scriptures, 'diligent' in other reading and using opportunities in conversation 'to promote each other's knowledge of Divine things'. Edwards warned that a person must not pursue knowledge 'chiefly for the sake of applause [or] to enable you to dispute with others'. Rather it should be sought for 'the benefit of your souls, and in order to practice'.[27]

Fuller recorded the impact reading the Hebrews message had on him in his diary, namely 'a desire to rise earlier, to read more and to make the discovery of truth into more of a business'.[28] The focus both on God and on practical experience was also important in Edwards' sermon entitled 'God the Best Portion of the Christian'. Edwards contended 'that there is no sign of sincerity so much insisted on in the Bible as this, that we deny ourselves, sell all, forsake the world, take up the cross and follow Christ whithersoever he goeth'.[29] With the help of these messages, Fuller was, in the language of Laws, beginning to 'look off to Jesus', as well as becoming more focused on practical Evangelical action. These and other works by Edwards were to provide important theological fuel which helped to fire the reshaping of his spirituality in the years immediately following 1789. Fuller was also reading John Owen during this period, for example his *Mortification of Sin* and also a work on 'spiritual mindedness'.[30] Of course Owen too can be described

---

25   Indeed, the 'Advertisement' to this 1st edn, *Practical Sermons: Never Before Published* (Edinburgh: M. Gray, 1798), p i, included a letter from Edwards Jr to Ryland. As the subtitle to this work indicates, Edwards' *Practical Sermons* had not previously appeared in America.

26   Ryland, *Andrew Fuller*, pp. 120-21.

27   For the text of these sermons see *Edwards Works*, Hickman (ed.), II, pp. 157-63; 104-107.

28   Ryland, *Andrew Fuller*, p. 121.

29   *Edwards Works*, Hickman (ed.), II, p. 107.

30   For Owen's famous *The Mortification of Sin in Believers* (1656), see J. Owen, *The Works of John Owen* (24 vols; W.H Goold ed.; London: Banner of Truth, 1965-68

(rightly!) as resolutely Christ centred. But Fuller's diary entries reveal an interesting trend. When he reflects on something from Owen, with his strong emphasis on rigorous self-examination, there is a tendency to introspection and unhappiness; when he reflects on Edwards, there is generally a much more optimistic tone.[31] This was almost certainly unconscious on Fuller's part. But he was clearly moving in Edwards' direction.

Parallel to his theological reading, there was also the return of some 'tender' times in prayer, especially when it was corporate prayer focused on the continuing monthly meetings for Revival (which of course had their roots in Edwards' *Humble Attempt*). Towards the end of 1791 he heard of 'some revival of religion about Walsgrave and Guilsborough', news that he passed on to his own people at the Kettering prayer meeting, expressing a desire that this might be a precursor to Revival amongst themselves. Writing about this particular time of prayer he said: 'Surely, if ever I wrestled with God in my life, I did so then, for more grace, for forgiveness, for the restoration of the joys of salvation.' He also adds a note that would become absolutely characteristic: 'O that God's being merciful to us and blessing us, might be the means of his way being made known upon the earth, and his saving health among all nations!'[32] It was this increasing world vision which provides one of the keys to the important change in his spirituality that was about to take place.

The Development of an Evangelical Spirituality

There is no doubt that from 1792 onwards there was a quite definite shift in the tenor of Fuller's spiritual life. References to 'joy', 'peace' and 'happiness' become common, in his diary and in other writings. He gains a far greater assurance of salvation, and the self-recriminatory

---

[1850-53]), VI, pp. 5-86. Owen on 'spiritual mindedness' is probably a reference to *The Grace and Duty of Being Spiritually Minded* (*Owen's Works*, VII, pp. 267-306).

31   E.g. Ryland, *Andrew Fuller*, pp. 120-21, although this point should not be exaggerated. Nevertheless, an analysis of Fuller's 'Diary and Spiritual Thoughts' confirms this impression.

32   Ryland, *Andrew Fuller*, p. 112. There were Particular Baptist churches in the Northamptonshire Association at both Walsgrave and Guilsborough. F.C. Lusty, *Walsgrave Baptist Church 1700-1950: A Brief Record of Two Hundred and Fifty Years Witness and Service* (Northampton: Billingham & Son, 1950), pp. 8-12, speaks (with a degree of exaggeration), of a 'glorious revival' taking place at Walsgrave at this time. One of the fruits if this was a large number of young men who became pastors or engaged in village preaching towards the end of the century.

tone fades out almost entirely. Unhappiness and doubt occasionally resurface, but very rarely, and all the evidence points to 1792-93 as being watershed years which brought about what can only be described as a lasting transformation in his spiritual life. What had led to this sea change in Fuller's spirituality?

One clue to what happened is in a diary entry dated 18 July 1794. Reflecting back on the previous two years he recorded that he had 'experienced perhaps as much peace and calmness of mind, as at any former period'. He continued:

> I have been enabled to walk somewhat more near to God than heretofore; and I find that there is nothing that affords such a preservative against sin. 'If we walk in the Spirit, we shall not fulfill the lusts of the flesh.' This passage has been of great use to me, ever since I preached from it, which was on June 3, 1792. The idea on which I then principally insisted was that sin is to be overcome, not so much by a direct or mere resistance of it, as by opposing other principles and considerations to it. This sentiment has been abundantly verified in my experience: so far as I have walked in the Spirit, so far has my life been holy and happy: and I have experienced a good degree of these blessings, compared with former times; though but a very small degree compared with what I ought to aspire after.[33]

This is worth quoting at length, firstly because it illustrates powerfully the very real change that had taken place, dated as beginning in 1792. The extract also highlights Fuller's experiential biblicism, with biblical truth empirically tested and 'verified' in his own experience. Scripture and Fuller's experience agreed – this was the way to be both 'holy and happy'. But most important, in terms of Fuller's spirituality, was the way he was now defining the path to spiritual growth positively (walking in the Spirit), rather than negatively (resistance of sin). Sin was still to be resisted, obviously, but this was not to be done through what Fuller now believed was as a morbid preoccupation with it, but rather by focusing elsewhere, on other 'principles and considerations'. What these 'principles and considerations' were becomes clear in the following extracts.

1792 was of course the year the BMS was founded, with Fuller taking on the role of the society's first secretary. The significance of this event, and how Fuller gave himself wholeheartedly to this work, have already been covered in detail in chapter six. But the BMS was also absolutely crucial in the remodelling of Fuller's spirituality. On 18 July 1794 he

---

33   Ryland, *Andrew Fuller*, p. 124. Cf. p. 227, Fuller to J. Ryland, 2 April 1795: 'Sin is to be overcome, not by maintaining a direct opposition to it, as by cultivating opposite principles.'

wrote the following in his diary:

> Within the last year or two, we have formed a Missionary Society; and have been
> enabled to send out two of our brethren to the East Indies. My heart has been
> greatly interested in this work. Surely I never felt more genuine love to God and
> to his cause in my life. I bless God that this work has been a means of reviving my
> soul. If nothing else comes of it, I and many others have obtained a spiritual
> advantage.[34]

Six months earlier he had written to Ryland: 'I have found the more I
do for Christ, the better it is with me. I never enjoyed so much the
pleasures of religion, as I have within the last two years, since we have
engaged in the Mission business. Mr Whitfield [sic] used to say, "The
more a man does for God, the more he may".'[35] The last comment is
significant because of what, for Fuller, was a rare reference to
Whitefield (note the spelling!). But far more important is the way both
these extracts specifically tie Fuller's changing spirituality to his activity
on behalf of the BMS. It was this, after many years of struggle, that
provided the decisive breakthrough in Fuller's quest for assurance and
happiness.

Why did his involvement with the BMS have such a significant and,
as Fuller believed, such a positive effect on his spirituality?
Undoubtedly Fuller's temperament should be mentioned here. A
number of the quotations in this chapter suggest that he was happier in
company than he was on his own, and happier too when he was actively
involved in *doing* something. This is confirmed by other comments,
both from Fuller himself and his friends. Also revealing is the fact that
he never had a 'study' in which to work, although there were rooms in
his house he could have used for this purpose. Throughout his life at
Kettering, the desk from which he did all his writing was in the sitting
room, and 'he worked with his family around him'.[36] The suspicion
must be that constitutionally he was far more suited to a spirituality
focused on activity than a contemplative one. As Morris commented
bluntly (and honestly): 'if spirituality consists in an aptness for spiritual
exercises...Mr Fuller was not eminent.'[37] But this on its own is not
sufficient explanation for what was happening. Fuller, like so many

---

34   Ryland, *Andrew Fuller*, p. 155.

35   Ryland, *Andrew Fuller*, p. 226. Letter dated 3 December 1793.

36   Morris, *Andrew Fuller*, 1st edn, p. 475; Laws, *Andrew Fuller*, p. 70: 'Under
such circumstances he penned all his letters to the missionaries...and generally
conducted all the work of the [BMS] committee.'

37   Morris, *Andrew Fuller*, 1st edn, p. 478. Morris was surveying the whole of
Fuller's ministerial career.

others of differing temperaments, was now being completely swept along in the Evangelical current. The cause of world-wide Revival, to which Fuller now gave himself in intense activity, was also a means to personal revival and the focus of a renewed, thoroughly Evangelical spirituality.

Fuller's New Approach to the Spiritual Life

Fuller drew together the key emphases of his new found spirituality in a circular letter written for the Northamptonshire Association in 1795, expounding his chosen themes with passion. This letter is well worth a detailed examination.[38] Fuller took as his title 'Why Christians in the Present Day Possess Less Joy than the Primitive Disciples', and he was quite clear as to the answers. The primary reason the early believers experienced more joy was their strong sense of assurance. Indeed, Fuller insisted that they enjoyed a 'settled persuasion of their interest in Christ'. He stated that: 'In all the New Testament we have scarcely an instance of a Christian being at a loss to perceive the evidence of his Christianity. What are called doubts and fears among us, and which make up so large a portion of our religious experiences, seem to have occupied scarcely any place amongst them.' Fuller continued to attack the High Calvinist spirituality that he believed was responsible for his own painful struggles:

> The language that we are in the habit of using, when speaking of our love, or faith, or obedience, betrays a sad defect in the exercise of these heavenly graces... I desire to love, I would believe, I wish to be obedient, are expressions which frequently occur in our prayers and hymns... Such language is unknown in the Scriptures, unless it be found in the character of the slothful.

Fuller had rarely been so bold, even daring to attack the High Calvinist hymnody prevalent in many Particular Baptist churches. Christians could and should be more certain, more definite. But where could this sense of assurance come from? Fuller was clear first of all that his reader's focus should shift, from a concentration on themselves (I desire, I would, I wish), to a concentration on the great truths of the gospel. The joy and peace the early Christians experienced was, first of all, through believing the good news. They believed in Christ, in his cross and in the promises of God regarding the future. In 'laying down

---

38   *Fuller's Works*, III, pp. 325-31. All the following quotations from 'Why Christians in the Present Day Possess Less Joy than the Primitive Disciples' are from these pages.

his life' Christ had delivered all that would believe 'from the wrath to come'. For Fuller, this gospel and these promises had not changed, nor had they lost any of their power, for Christ was the same, 'yesterday, today and forever'. Therefore the same joy and assurance was available, and through the same route. His readers needed to believe the objective truth of the gospel, and stop looking for subjective indicators within themselves that they were truly part of God's elect. To sum up, because Christ and his gospel had not changed, contemporary Christians could have the same assurance and joy as 'primitive' ones, if they maintained the same focus.

This note, that present assurance should be the normal experience of believers, was thoroughly Evangelical.[39] During the first 'Great Awakening', Jonathan Edwards would meet in his study with those who claimed to have undergone a decisive spiritual experience. If he was satisfied that this experience was genuine, he would assure them that they were converted.[40] Fuller's view was perhaps less focused on experience than Edwards or some other Evangelicals in that he tended to stress the objective work of Christ more than feelings. This was a line also taken by the Evangelical clergyman Henry Venn,[41] although feelings (the possession of the 'joy' that was spoken of in the association letter), were nevertheless important to Fuller. This more confident approach to assurance was one of the defining characteristics of eighteenth-century Evangelicalism. It was clearly a break from High Calvinism, but also represented a shift away from the Puritan view of assurance discussed earlier in this chapter. For the Puritans assurance was often the fruit of a long struggle; Fuller (despite his own earlier struggles), now believed that it should come through believing the promises of God. And where for the Puritans assurance had been 'a crown that few wear', for Fuller it should be the present possession of all believers.

The way to assurance and joy therefore, was through believing and being 'rooted and grounded' in the gospel. But Fuller then struck a second note, one that clearly reflected his own experience. Believing in Christ was not the only thing the 'primitive' Christians did. They believed the gospel – and then they went out and spread it. The early Christians were 'Commissioned to publish glad tidings to every creature, and persuaded that the cause in which they were engaged

---

39   Bebbington, *Evangelicalism*, p. 46; Gillett, *Trust and Obey*, pp. 47-51; D. Tidball, *Who are the Evangelicals: Tracing the Roots of Today's Movement* (London: Marshall Pickering, 1994), pp. 200-202.

40   Bebbington, *Evangelicalism*, pp. 47-48, links this view with Enlightenment empiricism.

41   As described by Bebbington, *Evangelicalism*, p. 45.

would sooner or later universally prevail, they laboured with courage and assiduity, and the work of the Lord prospered in their hands'. Moreover, Fuller was clear that for them, this had led to assurance and great joy: 'The primitive Christians were all intent on disseminating the gospel through the world; and it was in the midst of this kind of employment, and the persecutions which attended it, that they are said to have been "filled with joy and with the Holy Ghost".' Once again, Fuller drew straight lines from the experience of early Christians to those in his own day. His readers could and should follow the example of the church of the New Testament. If they did, then they too could expect similar joy.

Fuller tied his appeal to Evangelical action in the pursuit of conversions to his post-millennial eschatology which confidently expected a great 'turning to Christ' before his return. It was time to go forward in 'prayer, praise and joyful exertion'. But Fuller's major point was still quite simple: that joy came when believers stopped focusing on their own comfort and became 'swallowed up' in a vigorous concern for the salvation of others. Fuller once again drove this home with a strong challenge to any of his readers whose spirituality had been shaped by their High Calvinist milieu: 'If a portion of the time which we spend in ransacking for evidence in the mass of past experiences, were employed in promoting the cause of God in the world, and seeking the welfare of the souls and bodies of men, it would turn to a better account. In seeking the salvation of others we should find our own.'

For the sake of balance it is important to note that Fuller never completely repudiated self-examination. In a sermon entitled 'Advice to the Dejected' (not dated, but internal evidence makes it clear it must have been later than his 1792 watershed), he says he does not want to discourage 'all remembrances of past experiences', and criticizes preachers who 'cry down...all marks and signs of internal Christianity, taken from the work of sanctification in the soul.'[42] He continued to have a high regard for the Puritans, for example recommending in 1796 that the melancholic and depressive John Thomas read 'Dr Owen on the Mortification of Sin', and promising to send a copy to India for him.[43] But on the occasions where he was prepared to recommend some form of spiritual self-examination, he was careful to qualify it immediately with the sort of comments we see him making in his association letter.[44] There is a real sense in which, at least on this issue, he was not only leaving High Calvinism, but also leaving Puritanism.

Fuller concluded the association letter with the following appeal to

---

42   *Fuller's Works*, I, p. 234.

43   Fuller to J. Thomas, 16 May 1796, in Ryland, *Andrew Fuller*, p. 160.

44   See e.g., *Fuller's Works*, I, p. 471.

his readers' recent experience:

> We appeal to your own hearts, brethren, with respect to your late disinterested exertions for carrying the gospel amongst the heathen, we appeal to those of you especially who have had the undertaking most at heart, whether...you have not felt more of the joyful part of religion than you did before; yea, may we add, more than at any former period in your remembrance.

Fuller effectively challenged his readers to theological reflection on their recent experience of active commitment to the cause of world mission. All of this was of course deeply rooted in *his own* experience. In fact the whole letter is shot through with autobiography. Fuller is charting his own journey from an introspective, uncertain, unhappy and, he believed, an ultimately unholy piety to a God-centred, expansive, confident, joyful and supremely activist spirituality.

Before moving on it is interesting to reflect briefly on the inter-relationship between activism and assurance for Fuller. It is common for historians of eighteenth-century Evangelicalism to speak of how a confident knowledge of eternal security was, for men like Whitefield and Wesley, the essential motor for an activism that showed itself in intercessory prayer and evangelism.[45] For Fuller, an Evangelical whose life and career straddled the eighteenth and the nineteenth centuries, the relationship between assurance and activism was more complex, and if anything, reversed. Rather than assurance and 'joy unspeakable' leading to activism, activism in the service of the gospel was the key unlocking the door to joy and assurance. In highlighting this, this study seeks to make a contribution to an understanding of the dynamics involved in the development of Evangelical spirituality during this period.

The Main Themes of Fuller's Evangelical Spirituality

This chapter concludes with an examination of the main themes of Fuller's mature spirituality as it developed post 1792. To do this it is necessary to examine not only his private devotional practice as revealed in the diaries and in the journals of his missionary tours, but also his teaching on the Christian life. Fuller was increasingly to occupy an important public role as a sort of unofficial 'spiritual director' to missionaries and churches, a role maintained by means of his

---

45   Gillett, *Trust and Obey*, pp. 60-61, describes assurance as adding 'another octane to faith'; cf. Bebbington, *Evangelicalism*, p. 10, who speaks of the 'imperative to be up and doing'.

voluminous correspondence and frequent journeys.[46] Consequently relevant sermons and letters need also to be taken into account in highlighting what was most important for him as far as the spiritual life was concerned. In fact it becomes increasingly difficult to trace his spirituality through the diaries alone, as the frequency and nature of the entries in his diary and commonplace book change considerably from 1792 onwards. This in itself, of course, says something important about his new 'activist' focus. Surveying the range of relevant material, a number of closely related themes emerge.[47]

An Emphasis on the Bible and Prayer

Fuller's emphases on the Bible and prayer can be noted first. On 18 August 1814 Fuller wrote to Jabez Carey (1793-1862) in India. Jabez was the third and youngest of William Carey's sons, born just weeks before he finally set sail for India.[48] Jabez had followed his father in his commitment to the mission, and Fuller's letter to him was full of warmth, referring to Jabez as 'my dear young friend'. He had important advice to give: 'It will be a matter of great consequence that you be conversant with your Bible…[and] that you be much in prayer (dear Sutcliff said near his end, "I wish I had prayed more!").'[49] The Bible and prayer were absolutely fundamental to Fuller, and they were often joined in his thinking. To the missionaries James Chater, William Robinson and their respective partners, Fuller wrote of his own practice:

> I find it advantageous to read a part of the Scriptures to myself, before private prayer, and often turn it into prayer as I read it. Do not read the Scriptures merely as preachers, in order to find a text…but read them, that you may get good to your own souls.[50]

These were points that Fuller would regularly make, in his letters to missionaries and in public ministry. His desire for prayers that grew out

---

46   Morris, *Andrew Fuller*, 2nd edn, p. 45, compared Fuller's position amongst the Particular Baptist churches to that of a bishop.

47   For another survey of the spiritual themes most important to Fuller see Haykin (ed.), *Armies of the Lamb*, pp. 37-53. Haykin considers Fuller's spirituality by focusing on his missionary emphasis, the cross, his 'spiritual friendships' and spiritual renewal.

48   George, *Faithful Witness*, pp. 82-86.

49   Cited by Haykin (ed.), *Armies of the Lamb*, p. 264. Sutcliff had died earlier that year.

50   Fuller to Mr and Mrs Chater and Mrs and Mrs Robinson, 5 April 1806, in Ryland, *Andrew Fuller*, pp. 161-62.

of and were shaped by the scriptures themselves is typical of his high view of the Bible – Fuller was nothing if not a thoroughgoing biblicist. The significance of corporate prayer for Fuller is clear enough, particularly due to his involvement in the 'Call to Prayer'. But he also emphasized the importance of private prayer, as the above extracts indicate. In a message preached in London in 1797, Fuller contended that the 'prosperous soul' was one in which there was a balance between the 'retired' and 'active'. He continued:

> It is by retiring to our closets, reading the word of God in private, thinking and praying over it; by conversing with our own souls in secret, by dwelling on divine things...it is in these holy exercises that we may expect to meet a divine blessing, and to acquire such a savour of spirit, that when we go out into the world we shall carry the savour of Christ with us.[51]

Family prayers were also stressed in a number of his writings, and Fuller could challenge parents as to their responsibilities with passion. In another sermon preached in London, on 1 July 1800, he stated that: 'The godly parent has a very solemn and important charge, and he feels it to be such. It has been remarked more than once, where a child has been born and added to a family, "Now we have not only another body to provide for, but a soul to pray for."' He continued: 'Oh for the parent to be able to say, on his dying bed, "Be ye followers of me as I have been of Christ!" Oh for the parent to be able to say to his family, when taking leave of life, "The things that you have heard in me and seen of me, do!"'[52] The picture that emerges of the mature Fuller, is of someone who urged that a high place should be given Bible reading and prayer – in the corporate, family and personal spheres.

It is natural to question the extent to which Fuller's public teaching was reflected in his own private devotional practice. This is a particularly important area to open up given the material we looked at in chapter six, which suggested that later in life he became almost consumed by his work, particularly on behalf of the BMS. Piecing together a picture of Fuller's devotional life post 1792 is not an easy task. That Fuller in the 1780s gave himself daily to private and family prayers, as well as regularly setting aside longer times for prayer, fasting and Bible meditation, is well attested in his diary. Similar evidence for the later period is singularly lacking, as the nature and number of the

---

51   *Fuller's Works*, I, p. 406. The sermon was entitled 'Soul Prosperity' and delivered at the Old Jewry Chapel, London, 27 December 1797.

52   *Fuller's Works*, I, p. 472. The sermon was entitled 'Importance of Union of Public and Private Interests in the Service of God', and preached at New Bond Street Chapel, London.

diary entries change. The material relating to his tours with the BMS is also silent on these issues, with Fuller using his journal and letters to record details of his health, people he met, his preaching in different places and the amount of money raised for the mission.[53]

Of course it would be foolish to conclude, in the light of this, that Fuller did not give time to these things. In fact there are some clear references to the fact that Fuller maintained his private devotional life post 1792, as well as many hints. The letters to the various missionaries already quoted are relevant. Writing to John Thomas in India, in 1795 and 1796, he assured Thomas of his prayers. 'How often do I think of you' he wrote on Christmas Eve, 1795, 'especially on a Lord's day morning... My soul goes up to God for you'. With reference to all the India missionaries he exclaimed: 'Lord bless them, keep them, support them, succeed them.' Having heard from Samuel Pearce that Thomas was struggling with feelings of depression he later wrote: 'How could I weep on your account! Nay, before I write any more, I will go aside, and weep, and pray for you, to him who alone can deliver your soul from death and keep your feet from falling.'[54]

Further evidence concerning Fuller's spiritual life from this period comes from Gunton Fuller, who recorded that his father devoted a day to fasting and prayer before his second marriage to Ann Coles in 1794. He also reproduces Fuller's words to his errant son Robert in 1809, that he prayed 'continually' for him.[55] Doubtless many similar comments could have been made, but these things were not recorded in detail or with any frequency, at least in part because Fuller and his biographers were by this stage focusing on other things.[56] There are references from the 1780s of Fuller praying and meditating on scripture when travelling alone to a preaching engagement, and it is likely that this was a practice

---

53   See Ryland, *Andrew Fuller*, pp. 147-211, for the relevant sections.

54   Fuller to J. Thomas, 24 December 1795 and 16 May 1796, in Ryland, *Andrew Fuller*, pp. 158-60.

55   A.G. Fuller, *Men Worth Remembering*, pp. 71, 74.

56   See Ryland, *Andrew Fuller*, pp. 152 (prayer for the BMS) and 292-93 (An evening of prayer with his second wife and 'serious friends'), for some relevant references, also 'Reading the Scriptures', in *Fuller's Works*, III, pp. 788-89. The latter piece is potentially important evidence for Fuller's spiritual life post 1792. Fuller spoke of his own practice of rising early to read the Bible, mixing reading with prayer and reflection. 'Reading the Scriptures' is n.d. in *Fuller's Works*, but clearly appeared originally in one of the magazines to which Fuller contributed, although I have been unable to track it down. Probably it was written before the death of Pearce in 1799, as Fuller's friend is spoken of in the present tense, but it must have been after 1793, the year that the *Evangelical Magazine* was founded. All the other magazines to which Fuller contributed began life after this date.

he continued to make use of, perhaps increasingly so.[57] We might add that it is inherently unlikely that someone with his obvious integrity should teach certain things to others and then entirely neglect them in his own life. There can be little doubt that Fuller's devotional life was richer than the fragmentary and incomplete evidence suggests.

Nevertheless, we have to conclude that as his work increased to unmanageable proportions and as his health grew worse, he found regular private prayer and Bible reading increasingly more difficult. As we have seen, temperamentally Fuller was not contemplative. But he himself believed, as early as 1800, that he was in danger of neglecting not only 'my own family' but also 'my own vineyard, my own soul'.[58] On some of his BMS tours to Scotland, it appears he found it difficult to fit in time to sleep, let alone to pray. He was finding the balance between the 'retired' and the 'active' that he had urged on his London hearers in 1797 increasingly difficult to maintain for himself.

There were signs too, that this unceasing activity, which had initially brought him such happiness, was becoming so great a weight as to rob him of some of his joy. 'I sit down almost in despair', he wrote to Sutcliff in 1800: 'under this…load my heart has often of late groaned for rest.'[59] This is not typical, and Fuller's tone in most of his correspondence remained positive till the end. Also, his increasingly poor health must have been a major factor contributing to his sometimes feeling unhappy. But it is hard to avoid the impression that Fuller was just doing too much. At one stage, in 1807, he was feeling so overwhelmed that he wrote to Ryland saying 'I could almost wish I could shut myself up in a monastery'.[60] Fuller's attitude to Roman Catholics was colourful to say the least, and he is unlikely to have made the above remark lightly.[61] These feelings tended to come and go, but there is little doubt that the spiritual dynamic that Fuller had discovered, that activity in God's service led to increased joy, was sometimes stretched to breaking point.

---

57 Ryland, *Andrew Fuller*, p. 106.

58 A.G. Fuller, *Men Worth Remembering*, p. 91.

59 A.G. Fuller, *Men Worth Remembering*, pp. 91-92.

60 Ryland, *Andrew Fuller*, p. 249. The letter is dated 13 January 1807.

61 See e.g. Fuller's 'Commonplace Book', p. 15, for a reflection on 'the shocking immorality of popery'. In holding these views Fuller was, of course, typical of Protestant Dissenters of his age.

An Emphasis on Experience and the Cross

Returning to the evaluation of the emphases of Fuller's mature spirituality, we also need to note his stress on 'experimental religion', and his belief in the centrality of the cross of Christ. The stress on 'experience' and 'feeling' can be seen in many of the extracts we have already cited. For Fuller, true religion was 'felt' religion. This can be seen clearly in contrast to the Sandemanian Scotch Baptists, who we saw Fuller encountered on his missionary tours of Scotland. The majority of Scotch Baptists, with their intellectualized and dry understanding of faith, represented one of the alternative spiritualities on offer in the eighteenth-century market place. They must, according to Derek Murray, 'have appealed to those who were tired of looking for signs and motions of the heart, and who also had been the victims of over emotional preaching of the gospel'.[62] As already noted, Sandemanian views had heavily influenced the majority of Scotch Baptist churches. Fuller would have none of it, and his reasons were clear. As noted in chapter six, he believed they did not put sufficient emphasis on the exercise of the 'affections', and held to teaching that quenched the 'religion of the heart'.[63] His preaching in later life also contained an increasing emphasis on the Holy Spirit, and on the need for pastoral ministers, and others, to experience the felt presence of Christ.[64] For Fuller, this emphasis was non-negotiable.

But he was equally certain that experience had to be biblically based and focused on Christ and his cross. Gunton Fuller wrote that: 'If there was one theme on which he insisted...it was the sacrifice and mediation of Christ. Here he was at home, and again and again does he insist on it in his private records and his correspondence.'[65] For Fuller, the cross was 'the central point in which all the lines of evangelical truth meet and are united.'[66] In a sermon, entitled 'Conformity to the Death of Christ', Fuller made his own statement regarding the centrality of the cross of Christ: 'The death of Christ is a subject of so much importance

---

62   D.B. Murray, 'The Seventeenth and Eighteenth Centuries', in (ed.), D.W. Bebbington, *The Baptists in Scotland: A History* (Glasgow: Baptist Union of Scotland, 1988), p. 15; cf. J.S. Fisher, *Impelled by Faith: A Brief History of the Baptists in Scotland* (Stirling: Scottish Baptist History Project, 1996), pp. 2-3.

63   Ryland, *Andrew Fuller*, p. 170.

64   See *Fuller's Works*, I, pp. 504-505 for a sermon, 'The Influence of the Presence of Christ on a Minister'.

65   A.G. Fuller, *Men Worth Remembering*, p. 62.

66   *Calvinistic and Socinian Systems Compared* in *Fuller's Works*, II, p. 182. See Haykin (ed.), *Armies of the Lamb*, pp. 36-50, for this and other similar quotations.

in Christianity as to be essential to it...It is not so much a member of the body of Christian doctrine as the life blood that runs through the whole of it. The doctrine of the cross is the Christian doctrine.'[67]

As the first half of this study showed, Fuller's theology majored on the atonement, the saving work of Christ. As Fuller stated, the death of Christ was not that of a 'mere martyr'.[68] In a sermon on 'Preaching Christ' he urged gospel ministers to 'hold up Christ's atonement and mediation as the only ground of a sinner's hope'. It is the work of a Christian minister, he declared, 'to beat off self righteous hope...and to direct his hearers to the only hope set before them in the gospel'. He continued: 'Your business with the sins of mankind is to make use of them to convince your hearers of the corruption of their nature, and their need for a radical cure.'[69] The saving work of Christ on the cross had to be believed by the minister and preached with conviction, so that others too could experience what Fuller believed was their only hope.

But as well as emphasizing the atonement, he also stressed the cross as the motivation and standard for a godly Christian life. In the sermon on 'Conformity to the Death of Christ', Fuller emphasized that it was on the cross that love to God and love to men were supremely shown. 'Such was the example of Jesus', he stated, 'and such must be ours, if we be made conformable to him'. Moreover the spirit in which Christ endured his sufferings, with his prayer, 'Father forgive them, for they know not what they do', also spoke powerfully to Christians regarding their own attitudes and conduct.[70] The same themes were picked out in Fuller's missionary correspondence. In the letter to Chater and Robinson, cited earlier, he also wrote: 'Next to communion with your God and Saviour, cherish love to one another... To do this you must often think of the dying love of Christ towards you.' He continued: 'My dear brethren, know nothing but Jesus Christ and him crucified. Be this the summit of your ambition.'[71] The cross of Christ, therefore, was not only a sacrifice for sin which had to be embraced, but also an example of love to be imitated. As Derek Tidball has written: 'At the heart of Evangelical spirituality lies the atoning work of Christ. The Christian life is viewed primarily as a life that finds its origin in the cross and is lived in grateful response to it and humble imitation of it.'[72] Fuller

---

67   *Fuller's Works*, I, p. 310. The sermon is n.d..

68   *Fuller's Works*, I, p. 313.

69   *Fuller's Works*, I, pp. 501-504. This was preached at a minister's ordination. It is n.d. but must have been after 1806, as Fuller mentions Abraham Booth's death.

70   *Fuller's Works*, I, pp. 313-14.

71   Ryland, *Andrew Fuller*, p. 162.

72   D. Tidball, *The Message of the Cross* (Bible Speaks Today Bible Themes Series, 3; Leicester: IVP, 2000), p. 21. Gillett *Trust and Obey*, p. 66, highlights a stress

exemplified this, and the cross was a theme he returned to again and again.

An Emphasis on Conversion

The fact that Fuller pursued a 'conversionist' agenda should by now be obvious. But it is important to underline this once more in the context of his spirituality. Indeed, it should enjoy a central place. When Fuller prayed to God, it was, more often than not, for the 'Revival of religion' – in short, for conversions. When he worked for God, it was to bring about conversions, whether at home or overseas. When he reflected on the cross, it was primarily as the saving, atoning work of Christ which had to be preached evangelistically. His stress on evangelism undoubtedly played a key role in shaping the way he related to God. This evangelistic focus he urged on others. His conclusion to 'Conformity to the death of Christ' was typical. If Christ died to 'save sinners', then to conform to his death Christians must also seek the salvation of others. And this exhortation was not for ministers only, for 'the army of the Lamb is composed of the whole body of Christians'. Fuller urged that every disciple of Jesus should 'consider himself a missionary'. Though not all are called to preach all are called to serve and to '[recommend] the Saviour by a holy conversation'.[73]

Fuller's emphasis on conversion was also important for his views of baptism, which, he was clear, signified both a fundamental break with the forces of 'the world' and a radical new commitment to follow Christ. For this and for other reasons too, Fuller had a tenacious commitment to baptism, by immersion, for believers only. But equally important was the fact that he refused to make baptism itself his focus.[74] As he wrote to James Deakin, a deacon of the first Baptist church in Scotland to be organized along English lines, baptism was extremely significant, but it 'must not be the leading object in our ministrations'. Rather: 'Christ and him crucified must be our theme, and the turning of sinners to him...must be our object... If we are more concerned about an inferior matter than the spread of that kingdom for which our Redeemer died, then we really are sectarians, and shall come to nothing.'[75] What we can note here is this clear, strong commitment to conversions, an emphasis which shaped his spirituality.

---

on the cross as being at the 'heart of Evangelical spirituality'.

73   *Fuller's Works*, I, p. 315.
74   Cf. Haykin, 'Hazarding all for God at a Clap', pp. 185-95, especially p. 193.
75   Payne, 'Letters to James Deakin', p. 361.

Conclusion

This brief survey of Fuller's spirituality has highlighted a stress on the Bible and prayer, on the cross, and on experience, as defining themes for him. Moreover we have seen that these should not be considered as isolated strands but as closely woven parts of the whole. These of course were all key Evangelical characteristics, and this chapter has shown that Evangelicalism had permeated to the deepest level of Fuller's life. And yet this material has also suggested that if we want to highlight the dominant and defining note of Fuller's post 1792, BMS shaped spirituality, we need to return specifically to the theme of a God centred activity in pursuit of conversions, allied with a joyful Evangelical assurance of salvation. It was these activist and conversionist imperatives which in a very real sense defined the way that he related to God, and which summarized his lived spiritual experience. In a sermon preached in Norwich in 1810, entitled The 'Progress of the Gospel', he sounded the note that had become absolutely characteristic, and serves as a fitting conclusion not only to this chapter, but also to second half of this book. When you see a man 'God has raised up in order to spread the gospel in the earth', Fuller declared, then you see a man who has 'his heart full of spirituality'.[76]

---

76   *Fuller's Works*, III, p. 835.

CHAPTER EIGHT

Conclusion

I have...been enabled to love and serve him afresh

Fuller's *Works* include a sermon preached at the 'Old Jewry Chapel' in London in 1797 entitled 'Soul Prosperity' (referred to briefly in chapter seven). Fuller took 3 John 2 as his text and focused on the character of Gaius, the 'eminently pious and godly man' who was the recipient of the letter. Fuller stated that, for Gaius, 'the great principles of evangelical truth...afforded a constant spring of activity.' He continued: 'principles...lie at the bottom and source of affections and actions. If they be genuine, evangelical, and true, they are the spring of a holy life, and lie at the bottom of evangelical obedience.'[1] This study has sought to show that Fuller himself was an example of this dynamic in action, and it is hard to believe that his own experience did not inform his preaching at this point. Fuller had embraced what he termed here 'the great principles of evangelical truth', principles he had expounded to great effect in *The Gospel Worthy of Acceptation*. By the time *The Gospel Worthy* was finally published in 1785 this renewed theology had already become a 'spring' of 'evangelical obedience' for him, one which would determine the shape of his ministry for the rest of his life. First in thought and then in ministry, Fuller became an Evangelical.

Fuller's Movement from High Calvinism to Evangelicalism

This study has sought to map out in some detail the journey Fuller took as he abandoned High Calvinism and embraced Evangelical principles. This journey can be charted in each of the areas of his life and ministry surveyed in this study, beginning with theology and ending with spirituality, the last aspect of Fuller's life and thought to be decisively

---

1   *Fuller's Works*, I, p. 405.

transformed. In analysing why this movement took place, a cluster of interlocking factors have been noted. Important for Fuller, at almost every point, were the writings of Jonathan Edwards, both theological, philosophical and practical. The influence of Edwards was particularly marked as Fuller adopted the Edwardsean distinction between natural and moral inability in his theology, but it can also be seen in the effect the *Humble Attempt* had in broadening Fuller's evangelistic vision and in the way Edwards' sermons helped to refashion Fuller's spirituality. Fuller also came to be influenced by a number of theologians in the New Divinity school, followers of Edwards who went beyond him by embracing the Grotian governmental theory of the atonement. As Ivimey said, once Fuller had become 'acquainted with the writings of President Edwards, and the other New England divines...he drank deeply into them.'[2] The extent to which he leaned on Edwards and his disciples was one of the distinctive features of Fuller's Evangelicalism.

But this study has shown that a range of other factors were also crucial in bringing about changes in his theology and practice. Of particular note are Fuller's commitment to test everything by the Bible, and his desire for conversions. These typically Evangelical priorities provided a framework with which Fuller could sift and evaluate theological writing. For example when some of Edwards so-called 'improvers' set human philosophy on a level with the scriptures he would not follow them, and where they engaged in what Fuller considered esoteric metaphysical speculation he stated clearly his belief that they were being drawn away from the simplicity of the gospel. Fuller's Evangelical distinctives came to form the lens through which theology was viewed.

Fuller's Evangelicalism

As his career unfolded, Fuller consistently and increasingly displayed all of the hallmarks of Evangelicalism highlighted by Bebbington, namely crucicentrism, biblicism, conversionism and activism. That this 'quadrilateral of priorities'[3] was vital for Fuller has been emphasized repeatedly throughout this study, and much material could be cited to restate and reinforce this conclusion. One relevant passage not yet cited is found in the letter from Fuller to John Thomas in India, dated 16 May 1796. In it Fuller contrasted his new spirituality with his older practice:

> Within these [last] few years, my soul has not only recovered its former tone; but

---

2   *HEB*, IV, p. 437
3   Bebbington, *Evangelicalism*, p. 3.

blessed be God! a greater degree of spiritual strength than at any other period: and I think my engagement in the work of the mission has more than anything contributed to it. Before this I did little but pore over my misery; but since I have betaken myself to greater activity for God, my strength has been recovered, and my soul replenished. I have not been contented with ransacking for past evidences of love for God; but have been enabled to love and serve him afresh; looking for mercy to the Lamb of God, who taketh away the sin of the world.[4]

This single quotation illustrates a number of key points. First of all the movement from High Calvinism to Evangelicalism (in this instance in the realm of spirituality), is obvious. Fuller had left behind 'poring over his misery' and 'ransacking for past evidences of God's love'. He believed he had discovered a new approach which gave him 'a greater degree of spiritual strength' than ever before. Secondly, the four special marks of Evangelicalism all surface here. Fuller is both biblically based and focused on the cross of Christ ('the Lamb of God, who taketh away the sin of the world' [a direct quotation from John 1.29]). He is also conversionist ('the work of the mission') and, perhaps most obviously in this paragraph, activist ('I have betaken myself to greater activity'). Moreover the very fact that this letter was written to an overseas cross-cultural missionary, revealing a heartfelt concern for such activity, further marks Fuller out as an eighteenth-century Evangelical.[5] Bebbington's analysis of the characteristic tenets of Evangelicalism has provided the appropriate framework for this study of Fuller. Fuller's theology and practice were shaped by Evangelical forces and marked by Evangelical concerns.

In seeking to lay bare the driving force behind Fuller's life and ministry I have sometimes been tempted to argue, albeit tentatively, that for Fuller conversionism was paramount, and that it is this that provides the key to understanding his wide-ranging career. There is much evidence from this study which could be marshalled to support such a conclusion, particularly in the accounts of his pastoral ministry, work for the BMS and spirituality. His theology too was fashioned and re-fashioned in large measure by his evangelistic priorities, in particular his desire to safeguard at all costs the free offer of the gospel. Undoubtedly, both Fuller's ministry and his theology can be described as thoroughly evangelistic.

But following prolonged reflection, and a few false starts, I have drawn back from arguing that Fuller's commitment to evangelism was more important to him than the other three Evangelical distinctives, and

---

4   Fuller to J. Thomas, 16 May 1796, in Ryland, *Andrew Fuller*, p. 160.

5   Not forgetting the concern of someone like the Puritan Richard Baxter for this sort of work.

this for a number of reasons. Most important is that a strong case can also be made for the vital importance of the other three Evangelical priorities. As I have sought to show, Fuller believed wholeheartedly in what Peter T. Forsyth would later term 'the cruciality of the cross'.[6] It was the theme of his preaching, his theology and his private counsel. For Fuller the cross was 'the central point in which all lines of evangelical truth meet and are united'. Indeed, just as the sun is vital to the operation of the solar system so, according to Fuller, 'the doctrine of the cross is [vital] to the system of the gospel; it is the life of it.'[7] Writing to his father-in-law, William Coles, in June 1804, Fuller stated that the doctrine of the cross was so 'dear' to him he wished he would 'never preach another sermon but what shall bear some relation to it'.[8] But activism was also central, so much so that post 1792 he was almost consumed by his commitment to active Christian service. As Gunton Fuller recorded, even in 1815, just a few months before his death, he was still working at his desk 'upwards of twelve hours a day'.[9] As far as the Bible was concerned, for Fuller, everything sprang from the 'pure fountain' of the word of God.[10]

In fact for Fuller the four strands characteristic of Evangelicalism were so closely intertwined and interdependent it is often not easy to separate one from another. Fuller's activism was activism in pursuit of conversions; his theology of the atonement was based on the Bible and driven by the desire to see men and women coming to Christ. Rather than four isolated emphases, the stresses on the Bible, conversion, the cross and activity form, for Fuller, a 'four dimensional model of Evangelicalism',[11] a quadrilateral of priorities indeed, which *together* informed and shaped Fuller's life and ministry. It is, therefore, Bebbington's quadrilateral of priorities *taken as a whole* which

---

6   P.T. Forsyth, *The Cruciality of the Cross* (London: Independent Press, 2nd edn, 1948).

7   Fuller, *Calvinistic and Socinian Systems Compared*, in *Fuller's Works*, II, p. 182. Cf. the sermon 'God's Approbation of our Labours Necessary to the Hope of Success', preached at the Annual Meeting of Bedford Union, 6 May 1801, in *Fuller's Works*, I, p. 190: 'Christ crucified is the central point, in which all the lines of evangelical truth meet and are united. There is not a doctrine in the Scriptures but what bears an important relation to it.' See also Haykin, 'Particular Redemption in the Writings of Andrew Fuller', p. 110-11.

8   Fuller to W. Coles, June 1804, in A.G. Fuller, 'Andrew Fuller', in *Fuller's Works*, I, p. 83. The letter was written from Ireland, during Fuller's tour there on behalf of the BMS.

9   A.G. Fuller, *Andrew Fuller*, in *Fuller's Works*, I, p. 100.

10   From Fuller's 'covenant', Ryland, *Andrew Fuller*, 1st edn, pp. 203-204.

11   The phrase is Ian Randall's, *Evangelical Experiences*, p. 271.

constitutes the driving force behind Fuller's writing, speaking, general pastoral work, missionary activity and spiritual life. Seen in this light, Fuller's otherwise bewilderingly disparate career can be seen as a unity, with the same themes emerging repeatedly across the whole of his life and work.[12]

Fuller and the Revival of Eighteenth-Century Particular Baptist Life

This study has shown that Fuller's career and the Revival of eighteenth-century Particular Baptist life are inextricably intertwined. Indeed an analysis of Fuller's wide ranging ministry sheds considerable light on the revitalization of the churches which took place. This revitalization was highly significant, and it is no exaggeration to say that the Particular Baptists were transformed from an inward looking denomination in decline to one that was confident, outward looking and missionary minded. This transformation worked itself out in substantial numerical growth at home and, supremely, the formation of the BMS, arguably still the British Baptist denomination's 'greatest gift to the Church Universal'.[13] These were changes that the Bristol Baptist Academy (to which the denomination owed a great deal), had on its own been unable to effect. Although the work of the Academy forms one of the streams which fed the Revival of Particular Baptist life, the ministry of Fuller and his fellow Northamptonshire ministers undoubtedly marked a real turning point.[14]

I have sought to show that the Particular Baptist Revival was undoubtedly an Evangelical Revival. Once again, Jonathan Edwards was especially important in this story. The Revival of English Particular Baptist life consequently had a definite trans-atlantic dimension. There were signs that many thought that the Northamptonshire Particular

---

12   See the comments of the Congregationalist Thomas Toller in a sermon to his own church at Kettering the Sunday following Fuller's death as recorded in A.G. Fuller, *Andrew Fuller*, in *Fuller's Works*, I, pp. 103-104. Toller spoke of 'the variety and compass' of Fuller's writings, which nevertheless all bore 'on one grand point'. The 'grand point' Toller had in mind was the 'support of the radical principles of evangelical religion'.

13   This is Holmes' judgement, *God of Grace*, p. ix, with which it is hard to disagree.

14   As Morris perceptively put it, 'a *Western* Calvinist is a very different kind of animal from a Northamptonshire one'. J.W. Morris to J. Sutcliff, 19 November 1800, bound volume of original letters of Fawcett, Fuller, Morris, Ryland, 1773-1813, Angus Library, Oxford, cited by Stanley, *History of the BMS*, p. 19.

Baptists were over dependent on Edwards and revered him too highly. This ranged from the friendly caution of a John Newton to the outright hostility of a John Martin. Fuller and other key Northamptonshire ministers were keen to point out that they were not imitating Edwards. But they were quite happy to acknowledge their debt, and in doing so they were unrepentant.

The Importance of Fuller

This study has shown that Fuller was someone who helped to bring about this revitalization of Particular Baptist life. Many of his contemporaries and colleagues had little doubt of his importance in the overall story. After Fuller's death Robert Hall Jr paid tribute to his friend saying that Fuller 'endeared himself to his denomination by a long course of most useful labour'. Moreover: 'by his excellent works...as well as his devotion to the cause of missions, he laid the world under lasting obligations.' Joseph Belcher, the editor of the American edition of Fuller's works wrote in similar vein: 'Andrew Fuller was providentially raised up at a period when coldness benumbed some parts of the Christian church, and errors obscured the glory of others... The wonder is, that one short life should have accomplished so much.'[15] Later commentators have been no less fulsome. W.T. Whitley spoke of him as a 'great theologian', and E.A. Payne referred to 'Fullerism' as a 'revivifying impulse, north, south, east and west'.[16]

David Bebbington, in his Introduction to *The Gospel in the World*, describes Fuller as an 'outstanding but largely neglected theologian'.[17] If Fuller's theology has been neglected, then other aspects of his wide ranging work have received even less attention. This study has sought to draw the contours of Fuller's life and thought on the map of late-eighteenth and early-nineteenth Particular Baptist life, and thus make a significant and much needed contribution to the historiography of the period. In doing this I have continually sought to avoid hagiography, and to be aware too of how easy it is in a study of one particular person, to elevate their importance beyond what it actually was. Comments such as those in the previous paragraph, together with a myriad of others that could have been cited, undoubtedly run the risk, to varying degrees, of falling into this trap. Fuller was one of many significant individuals

---

15   For both these quotations, see A.G. Fuller, *Andrew Fuller*, in *Fuller's Works*, I, pp. 106-107.

16   See Clipsham, 'Development of a Doctrine', pp. 99-100.

17   D.W. Bebbington, 'Introduction', to Bebbington (ed.), *Gospel in the World*, p. 6.

involved in the revitalization of Calvinistic Baptist life, a Revival that was the result of a complex matrix of factors – theological, social and cultural. But I have sought to show in this study that there is historical justification for saying that Fuller was an absolutely central figure in the story of revitalization. This was particularly so with regards to theological renewal and the founding and subsequent growth of the BMS. It is no exaggeration to say that Fuller has a vital place, not only in the story of the Revival of eighteenth-century Particular Baptist life, but also in the spread of the Christian faith around the globe.

Bibliography

PRIMARY SOURCES – MANUSCRIPTS

Angus Library, Regents Park College, Oxford

Typescript Andrew Fuller Letters, transcribed by E.A. Payne (4/5/1 and 4/5/2)
Andrew Fuller Letters to John Saffery (II/273)
Andrew Fuller Letter to William Wilberforce, 5 December 1801 (II/200)
Bound Volume of Andrew Fuller Letters to W. Carey, J. Marshman, W. Ward and other
BMS Missionaries, 1795-1815, transcribed in India, with an index compiled by A.
Gunton Fuller (3/170)

Bristol Baptist College Library

'Colonel Bie Letter to Andrew Fuller' (OS G 97 B)
Fuller, A., 'Book of Miscellaneous Writings [including Fuller's "List of Books" from
1798, and a "Meditation" by Ann Fuller]' (G 95 b)
— 'Commonplace Book [first entry 22 June 1798]' (95 a)
— 'Diary and Spiritual Thoughts [1784-1801]' (G 95 b)
— 'Letter to an un-named missionary and his colleagues at Serampore [7 January
1813]' (G 96 Box D)
— 'Fuller Sermons…in shorthand, with occasional meditations in longhand [Books
1-5 bound in 1 vol.]' (G 95 A)
— 'Subscribers' list and notes about collection for BMS, plus some Greek grammar'
(G 95 b)
'John Ryland Jr Letter to Andrew Fuller' (G 97 B Box A)
'Letters to and from Andrew Fuller and Others of the Fuller Family' (G 95 B)

Fuller Baptist Church, Kettering

The Church Book of Kettering Baptist Church (The 'Little Meeting'), 1773-1815
Diary of George Wallis
Fuller Chapel Letters (Letters to Andrew Fuller), vol. 1 (1-34), vol. 2 (35-71)

County Records Office, Cambridge

Fuller, A., 'A Narration of the dealings of God in a way of Providence with the Baptist
Church at Soham from the year 1770' (NC/B - Soham R70/20)

Copies of annual letters of Soham Baptist Church to the Northamptonshire Association
   1776-83 (NC/B - Soham R70/20)
Soham Baptist Church Book, 1770-1833 (with records before 1840 transcribed from the
   'old church book') (NC/B - Soham)

PRIMARY SOURCES – BOOKS AND BOOKLETS

Bellamy, J., *True Religion Delineated; or, Experimental Religion... Set in a Scriptural
   and Rational Light*, with a 'Recommendatory Preface' by A. Fuller (London: T.
   Hamilton, 3rd edn, 1809)
Bennett, J. and Bogue, D., *A History of the Dissenters During the Last 30 years*
   (London, 1839)
Booth, A., *The Collected Works of Abraham Booth, With Some Account of his Life and
   Writings* (3 vols; London, 1813)
Brooks, T., *Heaven on Earth* (Edinburgh: Banner of Truth, 1961[1645])
Bunyan, J., *Grace Abounding to the Chief of Sinners* (Harmondsworth, Middlesex:
   Penguin, 1987 [1666])
Button, W., *Remarks on a Treatise Entitled The Gospel of Christ Worthy of All
   Acceptation* (London, 1785)
Carey, E., *Memoir of William Carey, DD* (London: Jackson and Walford, 1836)
Carey, W., *An Enquiry into the Obligations for Christians to use Means for the
   Conversion of the Heathens* (London: Kingsgate Press, 1961 [1792])
Edwards, J., *The Works of Jonathan Edwards* (ed. E. Hickman; 2 vols; Edinburgh:
   Banner of Truth, 1974 [1834])
— *The Freedom of the Will*, in *The Works of Jonathan Edwards*, vol. I, ed. P.
   Ramsey (New Haven: Yale University Press, 1985 [1754])
— *The Life of David Brainerd*, in *The Works of Jonathan Edwards*, vol. VII, ed. N.
   Pettit (New Haven: Yale University Press, 1985 [1749])
— *Practical Sermons: Never Before Published* (Edinburgh: M. Gray, 1798)
Fawcett, Jr J., *An Account of the Life, Ministry and Writings of the Late Rev John
   Fawcett, DD* (London: Baldwin, Craddock and Joy, 1818)
Fuller, A., *The Complete Works of the Rev Andrew Fuller, With a Memoir of his Life by
   the Rev. Andrew Gunton Fuller* (ed. A.G. Fuller; rev. ed. J. Belcher; 3 vols;
   Harrisonburg, Virginia: Sprinkle Publications, 3rd edn, 1988 [1845])
— *The Gospel Worthy of All Acceptation* (Northampton: T. Dicey, 1st edn, 1785)
Fuller, A.G., *Men Worth Remembering: Andrew Fuller* (London: Hodder and
   Stoughton, 1882)
Gill, J., *The Cause of God and Truth* (London, 1855 [1735-38])
— *The Doctrines of God's Everlasting Love to His Elect... Stated and Defended. In
   a Letter to Dr Abraham Taylor* (London, 1752)
— *An Exposition of the Old* Testament (4 vols; London: Matthews and Leigh, 1810)
— *Sermons and Tracts* (3 vols; London, 1778)
Haldane, A., *The Lives of Robert and James Haldane*, (London: Hamilton and Adams,
   3rd edn, 1853)
Hall, Sr R., *The Complete Works of the Late Robert Hall* (ed. J.W. Morris; London,
   1828)

Hall, Jr R., *The Works of Robert Hall* (ed. O. Gregory; 6 vols; London: Holdsworth & Ball, 1833)

Hopkins, S., *The Memoirs of Miss Susanna Anthony, who died at Newport, Rhode Island, June 23, 1791*, with a 'Recommendatory Preface', by J. Ryland Jr, A. Fuller and J. Sutcliff (J.W. Morris: Clipstone, 1803)

Ivimey, J., *A History of the English Baptists* (4 vols; London: Hinton, Holdsworth & Ball, 1811-30)

— *The Perpetual Intercession of Christ for his Church: A Source of Consolation under the Loss of Useful Ministers* (London: T. Gardiner & Son, 1815)

Marshman, J.C., *The Story of Carey, Marshman and Ward, The Serampore Missionaries* (London: Alexander Strahan, 1864)

Martin, J., *Thoughts On The Duty Of Man Relative To Faith In Jesus Christ, In Which Mr Andrew Fuller's Leading Propositions On This Subject Are Considered* (London, 1788-91)

Morris, J.W., *Memoirs of the Life and Death of the Rev. Andrew Fuller* (High Wycombe, 1st edn, 1816; London: Wightman and Cramp, 2nd edn, 1826)

Owen, J., *The Works of John Owen*, (24 vols; ed. W.H Goold; London: Banner of Truth, 1965-68 [1850-53])

Periodical Accounts Relative to the Baptist Missionary Society, 1, (Clipstone: J.W. Morris, 1800 [1794])

Pratt, J.H. (ed.), *The Thought of the Evangelical Leaders: Notes of the Discussions of The Eclectic Society London During the Years 1798-1814* (Edinburgh: Banner of Truth, 1978 [1856])

Pritchard, G., *Memoir of the Life and Writings of the Rev. Joseph Ivimey* (London: George Wightman, 1835)

Rippon, J., *The Baptist Annual Register*, vol. I (London: Dilly, Button and Thomas, 1793); vol. III (London: Button, Conder, Brown et al, 1801)

— *A Brief Memoir of the Life and Writings of the Late Rev. John Gill, DD* (London: John Bennett, 1838)

Ryland, Jr J., *The Work of Faith, the Labour of Love, and the Patience of Hope Illustrated in the Life and Death of the Rev. Andrew Fuller* (London: Button and Son, 1st edn, 1816; London: Button and Son, 2nd edn, 1818)

Scott, J., *The Life of Thomas Scott* (London: Seeley, 1836)

Taylor, A., *Memoirs of the Rev Dan Taylor* (London: Baynes and Son, 1820)

Taylor, D., *Observations on the Rev Andrew Fuller's Late Pamphlet Entitled The Gospel of Christ Worthy of All Acceptation* (St Ives, Cambridgeshire, 1786)

— *Observations on the Rev. Andrew Fuller's Reply to Philanthropos* (St Ives, Cambridgeshire, 1788)

— *The Friendly Conclusion Occasioned by the Letters of 'Agnostos'* (London, 1790)

Wallin, B., *The Christian Life, In Divers of its Branches Described and Recommended* (2 vols; London, 1746)

Ward, W.R., *A Sketch of the Character of the Late Rev Andrew Fuller* (Bristol: J.G. Fuller, 1817)

SECONDARY SOURCES – BOOKS AND BOOKLETS

Atkinson, D.J and D.H. Field (eds), *New Dictionary of Christian Ethics and Pastoral Theology* (Leicester: IVP, 1995)

Bebbington, D.W., *Evangelicalism in Modern Britain: A History from the 1730s to the 1980s* (London: Unwin Hyman, 1989)

— (ed.), *The Baptists in Scotland: A History* (Glasgow: Baptist Union of Scotland, 1988)

— (ed.), *The Gospel in the World: International Baptist Studies* (Studies in Baptist History and Thought, 1; Carlisle: Paternoster, 2002)

Berkhof, L., *Systematic Theology* (Edinburgh: Banner of Truth, 1981 [1949])

Binfield, C., *Pastors and People: The Biography of a Baptist Church, Queen's Road, Coventry* (Coventry: Alan Sutton, 1984)

Brady, S. and H.H. Rowden (eds), *For Such a Time as This* (London: Scripture Union, 1996)

Briggs, J.H.Y., *English Baptists of the Nineteenth Century* (A History of the English Baptists, 3; Didcot: Baptist Historical Society, 1994)

Brown, F.K., *Fathers of the Victorians* (Cambridge: Cambridge University Press, 1961)

Brown, R., *The English Baptists of the Eighteenth Century* (A History of the English Baptists, 2; London: Baptist Historical Society, 1986)

Cameron, N.M. de S. (ed.), *Dictionary of Scottish Church History and Theology* (Edinburgh: T. & T. Clark, 1993)

Carey, S.P., *Memoir of William Carey, DD* (London: Hodder and Stoughton, 1923)

— *Samuel Pearce M.A., The Baptist Brainerd* (London: Carey Kingsgate Press, 3rd edn, n.d.)

Carson, D.A., *The Gagging of God: Christianity Confronts Pluralism* (Leicester: IVP, 1996)

— *New Testament Commentary Survey* (Leicester: IVP, 5th edn, 2001)

Chadwick, O., *The Spirit of the Oxford Movement* (Cambridge: Cambridge University Press, 1990)

Cockerton, J., *Essentials of Evangelical Spirituality* (Grove Spirituality Series, 49; Nottingham: Grove Books, 1994)

Conforti, J.A., *Samuel Hopkins and the New Divinity Movement* (Grand Rapids: Eerdmans, 1981)

Cox, F.A., *History of the Baptist Missionary Society from 1792 to 1842* (2 vols; London: T. Ward and G. & J. Dyer, 1842)

Crawford, M.J., *Seasons of Grace, Colonial New England's Revival Tradition in its British Context* (Oxford: Oxford University Press, 1991)

Culross, J., *The Three Rylands* (London: Elliot Stock, 1897)

De Jong, J.A., *As The Waters Cover the Sea, Millennial Expectations in the Rise of Anglo-American Missions, 1640-1810* (Kampen: J.H. Kok NV, 1970)

Ditchfield, G.M., *The Evangelical Revival* (Introductions to History; London: UCL Press, 1998)

Dix, K., *Strict and Particular: English Strict and Particular Baptists in the Nineteenth Century* (Didcot: Baptist Historical Society, 2001)

Dudley-Smith, T., *John Stott: The Making of a Leader* (Leicester: IVP, 1999)

Eden, M. and D.F. Wells (eds), *The Gospel in the Modern World: A Tribute to John Stott* (Leicester: IVP, 1991)

Ella, G.M., *Law and Gospel in the Theology of Andrew Fuller* (Eggleston, Co. Durham: Go Publications, 1996)

Elwyn, T.S.H., *The Northamptonshire Baptist Association* (London: Carey Kingsgate Press, 1964)

Ferguson, S.B., *John Owen on the Christian Life* (Edinburgh: Banner of Truth, 1987)
— and D.F. Wright (eds), *New Dictionary of Theology* (Leicester: IVP, 1988)

Ferm, R.L., *Jonathan Edwards the Younger: A Colonial Pastor* (Grand Rapids: Eerdmans, 1976)

Fisher, J.S., *Impelled by Faith: A Brief History of the Baptists in Scotland* (Stirling: Scottish Baptist History Project, 1996)

Forsyth, P.T., *The Cruciality of the Cross* (London: Independent Press, 2nd edn, 1948)

Foster, F.H., *A Genetic History of the New England Theology* (Chicago: Univ. Chicago Press, 1907)

Fuller, J.G., *A Brief History of the Western Association* (Bristol: I. Hemmans, 1843)

Fuller, T.E., *A Memoir of the Life and Writings of Andrew Fuller* (Bunyan Library, 11; London: J. Heaton, 1863)

Gillett, D., *Trust and Obey: Explorations in Evangelical Spirituality* (London: Darton, Longman and Todd, 1993)

George, T., *Faithful Witness: The Life and Mission of William Carey* (Leicester: IVP, 1991)
— and D.S. Dockery (eds), *Baptist Theologians* (Nashville, TN: Broadman Press, 1990)

Greenall, R.L. (ed.), *The Kettering Connection: Northamptonshire Baptists and Overseas Mission* (Leicester: Department of Adult Education, University of Leicester, 1993)

Hatch N.O. and H.S. Stout (eds), *Jonathan Edwards and the American Experience* (Oxford: Oxford University Press, 1988)

Haykin, M.A.G. (ed.), *The Apologetic Ministry of Andrew Fuller* (Studies in Baptist History and Thought, 6; Carlisle: Paternoster, forthcoming, 2003)
— *The Armies of the Lamb: The Spirituality of Andrew Fuller* (Classics of Reformed Spirituality, 3; Dundas, Ontario: Joshua Press, 2001)
— (ed.), *The British Particular Baptists, 1638-1910* (2 vols; Springfield, Missouri: Particular Baptist Press, 1998-2000)
— (ed.), *The Life and Thought of John Gill (1697-1771): A Tercentennial Appreciation* (Leiden: Brill, 1997)
— *One Heart and Soul: John Sutcliff of Olney, his Friends and his Times* (Durham: Evangelical Press, 1994)

Haroutunian, J., *Piety versus Moralism: The Passing of the New England Theology* (New York: Harper and Row, 1970)

Hemmens, H.L., E.A. Payne, B.G. Griffith et al, *Baptist Missionary Society Ter-Jubilee Celebrations, 1942-4: Programmes of Meetings and Services...With some of the Sermons and Speeches And a Statement of Contributions to the Celebrations Fund* (London: Baptist Missionary Society, 1945)

Hindmarsh, B., *John Newton and the English Evangelical Tradition: Between the Conversions of Wesley and Wilberforce* (Oxford: Clarenden Press, 1996)

Holmes, S.R., *God of Grace and God of Glory: An Account of the Theology of Jonathan Edwards* (Edinburgh: T. & T. Clark, 2000)

Hudson, W.S. (ed.), *Baptist Concepts of the Church* (Philadelphia: Judson Press, 1959)

Hughes, G.W., *With Freedom Fired: The Story of Robert Robinson, Cambridge Nonconformist* (London: Carey Kingsgate Press, 1955)

Hylson-Smith, K.R., *The Churches in England from Elizabeth I to Elizabeth II.* 2: *1689-1833* (London: SCM Press, 1997)

Jeffrey, D.L. (ed.), *English Spirituality in the Age of Wesley* (Grand Rapids: Eerdmans, 1987)

Laws, G., *Andrew Fuller: Pastor, Theologian, Ropeholder* (London: Kingsgate Press, 1942)

Lee, S.H., *The Philosophical Theology of Jonathan Edwards* (Princeton: Princeton University Press, 1988)

Lewis, C.B., *The Life of John Thomas* (London: Macmillan, 1873)

Lewis, D.M. (ed.), *Dictionary of Evangelical Biography 1730-1860* (2 vols; Oxford: Blackwell, 1995)

Lovegrove, D.W., *Established Church, Sectarian People: Itinerancy and the Transformation of English Dissent, 1780-1830* (Cambridge: Cambridge University Press, 1988)

Lusty, F.C., *Walsgrave Baptist Church 1700-1950: A Brief Record of Two Hundred and Fifty Years Witness and Service* (Northampton: Billingham & Son, 1950)

Manley, K.R., *'Redeeming Love Proclaim': John Rippon and the Particular Baptists* (Studies in Baptist History and Thought, 12; Carlisle: Paternoster, forthcoming, 2003).

McGrath, A.E., *Christian Spirituality* (Oxford: Blackwell, 1999)

— *Evangelicalism and the Future of Christianity* (London: Hodder & Stoughton, 1996)

Meek, D.E., *A Mind for Mission: Essays in Appreciation of the Rev. Christopher Anderson 1782-1852* (Edinburgh: Scottish Baptist History Project, 1992)

Murray, I.H., *Jonathan Edwards: A New Biography* (Edinburgh: Banner of Truth, 1987)

— *The Puritan Hope: Revival and the Interpretation of Prophecy* (Edinburgh: Banner of Truth, 1971)

Naylor, P., *Calvinism, Communion and the Baptists: A Study of English Calvinistic Baptists From the Late 1600s to the Early 1800s* (Studies in Baptist History and Thought, 7; Carlisle: Paternoster, forthcoming, 2003)

— *Picking up a Pin for the Lord: English Particular Baptists from 1688 to the Early Nineteenth Century* (Durham: Grace Publications Trust, 1992)

Neill, S., *A History of Christian Missions* (Pelican History of the Church, 6; Harmondsworth, Middlesex: Penguin, 1964)

Nettles, T.J., *By His Grace and For His Glory: A Historical, Theological and Practical Study of the Doctrines of Grace in Baptist Life* (Grand Rapids: Baker, 1986)

Noll, M. A., Christianity in the USA and Canada (Grand Rapids: Eerdmans / London: SPCK, 1992)

— *Turning Points, Decisive Moments in the History of Christianity* (Leicester: IVP, 1997)

— D.W. Bebbington and G.A. Rawlyk (eds), *Evangelicalism: Comparative Studies in Popular Protestantism in North America, The British Isles and Beyond, 1700-1990* (Oxford: Oxford University Press, 1994)

Packer, J.I., *Among God's Giants: The Puritan Vision of the Christian Life* (Eastbourne: Kingsway, 1991)

Parsons, K.A.C. (ed.), *The Book of the Independent Church (Now Pound Lane Baptist), Isleham 1693-1805* (Cambridge: Cambridge Antiquarian Records Society, 1984)

Payne, E.A., *The Baptist Union: A Short History* (London: Carey Kingsgate Press, 1959)

— *The Free Church Tradition in the Life of England* (London: Hodder and

Stoughton, 4th edn, 1965)

— *The Prayer Call of 1784* (London: Kingsgate Press, 1941)

Porter, R., *Enlightenment: Britain and the Creation of the Modern World* (London: Penguin, 2000)

Porter, S.E. and A.R. Cross (eds), *Baptism, the New Testament and the Church: Historical and Contemporary Essays in Honour of R.E.O White* (JSNTSupp Series, 171; Sheffield: Sheffield Academic Press, 1999)

Potts, E.D., *British Baptist Missionaries in India, 1793-1837* (Cambridge: Cambridge University Press, 1967)

Rack, H.D., *Reasonable Enthusiast: John Wesley and the Rise of Methodism* (Epworth: London, 1989)

Randall, I.M., *Evangelical Experiences: A Study in the Spirituality of English Evangelicalism 1918-1939* (Studies in Evangelical History and Thought; Carlisle: Paternoster, 1999)

Rawlyk, G.A. and M.A. Noll (eds), *Amazing Grace, Evangelicalism in Australia, Britain, Canada and the United States* (Grand Rapids: Baker, 1993)

Rinaldi, F.W., *'The Tribe of Dan': The New Connexion of General Baptists 1770-1891* (Studies in Baptist History and Thought, 10; Carlisle: Paternoster, forthcoming, 2003)

Sell, A.P.F., *The Great Debate: Calvinism, Arminianism and Salvation* (Worthing: H.E. Walter, 1982)

Sheldrake, P., *Spirituality and History* (London: SPCK, 1991)

Stephens, L. and S. Lee (eds), *Dictionary of National Biography, from the Earliest Times to 1900* (21 vols; Oxford: Oxford University Press, 1921-22)

Tidball, D., *The Message of the Cross* (Bible Speaks Today Bible Themes Series, 3; Leicester: IVP, 2000)

— *Who are the Evangelicals: Tracing the Roots of Today's Movement* (London: Marshall Pickering, 1994)

Toon, P., *The Emergence of Hyper Calvinism in English Nonconformity 1689-1765* (London: Olive Tree, 1967)

Stanley, B., *The History of the Baptist Missionary Society, 1792-1992* (Edinburgh: T. & T. Clark, 1992)

Streather, G.T., *Memorials of the Independent Chapel at Rothwell* (Rothwell: Rothwell United Reformed Church, 1994)

Stout, H.S., *The Divine Dramatist: George Whitefield and the Rise of Modern Evangelicalism* (Grand Rapids: Eerdmans, 1991)

Tull, J.E., *Shapers of Baptist Thought* (Valley Forge: Judson Press, 1972)

Underwood, A.C., *A History of the English Baptists* (London: Kingsgate Press, 1947)

Warfield, B.B., 'Edwards and the New England Theology', in *The Works of Benjamin B Warfield. 9: Studies in Theology* (10 vols; Grand Rapids: Baker, 1991)

Watts, M.R., *The Dissenters. 1: From the Reformation to the French Revolution* (Oxford: Clarenden Press, 1978)

— *The Dissenters. 2: The Expansion of Evangelical Nonconformity* (Oxford: Clarendon Press, 1995)

Vedder, H.C., *A Short History of the Baptists* (Valley Forge: Judson Press, 1907)

Whitley, W.T., *The Baptists of London 1612 -1928* (London: Kingsgate Press, 1928)

— *Calvinism and Evangelism in England and Especially Among the Baptists* (London: Kingsgate Press, 1933)

— *A History of English Baptists* (London: Charles Griffin, 1923)

Wolfe, J. (ed.), *Evangelical Faith and Public Zeal: Evangelicals in Society in Britain 1780-1980* (London: SPCK, 1995)

SECONDARY SOURCES – ARTICLES

Amey, B., 'Baptist Missionary Society Radicals', *BQ* 26.8 (October, 1976), pp. 363-76

Baines, A.H.J., 'The Pre-History of Regents Park College', *BQ* 36.4 (October, 1995), pp. 191-201

Brackney, W.H., 'The Baptist Missionary Society in Proper Context: Some Reflections on the Larger Voluntary Religious Tradition', *BQ* 34.8 (October, 1992), pp. 364-77

Champion, L.G., 'Evangelical Calvinism and the Structures of Baptist Church Life', *BQ* 28.5 (January, 1980), pp. 196-208

Clipsham, E.F., 'Andrew Fuller and the Baptist Mission', *Foundations* 10.1 (January, 1967), pp. 4-18

— 'Andrew Fuller and Fullerism: A Study in Evangelical Calvinism', *BQ* 20.1-4 (1963); '1. The Development of a Doctrine'; pp. 99-114; '2. Fuller and John Calvin', pp. 147-54; '3. The Gospel Worthy of All Acceptation', pp. 215-25; '4. Fuller as a Theologian', pp. 269-76

Davies, R.E., 'The Great Commission from Christ to Carey', *Evangel* 14.2 (1996), pp. 46-49

Ella, G.M., 'John Gill and the Charge of Hyper-Calvinism', *BQ* 36.4 (October, 1995), pp. 166-77

Elwyn, T.S.H., 'Particular Baptists of the Northamptonshire Association as Reflected in the Circular Letters, 1765-1820', Part 1, *BQ* 36.8 (October, 1996), pp. 368-81; Part 2, 37.1 (January, 1997), pp. 3-19

Gordon, G., 'The Call of Dr John Ryland Jr', *BQ* 34.5 (January, 1992), pp. 214-27

Haykin, M.A.G., 'A Habitation of God, Through The Spirit: John Sutcliff (1752-1814) and the Revitalization of the Calvinistic Baptists in the Late Eighteenth Century', *BQ* 34.7 (July, 1992), pp. 304-19

— 'The Baptist Identity: A View From the Eighteenth Century', *Evangelical Quarterly* 67.2 (1995), pp. 137-152

— 'The Elder Robert Hall and his Help to Zion's Travellers', *Banner of Truth Magazine* 343 (April, 1992), pp. 17-20; 344 (May, 1992), pp. 22-27

— 'Hazarding all for God at a Clap: The Spirituality of Baptism Among British Calvinistic Baptists', *BQ* 38.4 (October, 1999), pp. 185-95

— '"The Oracles of God": Andrew Fuller and the Scriptures', *The Churchman* 103.1 (1989), pp. 60-76

Holmes, S.R., 'Edwards on the Will', *International Journal of Systematic Theology* 1.3 (1999), pp. 266-85

Hulcoop, S. and S. Newens, 'John Davis, Minister at Waltham Abbey 1764-1795', *BQ* 39.8 (October, 2002), pp. 409-410

James, S., 'Revival and Renewal in Baptist Life: The Contribution of William Steadman (1764-1837)', *BQ* 37. 6 (April, 1998), pp. 263-82

Killingray, D., 'Black Christian Biography', *Christianity and History Forum Newsletter* (Autumn, 2002), pp. 12-21

Kirkby, A.H., 'Andrew Fuller, Evangelical Calvinist', *BQ* 15.5 (January, 1954), pp. 195-202

Langley, A.S., 'Baptist Ministers in England About 1750 A.D.', *Transactions of the Baptist Historical Society* 6 (1910-11), pp. 138-57

Milner, J., 'Andrew Fuller', *Reformation Today*, 17 (Jan-Feb, 1974), pp. 18-29

Nuttall, G.F., 'The Baptist Churches and Their Ministers: Rippon's Baptist Annual Register', *BQ* 30.8 (October, 1984), pp. 383-87

— 'Letters from Robert Hall to John Ryland, 1791-1824', *BQ* 34.3 (July, 1991), pp. 127-31

— 'Northamptonshire and The Modern Question: A Turning Point in Eighteenth-Century Dissent', *Journal of Theological Studies* 16.1 (April, 1965), pp. 101-123

— 'The State of Religion in Northamptonshire (1793) by Andrew Fuller', *BQ* 29.4 (October, 1981), pp. 177-79

O'Brien [Durden], S., 'A Transatlantic Community of Saints: The Great Awakening and the First Evangelical Network, 1735-1755', *American Historical Review* 91 (1986), pp. 812-24

Oliver, R.W., 'George Whitefield and the English Baptists', *Grace Magazine* 5 (October, 1970), pp. 9-12

Payne, E.A., 'Abraham Booth, 1734-1806', *BQ* 26.1 (January, 1975), pp. 28-42

— 'Andrew Fuller and James Deakin, 1803', *BQ* 7 (1934-35), pp. 326-33

— 'Andrew Fuller as Letter Writer', *BQ* 15.7 (July, 1954), pp. 290-96

— 'Carey and his Biographers', *BQ* 19.1 (January, 1961), pp. 4-12

— 'John Dyer's Memoir of Carey', *BQ* 22.6 (April, 1968), pp. 326-27

— 'Letters to James Deakin', *BQ* 7 (1934-35), pp. 361-73

— 'Some Samuel Pearce Documents', *BQ* 18.1 (January, 1959), pp. 26-34

— 'Some Sidelights on Pearce and His Friends', *BQ* 7 (1934-35), pp. 270-75

Potts, E.D., '"I throw away the guns to preserve the ship:" A Note on the Serampore Trio', *BQ* 20.3 (July, 1963), pp. 115-117

Read, S., 'Further Information on the Ryland Family', *BQ* 36.4 (October, 1995), pp. 202-203

Robison, O.C., 'The Legacy of John Gill', *BQ* 24.3 (July, 1971), pp. 111-25

Sellers, I., 'John Howard Hinton, Theologian', *BQ* 33.3 (July, 1989), pp. 119-32

Smith, A.C., 'The Spirit and Letter of Carey's Catalytic Watchword: A Study in the Transmission of Baptist Tradition', *BQ* 33.5 (January, 1990), pp. 226-37

Ward, W.R., 'Baptists and the Transformation of the Church, 1780-1830', *BQ* 25.4 (October 1973), pp. 167-84

Whitley, W.T., 'Baptist Board Minutes, 1750-1820', *Transactions of the Baptist Historical Society* 6 (1918-19), pp. 72-127

— 'The Baptist Interest under George I', *Transactions of the Baptist Historical Society* 2 (1910-11), pp. 95-109

SECONDARY SOURCES - THESES

Archer, R.W.F., 'The Evangelistic Ministry of John Bunyan (1655-1688)' (MPhil thesis, University of Wales, 1995)

Coppenger, R.A., 'Abraham Booth, 1734-1806: A Study of his Thought and Work'

(PhD thesis, Edinburgh University, 1953)

Hayden, R., 'Evangelical Calvinism Among Eighteenth Century Particular Baptists with Particular Reference to Bernard Foskett, Hugh and Caleb Evans and the Bristol Baptist Academy 1690-1791' (PhD thesis, Keele University, 1991)

Kirkby, A.H., 'The Theology of Andrew Fuller in its Relation to Calvinism' (PhD thesis, Edinburgh University, 1956)

Manley, K.R., 'John Rippon D.D. (1751-1836) and the Particular Baptists' (DPhil thesis, University of Oxford, 1967)

Morden, P.J., 'Andrew Fuller (1754-1815) and the Revival of Eighteenth Century Particular Baptist Life' (MPhil thesis, University of Wales [Spurgeon's College], 2000)

Oliver, R.W., 'The Emergence of a Strict and Particular Baptist Community Among the English Calvinistic Baptists, 1770-1850' (DPhil thesis, CNAA [London Bible College], 1986)

Rinaldi, F.W., '"The Tribe of Dan": The New Connexion of General Baptists 1770 - 1891. A study in the transition from revival movement to established denomination' (PhD thesis, Glasgow University, 1996)

Robison, O.C., 'The Particular Baptists in England: 1760-1820' (DPhil thesis, University of Oxford, 1963)

South, T.J., 'The Response of Andrew Fuller to the Sandemanian View of Saving Faith' (ThD Thesis, Mid-America Baptist Theological Seminary, 1993)

Young, D.L., 'The Place of Andrew Fuller in the Developing Modern Missions Movement' (DPhil thesis, Southwestern Baptist Theological Seminary, 1981)

Index

Studies in Baptist History and Thought

An established series of doctoral theses of high
academic standard
(All titles paperback, 229 x 152mm)

David Bebbington and Anthony R. Cross (eds)
Baptist Identities
International Studies from the Seventeenth to the Twentieth Centuries
This volume of essays comprises the papers from the Third International
Conference on Baptist Studies held in Prague in July 2003.
2004 / ISBN 1-84227-215-2

David Bebbington and Anthony R. Cross (eds)
Global Baptist History
(provisional title)
This volume of essays comprises the papers from the Second International
Conference on Baptist Studies held in Wake Forest North Carolina, July
2000.
2004 / ISBN 1-84227-214-4

David Bebbington (ed.)
The Gospel in the World
International Baptist Studies
This volume of essays deals with a range of subjects spanning Britain, North
America, Europe, Asia and the Antipodes. Topics include studies on
religious tolerance, the communion controversy and the development of the
international Baptist community, and concludes with two important essays
on the future of Baptist life that pay special attention to the United States.
2002 / ISBN 1-84227-118-0 / xiii + 362pp

Anthony R. Cross
Baptism and the Baptists
Theology and Practice in Twentieth-Century Britain
At a time of renewed interest in baptism, Baptism and the Baptists is a
detailed study of twentieth-century baptismal theology and practice and the
factors which have influenced its development.
2000 / ISBN 0-85364-959-6 / xx + 530pp

Anthony R. Cross and Philip E. Thompson (eds)
Baptist Myths
This collection of essays examines some of the 'myths' in Baptist history and theology: these include the idea of development in Baptist thought, studies in the church, baptismal sacramentalism, community, spirituality, soul competency, women, the civil rights movement and Baptist landmarkist ecclesiology, Baptist bishops, creeds and the Bible, and overseas missions.

2004 / ISBN 1-84227-122-9

Anthony R. Cross and Philip E. Thompson (eds)
Baptist Sacramentalism
This collection of essays includes historical and theological studies in the sacraments from a Baptist perspective. Subjects explored include the physical side of being spiritual, baptism, the Lord's supper, the church, ordination, preaching, worship, religious liberty and the issue of disestablishment.

2003 / ISBN 1-84227-119-9 / xvi + 280pp

Paul S. Fiddes
Tracks and Traces
Baptist Identity in Church and Theology
This is a comprehensive, yet unusual, book on the faith and life of Baptist Christians. It explores the understanding of the church, ministry, sacraments and mission from a thoroughly theological perspective. In a series of interlinked essays, the author relates Baptist identity consistently to a theology of covenant and to participation in the triune communion of God.

2003 / ISBN 1-84227-120-2 / xvi + approx. 304pp

Stanley K. Fowler
More Than a Symbol
The British Baptist Recovery of Baptismal Sacramentalism
Fowler surveys the entire scope of British Baptist literature from the seventeenth-century pioneers onwards. He shows that in the twentieth century leading British Baptist pastors and theologians recovered an understanding of baptism that connected experience with soteriology and that in doing so they were recovering what many of their forebears had taught.

2002 / ISBN 1-84227-052-4 / xvi + 276pp

Michael A.G. Haykin (ed.)
Fuller as an Apologist
One of the greatest Baptist theologians of the eighteenth and early nineteenth-centuries, Andrew Fuller has not had justice done to him. There is little doubt that Fuller's theology lay behind the revitalization of the Baptists in the late eighteenth century and the first few decades of the nineteenth. This collection of essays fills a much needed gap by examining a major area of Fuller's thought, his work as an apologist.
2003 / ISBN 1-84227-171-7

Michael A.G. Haykin
Studies in Calvinistic Baptist Spirituality
In a day when spirituality is in vogue and Christian communities are looking for guidance in this whole area, there is wisdom in looking to the past to find untapped wells. The Calvinistic Baptists, heirs of the rich ecclesial experience in the Puritan era of the seventeenth century, but, by the end of the eighteenth century, also passionately engaged in the catholicity of the Evangelical Revivals, are such a well. This collection of essays, covering such things the Lord's Supper, friendship and hymnody, seeks to draw out the spiritual riches of this community for reflection and imitation in the present day.
2004 / ISBN 1-84227-229-2

Brian Haymes, Anthony R. Cross and Ruth Gouldbourne
On Being the Church
Revisioning Baptist Identity
The aim of the book is to re-examine Baptist theology and practice in the light of the contemporary biblical, theological, ecumenical and missiological context drawing on historical and contemporary writings and issues. It is not a study in denominationalism but rather seeks to revision historical insights from the believers' church tradition for the sake of Baptists and other Christians in the context of the modern-postmodern context.
2005 / ISBN 1-84227-121-0

Ken R. Manley
From Woolloomooloo to 'Eternity'
A History of Baptists in Australia
From their beginnings in Australia in 1831 with the first baptisms in Woolloomoolloo Bay in 1832, this pioneering study describes the quest of Baptists in the different colonies (states) to discover their identity as Australians and Baptists. Although institutional developments are analyzed and the roles of significant individuals traced, the major focus is on the social and theological dimensions of the Baptist movement.
2004 / ISBN 1-84227-194-6

Ken R. Manley
'Redeeming Love Proclaim'
John Rippon and the Baptists
A leading exponent of the new moderate Calvinism which brought new life to many Baptists, John Rippon (1751-1836) helped unite the Baptists at this significant time. His many writings expressed the denomination's growing maturity and mutual awareness of Baptists in Britain and America, and exerted a long-lasting influence on Baptist worship and devotion. In his various activities, Rippon helped conserve the heritage of Old Dissent and promoted the evangelicalism of the New Dissent
2003 / ISBN 1-84227-193-8

Peter J. Morden
Offering Christ to the World
Andrew Fuller and the Revival of English Particular Baptist Life
Andrew Fuller (1754-1815) was one of the foremost English Baptist ministers of his day. His career as an Evangelical Baptist pastor, theologian, apologist and missionary statesman coincided with the profound revitalization of the Particular Baptist denomination to which he belonged. This study examines the key aspects of the life and thought of this hugely significant figure, and gives insights into the revival in which he played such a central part.
2003 / ISBN 1-84227-141-5 / xx + 202pp

Peter Naylor
Calvinism, Communion and the Baptists
A Study of English Calvinistic Baptists
from the Late 1600s to the Early 1800s
Dr Naylor argues that the traditional link between 'high-Calvinism' and 'restricted communion' is in need of revision. He examines Baptist communion controversies from the late 1600s to the early 1800s and also the theologies of John Gill and Andrew Fuller.
2003 / ISBN 1-84227-142-3 / xx + 266pp

Frank Rinaldi
'The Tribe of Dan'
A Study of the New Connexion of General Baptists 1770-1891
'The Tribe of Dan' is a thematic study which explores the theology, organizational structure, evangelistic strategy, ministry and leadership of the New Connexion of General Baptists as it experienced the process of institutionalization in the transition from a revival movement to an established denomination.
2004 / ISBN 1-84227-143-1

Peter Shepherd
The Making of a Modern Denomination
John Howard Shakespeare and the English Baptists 1898-1924
John Howard Shakespeare introduced revolutionary change to the Baptist denomination. The Baptist Union was transformed into a strong central institution and Baptist ministers were brought under its control. Further, Shakespeare's pursuit of church unity reveals him as one of the pioneering ecumenists of the twentieth century.

2001 / ISBN 1-84227-046-X / xviii + 220pp

Brian Talbot
The Search for a Common Identity
The Origins of the Baptist Union of Scotland 1800 1870
In the period 1800 to 1827 there were three streams of Baptists in Scotland: Scotch, Haldaneite and 'English' Baptist. A strong commitment to home evangelization brought these three bodies closer together, leading to a merger of their home missionary societies in 1827. However, the first three attempts to form a union of churches failed, but by the 1860s a common understanding of their corporate identity was attained leading to the establishment of the Baptist Union of Scotland.

2003 / ISBN 1-84227-123-7

Philip E. Thompson
The Freedom of God
Towards Baptist Theology in Pneumatological Perspective
This study contends that the range of theological commitments of the early Baptists are best understood in relation to their distinctive emphasis on the freedom of God. Thompson traces how this was recast anthropocentrically, leading to an emphasis upon human freedom from the nineteenth century onwards. He seeks to recover the dynamism of the early vision via a pneumatologically oriented ecclesiology defining the church in terms of the memory of God.

2004 / ISBN 1-84227-125-3

Linda Wilson
Marianne Farningham
A Study in Victorian Evangelical Piety
Marianne Farningham, of College Street Baptist Chapel, Northampton, was a household name in evangelical circles in the later nineteenth century. For over fifty years she produced comment, poetry, biography and fiction for the popular Christian press. This investigation uses her writings to explore the beliefs and behaviour of evangelical Nonconformists, including Baptists, during these years.

2004 / ISBN 1-84227-124-5

Other Paternoster titles
relating to Baptist history and thought

Paul Beasley-Murray
Fearless for Truth
A Personal Portrait of the Life of George Beasley-Murray
Without a doubt George Beasley-Murray was one of the greatest Baptists of the twentieth century. A long-standing Principal of Spurgeon's College, he wrote more than twenty books and made significant contributions in the study of areas as diverse as baptism and eschatology, as well as writing highly respected commentaries on the Book of Revelation and John's Gospel.

2002 / ISBN 1-84227-134-2 / xii + 244pp

David Bebbington
Holiness in Nineteenth-Century England
David Bebbington stresses the relationship of movements of spirituality to changes in the cultural setting, especially the legacies of the Enlightenment and Romanticism. He shows that these broad shifts in ideological mood had a profound effect on the ways in which piety was conceptualized and practised. Holiness was intimately bound up with the spirit of the age.

2000 / ISBN 0-85364-981-2 / viii + 98pp

Anthony R. Cross (ed.)
Ecumenism and History
Studies in Honour of John H.Y. Briggs
This collection of essays examines the inter-relationships between the two fields in which Professor Briggs has contributed so much: history - particularly Baptist and Nonconformist - and the ecumenical movement. With contributions from colleagues and former research students from Britain, Europe and North America, Ecumenism and History provides wide-ranging studies in important aspects of Christian history, theology and ecumenical studies.

2002 / ISBN 1-84227-135-0 / xx + 362pp

Keith E. Eitel
Paradigm Wars
The Southern Baptist International Mission Board
Faces the Third Millennium
The International Mission Board of the Southern Baptist Convention is the
largest denominational mission agency in North America. This volume
chronicles the historic and contemporary forces that led to the IMB's recent
extensive reorganization, providing the most comprehensive case study to
date of a historic mission agency restructuring to continue its mission
purpose into the twenty-first century more effectively.
2000 / ISBN 1-870345-12-6 / x + 139pp

Mark Hopkins
Baptists, Congregationalists, and Theological Change
Some Late Nineteenth Century Leaders and Controversies
2003 / ISBN 1-84227-150-4

Donald M. Lewis
Lighten Their Darkness
The Evangelical Mission to Working-Class London, 1828-1860
This is a comprehensive and compelling study of the Church and the
complexities of nineteenth-century London. Challenging our understanding
of the culture in working London at this time, Lewis presents a well-
structured and illustrated work that contributes substantially to the study of
evangelicalism and mission in nineteenth-century Britain.
2001 / ISBN 1-84227-074-5 / xviii + 371pp

Meic Pearse
The Great Restoration
The Religious Radicals of the 16th and 17th Centuries
Pearse charts the rise and progress of continental Anabaptism - both
evangelical and heretical - through the sixteenth century. He then follows the
story of those English people who became impatient with Puritanism and
separated - first from the Church of England and then from one another - to
form the antecedents of later Congregationalists, Baptists and Quakers.
1998 / ISBN 0-85364-800-X / xii + 320pp

Charles Price and Ian M. Randall
Transforming Keswick
Transforming Keswick is a thorough, readable and detailed history of the
convention. It will be of interest to those who know and love Keswick, those
who are only just discovering it, and serious scholars eager to learn more
about the history of God's dealings with his people.
2000 / ISBN 1-85078-350-0 / 288pp

Ian M. Randall
Educating Evangelicalism
The Origins, Development and Impact of London Bible College
London Bible College has been at the centre of theological education in
Britain for over fifty years. Through its staff and former students it has had
a significant influence on post-war evangelical life and has in turn been
shaped by evangelical currents. This book is the story of LBC's sometimes
difficult progress through the changing tides of evangelical opinion and
support to its current position as a touchstone for the finest in distinctly
evangelical scholarship.
2000 / ISBN 0-85364-873-5 / xx + 320pp

Ian M. Randall
One Body in Christ
The History and Significance of the Evangelical Alliance
In 1846 the Evangelical Alliance was founded with the aim of bringing
together evangelicals for common action. This book uses material not
previously utilized to examine the history and significance of the
Evangelical Alliance, a movement which has remained a powerful force for
unity. At a time when evangelicals are growing world-wide, this book offers
insights into the past which are relevant to contemporary issues.
2001 / ISBN 1-84227-089-3 / xii + 394pp

Ian M. Randall
Evangelical Experiences
A Study in the Spirituality of English Evangelicalism 1918-1939
This book makes a detailed historical examination of evangelical spirituality
between the First and Second World Wars. It shows how patterns of devotion
led to tensions and divisions. In a wide-ranging study, Anglican, Wesleyan,
Reformed and Pentecostal-charismatic spiritualities are analysed.
1999 / ISBN 0-85364-919-7 / xii + 310pp

Ian M. Randall
Spirituality and Social Change
The Contribution of F.B. Meyer (1847-1929)
2003 / ISBN 1-84227-195-4

Alan P.F. Sell and Anthony R. Cross (eds)
Protestant Nonconformity in the Twentieth Century
In this collection of essys scholars representative of a number of
Nonconformist traditions reflect thematically on Free Church life and
witness during the twentieth century. Among the subjects reviewed are
biblical studies, theology, worship, evangelism and spirituality, and
ecumenism. Over and above its immediate interest, this collection provides
a marker to future scholars and others wishing to know how some of their
forebears assessed Nonconformity's contribution to a variety of fields
during the century leading up to Christianity's third millennium.
2003 / ISBN 1-84227-221-7 / x + 388pp

Linda Wilson
Constrained by Zeal
Female Spirituality amongst Nonconformists 1825-1875
Dr Wilson investigates the neglected area of Nonconformist female
spirituality. Against the background of separate spheres she analyses the
experience of women from four denominations, and argues that the churches
provided a 'third sphere' in which they could find opportunities for
participation.
2000 / ISBN 0-85364-972-3 / xvi + 293pp

Nigel G. Wright
Disavowing Constantine
*Mission, Church and the Social Order in the Theologies of John Howard
Yoder and Jürgen Moltmann*
This book is a timely restatement of a radical theology of church and state
in the Anabaptist and Baptist tradition. Dr Wright constructs his argument in
dialogue and debate with Yoder and Moltmann, major contributors to a free
church perspective.
2000 / ISBN 0-85364-978-2 /xv + 251pp

Nigel G. Wright
New Baptists, New Agenda
New Baptists, New Agenda is a timely contribution to the growing debate
about the health, shape and future of the Baptists. It considers the steady
changes that have taken place among Baptists in the last decade – changes
of mood, style, practice and structure - and encourages us to align these
current movements and questions with God's upward and future call. He
contends that the true church has yet to come: the church that currently
exists is an anticipation of the joyful gathering of all who have been called
by the Spirit through Christ to the Father.
2002 / ISBN 1-84227-157-1 / x + 161pp

PATERNOSTER PRESS

The Paternoster Press,
PO Box 300, Carlisle, Cumbria CA3 0QS, United Kingdom
Web: www.paternoster-publishing.com